First Workshop on Knowledge Graphs and Large Language Models (KaLLM 2024)

Bangkok, Thailand
15 August 2024

ISBN: 979-8-3313-0165-1

Printed from e-media with permission by:

Curran Associates, Inc.
57 Morehouse Lane
Red Hook, NY 12571

CURRAN ASSOCIATES INC. proceedings.com

Some format issues inherent in the e-media version may also appear in this print version.

Association for Computational Linguistics
209 N. Eighth Street
Stroudsburg, Pennsylvania 18360

Phone: 1-570-476-8006
Fax: 1-570-476-0860

acl@aclweb.org

Additional copies of this publication are available from:

Curran Associates, Inc.
57 Morehouse Lane
Red Hook, NY 12571 USA
Phone: 845-758-0400
Fax: 845-758-2633
Email: curran@proceedings.com
Web: www.proceedings.com

KaLLM 2024

The First Workshop on Knowledge Graphs and Large Language Models

Proceedings of the Workshop

August 15, 2024

The KaLLM organizers gratefully acknowledge the support from the following sponsors.

Best Paper Award by

Bloomberg

Engineering

Association for Computational Linguistics (ACL)
317 Sidney Baker St. S
Suite 400 - 134
Kerrville, TX 78028
USA
Tel: +1-855-225-1962
acl@aclweb.org

Introduction

Welcome to KaLLM 2024, the first workshop on Knowledge Graphs and Large Language Models.

Large Language Models (LLMs) have revolutionised the field of Natural Language Processing (NLP) by improving contextual understanding, zero-shot and few-shot learning, text generation, and question answering. However, LLMs have limitations such as accuracy, bias, interpretability, and context. They often produce factually inaccurate information, struggle to understand complex contexts, and may unintentionally produce biased or stereotyped information. KGs, on the other hand, have high-quality explicit knowledge, symbolic reasoning potential, and the ability to evolve with new knowledge, making them essential for various applications. The intersection of LLMs and KGs has sparked significant interest and innovation in NLP. LLM-enhanced KGs can be introduced into pre-training and inference stages to provide external knowledge and assess interpretability. LLM-augmented KGs are designed to improve coverage and ease the use of KGs in various tasks, including embedding learning, completion, construction, KG-to-text generation, and KGQA. Combining the benefits of LLMs and KGs can also improve performance in knowledge representation.

KaLLM 2024 intends to provide a platform for researchers, practitioners, and industry professionals to explore the synergies between LLMs and KGs. We aim to provide a space for the LLM community and the community of KG researchers to interact and explore how these two communities could collaborate and support one another. The goal of the workshop is to seize on the tremendous opportunities arising from investigating cutting-edge approaches, addressing challenges and limitations, and applications in different domains.

We received a total of 18 submissions; 1 non-archival and 17 archival. 1 archival submission was withdrawn as the topic did not fit the workshop. We accepted the non-archival submission and 13 out of the 16 archival submissions. We used reviewers' recommendations and scores to shortlist a set of three papers nominated for the Best Paper Award.

The program will feature oral presentations of the three papers nominated for best papers, and poster presentations of all accepted papers. We are also excited to have invited talks by four speakers: Xin Luna Dong (Meta Reality Labs), Marko Grobelnik (Jozef Stefan Institute), Heng Ji (University of Illinois Urbana-Champaign) and Ivan Titov (University of Edinburgh).

Organizing Committee

General Chairs

Russa Biswas, Aalborg University, Denmark
Lucie-Aimée Kaffee, HuggingFace, Germany
Oshin Agarwal, Bloomberg LP, USA
Pasquale Minervini, University of Edinburgh, UK
Sameer Singh, University of California Irvine, USA
Gerard de Melo, University of Potsdam, Germany

Program Committee

Reviewers

Nikita Bhutani, Megagon Labs Inc
Margarita Bugueño, Hasso Plattner Institute
Yiyi Chen, Aalborg University
Daniel Garijo, Universidad Politécnica de Madrid
Shrestha Ghosh, Max-Planck Institute for Informatics
Paul Groth, University of Amsterdam
Stefan Heindorf, Paderborn University
Fabian Hoppe, Vrije Universiteit Amsterdam
Filip Ilievski, Vrije Universiteit Amsterdam
Jan-Christoph Kalo, University of Amsterdam
Mayank Kejriwal, University of Southern California
Maria Koutraki, Leibniz University of Hannover
Pengwei Li, Meta
Matteo Lissandrini, University of Verona
Daniele Metilli, University College London
Swati Padhee, Wright State University
Heiko Paulheim, University of Mannheim
Simon Razniewski, Technische Universität Dresden
Sneha Singhania, Max-Planck Institute for Informatics
Mary Ann Tan, Karlsruhe Institute of Technology
Rosni Vasu, University of Zurich

Keynote Talk

The Journey to A Knowledgeable Assistant with Retrieval-Augmented Generation (RAG)

Xin Luna Dong
Meta Reality Labs

Abstract: For decades, multiple communities (Database, Information Retrieval, Natural Language Processing, Data Mining, AI) have pursued the mission of providing the right information at the right time. Efforts span web search, data integration, knowledge graphs, question answering. Recent advancements in Large Language Models (LLMs) have demonstrated remarkable capabilities in comprehending and generating human language, revolutionizing techniques in every front. However, their inherent limitations such as factual inaccuracies and hallucinations make LLMs less suitable for creating knowledgeable and trustworthy assistants.
This talk describes our journey in building a knowledgeable AI assistant by harnessing LLM techniques. We start with our findings from a comprehensive set of experiments to assess LLM reliability in answering factual questions and analyze performance variations across different knowledge types. Next, we describe our federated Retrieval-Augmented Generation (RAG) system that integrates external information from both the web and knowledge graphs for trustworthy text generation on real-time topics like stocks and sports, as well as on torso-to-tail entities like local restaurants. Additionally, we brief our explorations on extending our techniques towards multi-modal, contextualized, and personalized Q&A. We will share our techniques, our findings, and the path forward, highlighting how we are leveraging and advancing the decades of work in this area.

Bio: Xin Luna Dong is a Principal Scientist at Meta Reality Labs, leading the ML efforts in building an intelligent personal assistant. She has spent more than a decade building knowledge graphs, such as the Amazon Product Graph and the Google Knowledge Graph. She has co-authored books Machine Knowledge: Creation and Curation of Comprehensive Knowledge Basesand "Big Data Integration". She was named an ACM Fellow and an IEEE Fellow for significant contributions to knowledge graph construction and data integration", awarded the VLDB Women in Database Research Award and VLDB Early Career Research Contribution Award. She serves in the PVLDB advisory committee, was a member of the VLDB endowment, a PC co-chair for KDD'2022 ADS track, WSDM'2022, VLDB'2021, and Sigmod'2018.

Keynote Talk

Extracting Common Sense World Models from LLMs

Marko Grobelnik
AiLab, Jozef Stefan Institute

Abstract: LLMs are often criticized for not operating with a notion of world models, which could provide robustness, explainability, and multi-hop reasoning. In this keynote, we will show the methodology and concrete examples of how to extract non-trivial symbolic world models from LLMs for an arbitrary domain. The extracted world models will be represented in an operational first-order logic; concretely in the Prolog programming language, in its basic and probabilistic versions. In the second step, the extracted world models will be used to ground textual data into the semantics of world models to enable reasoning, explanation, and possibly efficient agent communication operating with explicit representations. The approach aims to integrate black-box LLM representations with transparent symbolic representations close to humans without significant loss of information for practical applications.

Bio: Marko Grobelnik is a researcher in the field of Artificial Intelligence (AI). Focused areas of expertise are Machine Learning, Data/Text/Web Mining, Network Analysis, Semantic Technologies, Deep Text Understanding, and Data Visualization. Marko co-leads Artificial Intelligence Lab at Jozef Stefan Institute, cofounded UNESCO International Research Center on AI (IRCAI), and is the CEO of Quintelligence.com specialized in solving complex AI tasks for the commercial world. He collaborates with major European academic institutions and major industries such as Bloomberg, British Telecom, European Commission, Microsoft Research, New York Times, OECD. Marko is co-author of several books, co-founder of several start-ups and is/was involved into over 100 EU funded research projects in various fields of Artificial Intelligence. Significant organisational activities include Marko being general chair of LREC2016 and TheWebConf2021 conferences. Marko represents Slovenia in OECD AI Committee (AIGO/ONEAI), in Council of Europe Committee on AI (CAHAI/CAI), NATO (DARB), and Global Partnership on AI (GPAI). In 2016 Marko became Digital Champion of Slovenia at European Commission.

Keynote Talk

Making Large Language Model's Knowledge More Accurate, Organized, Up-to-date and Fair

Heng Ji
University of Illinois Urbana-Champaign

Abstract: Large language models (LLMs) have demonstrated remarkable performance on knowledge reasoning tasks, owing to their implicit knowledge derived from extensive pretraining data. However, their inherent knowledge bases often suffer from disorganization and illusion, bias towards common entities, and rapid obsolescence. Consequently, LLMs frequently make up untruthful information, exhibit resistance to updating outdated knowledge, or struggle with generalizing across multiple languages. In this talk I will discuss our recent research efforts at tackling these challenges. I will begin by presenting theoretical and empirical analyses that illuminate when and why LLMs frequently produce factual errors and struggle to determine knowledge updating boundary in order to reach "ripple effect". Our investigations reveal several underlying causes. First, LLMs acquire implicit knowledge primarily through attention-weighted associations between words, rather than explicit understanding of concepts, entities, attributes, relations, events, semantic roles, and logics. Second, frequent word associations overshadow uncommon ones due to training data imbalance and wide context, particularly in contexts involving dynamic events. Third, counter-intuitive updating behaviors are elucidated through a novel gradient similarity metric. Fourth, LLMs are often unaware of real-world events occurring after their pretraining phase, complicating the anchoring of related knowledge updates. While existing methods focus largely on updating entity attributes, our research underscores the necessity of updating factual knowledge—such as participants, semantic roles, time, and location—based on real-world events. We propose a novel framework for knowledge updating in LLMs that leverages event-driven signals to identify factual errors preemptively and introduce a training-free self-contrastive decoding approach to mitigate inference errors.

Bio: Heng Ji is a professor at Computer Science Department, and an affiliated faculty member at Electrical and Computer Engineering Department and Coordinated Science Laboratory of University of Illinois Urbana-Champaign. She is an Amazon Scholar. She is the Founding Director of Amazon-Illinois Center on AI for Interactive Conversational Experiences (AICE). She received her B.A. and M. A. in Computational Linguistics from Tsinghua University, and her M.S. and Ph.D. in Computer Science from New York University. Her research interests focus on Natural Language Processing, especially on Multimedia Multilingual Information Extraction, Knowledge-enhanced Large Language Models and Vision-Language Models. She was selected as a Young Scientistby the World Laureates Association in 2023 and 2024. She was selected as Young Scientistand a member of the Global Future Council on the Future of Computing by the World Economic Forum in 2016 and 2017. She was named as part of Women Leaders of Conversational AI (Class of 2023) by Project Voice. The other awards she received include two Outstanding Paper Awards at NAACL2024, AI's 10 to WatchAward by IEEE Intelligent Systems in 2013, NSF CAREER award in 2009, PACLIC2012 Best paper runner-up, Best of ICDM2013paper award, Best of SDM2013paper award, ACL2018 Best Demo paper nomination, ACL2020 Best Demo Paper Award, NAACL2021 Best Demo Paper Award, Google Research Award in 2009 and 2014, IBM Watson Faculty Award in 2012 and 2014 and Bosch Research Award in 2014-2018. She was invited to testify to the U.S. House Cybersecurity, Data Analytics, IT Committee as an AI expert in 2023. She was selected to participate in DARPA AI Forward in 2023. She was invited by the Secretary of the U.S. Air Force and AFRL to join Air Force Data Analytics Expert Panel to inform the Air Force Strategy 2030, and invited to speak at the Federal Information Integrity RD Interagency Working Group (IIRD IWG) briefing in 2023. She is the lead of many multi-institution projects and tasks, including the U.S. ARL projects on information fusion and knowledge networks construction, DARPA ECOLE MIRACLE team, DARPA KAIROS RESIN team and DARPA DEFT Tinker Bell team. She has coordinated the NIST TAC Knowledge Base Population task 2010-2020. She is the Chief Editor of Data Intelligence Journal. She served as the associate editor for IEEE/ACM Transaction on Audio, Speech, and Language Processing, and the Program Committee Co-Chair of many conferences including NAACL-HLT2018 and AACL-IJCNLP2022. She was elected as the North American Chapter of the Association for Computational Linguistics (NAACL) secretary 2020-2023. Her research has been widely supported by the U.S. government agencies (DARPA, NSF, DoE, ARL, IARPA, AFRL, DHS) and industry (Amazon, Google, Bosch, IBM, Disney).

Keynote Talk

Understanding and Navigating Human Control and Transparency in LLMs

Ivan Titov
University of Edinburgh

Abstract: Language models are an exciting technology that has transformed our field and used by millions of people daily. However, both users and researchers often find themselves puzzled by LLM's responses and struggle to understand the underlying decision processes or attribute their responses to specific data sources. I will talk about our work which tries to enhance the transparency of these models for human users, ensure their behavior is systematic, and uncover the sources of their decisions. This transparency should enable finer control of these models, including model editing, the unlearning of undesirable behaviors or data sources, integration of extra information (e.g., in the form of knowledge bases).
In this talk, I will discuss the approaches my group (as well as colleagues) have been developing, highlighting not only methods but also some cautious lessons learned along the way. This includes pitfalls in data attribution and the challenges of guiding model responses with human rationale. Although progress in these areas may seem slow and sometimes illusory, it is a crucial direction, given the growing reliance on collaboration between humans and large language models. I also hope to convince you that this area holds a diverse range of intriguing open problems for us, researchers, to explore.

Bio: Ivan Titov is a Full Professor at the University of Edinburgh, UK, and also a faculty member at the University of Amsterdam, Netherlands. Ivan's current interests lie in making deep learning models interpretable, robust, and controllable, or more generally in machine learning for NLP. He has received awards at leading NLP conferences. Ivan has been a program co-chair of ICLR 2021 and CoNLL 2018, and has served on the editorial boards of the Transactions of the ACL, Journal of Artificial Intelligence Research, and Journal of Machine Learning Research, and on the advisory board of the European chapter of ACL. Ivan is an ELLIS fellow and co-directs the ELLIS NLP program and Edinburgh ELLIS unit. Ivan's research group has been supported by personal fellowships (e.g., ERC, Dutch Vici, and Vidi grants) as well as industrial funding (e.g., Google, SAP, Booking.com and Amazon).

Table of Contents

Program

Thursday, August 15, 2024

09:00 - 09:15 *Opening Remarks*

09:15 - 10:00 *Invited Talk by Xin Luna Dong*

10:00 - 10:30 *Spotlight Paper Presentations*

Multi-hop Database Reasoning with Virtual Knowledge Graph
Juhee Son, Yeon Seonwoo, Alice Oh, James Thorne and Seunghyun Yoon

Zero- and Few-Shots Knowledge Graph Triplet Extraction with Large Language Models
Andrea Papaluca, Daniel Krefl, Sergio José Rodríguez Méndez, Artem Lensky and Hanna Suominen

KGAST: From Knowledge Graphs to Annotated Synthetic Texts
Nakanyseth Vuth, Gilles Sérasset and Didier Schwab

10:30 - 11:00 *Break*

11:00 - 11:45 *Invited Talk by Marko Grobelnik*

11:45 - 13:00 *Poster Session I*

13:00 - 14:00 *Break*

14:00 - 14:45 *Invited Talk by Heng Ji*

14:45 - 15:30 *Invited Talk by Ivan Titov*

15:30 - 16:00 *Break*

16:00 - 16:45 *Poster Session II*

16:45 - 17:00 *Closing Remarks*

Thursday, August 15, 2024 (continued)

Multi-hop Database Reasoning with Virtual Knowledge Graph

Juhee Son[1], **Yeon Seonwoo**[1], **Seunghyun Yoon**[2], **James Thorne**[1], **Alice Oh**[1]
[1]KAIST, [2]Adobe
{sjh5665, yeon.seonwoo, thorne}@kaist.ac.kr,
syoon@adobe.com, alice.oh@kaist.edu

Abstract

Application of LLM to database queries on natural language sentences has demonstrated impressive results in both single and multi-hop scenarios. In the existing methodologies, the requirement to re-encode query vectors at each stage for processing multi-hop queries presents a significant bottleneck to the inference speed. This paper proposes **VKGFR** (**V**irtual **K**nowledge **G**raph based **F**act **R**etriever) that leverages large language models to extract representations corresponding to a sentence's knowledge graph, significantly enhancing inference speed for multi-hop reasoning without performance loss. Given that both the queries and natural language database sentences can be structured as a knowledge graph, we suggest extracting a Virtual Knowledge Graph (VKG) representation from sentences with LLM. Over the pre-constructed VKG, our VKGFR conducts retrieval with a tiny model structure, showing performance improvements with higher computational efficiency. We evaluate VKGFR on the WikiNLDB and MetaQA dataset, designed for multi-hop database reasoning over text. The results indicate 13x faster inference speed on the WikiNLDB dataset without performance loss.

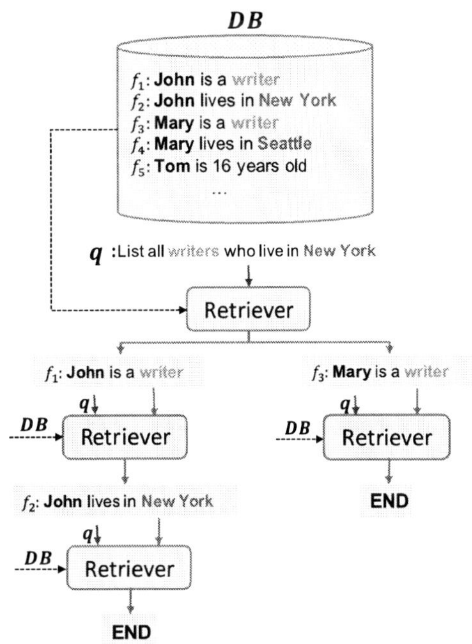

Figure 1: Illustration of the multi-hop reasoning procedure for answering the database query. The retriever searches related facts in the database per each reasoning step. As the database sizes increases, the number of facts used for multi-hop reasoning increases, so the number of retriever's operation gets higher.

1 Introduction

If open-domain question-answering models could accurately reason with large-scale facts in databases, it would make it feasible to substitute or augment existing database management systems with NLP technology (Thorne et al., 2021b). Several benchmarks have been proposed (Weston et al., 2016a; Dua et al., 2019; Thorne et al., 2021a), which range in size and complexity and require systems to conduct discrete reasoning (incorporating numerical operations like counting and argmax) by collating multiple facts within the database. To facilitate the reasoning at the scale of databases, NLP systems are required to access numerous sets of relevant sentences, often in combination with multi-hop retrieval (Figure 1).

For open-domain NLP systems to reason over only the relevant subset of facts from a corpus, a two-stage architecture of retrieval and reasoning is typically used (Petroni et al., 2021). However, challenges in database-style reasoning require additional complexity with retrieving non-redundant sets of tens or hundreds of facts. For the WikiNLDB benchmark, Thorne et al. (2021a) proposed an incremental retrieval architecture called

Proceedings of the 1st Workshop on Knowledge Graphs and Large Language Models (KaLLM 2024), pages 1–11
August 15, 2024 ©2024 Association for Computational Linguistics

SSG (Support Set Generator) built on sentence-BERT (Reimers and Gurevych, 2019). The inference speed of the SSG is not scalable because it encodes query vectors for each reasoning step in multi-hop retrieval through the transformer (Vaswani et al., 2017), causing computation inefficiency. As the size of the database increases, retrieval slows down significantly. For example, with 25 facts in the database, SSG processes 21.51 queries per second, but as the number of facts increases to 1000, SSG only processes 1.46 queries per second.

In this paper, we propose **VKGFR** (**V**irtual **K**nowledge **G**raph based **F**act **R**etriever) which significantly improves the inference speed and retrieval performance. Since the WikiNLDB dataset can be represented in the knowledge graph structure, we suggest constructing a virtual knowledge graph (Wang et al., 2017, VKG) for fact retrieval with LLM. The VKG embedding provides compressed vectorized representations of facts and queries and can be pre-indexed, enabling efficient and accurate multi-hop retrieval. Recent works have used VKG to predict target entities from knowledge bases (Dhingra et al., 2020; Sun et al., 2021) or retrieve facts to claim verification (de Jong et al., 2021). However, the number of reasoning steps and hop lengths are predetermined for these specific tasks, making it challenging to adapt them directly to database reasoning. Applying the VKG to the database reasoning task is non-trivial because it requires various hops of reasoning, and the candidates per each reasoning step are not known a priori, and our work is the first to employ VKG for database reasoning.

We evaluate VKGFR on WikiNLDB, a database reasoning task consisting of various sizes of database facts and corresponding queries, and MetaQA (Zhang et al., 2018), a conventional multi-hop QA dataset over the knowledge base. VKGFR performs best compared with several other VKG-based models and multi-hop dense retrieval models (Xiong et al., 2021; Lee et al., 2021) on both datasets. Furthermore, VKGFR shows at least 4.7 times faster inference time than SSG in all database sizes of WikiNLDB (Figure 6). We conduct an ablation study with different types of entity embedding and model structure, and our approach shows the best performance. Our main contribution is to propose a significantly more efficient and accurate VKG-based retriever enabling natural language database reasoning.

Facts

- John is a writer who lives in Seoul, 35 years old
- Marry is 18 year old girl graduated from Boston school
- James is a 40 years old lawyer graduated from Harvard law school

Queries

- **Argmax**: Who is the oldest person?
- **Set**: List all writers lives in New York.
- **Count**: How many people live in Seoul?
- **Bool**: Did James graduate from Harvard?

Figure 2: Examples of facts included in natural language databases and database queries. The highlighted texts are entities important for reasoning on the database.

2 Background

2.1 Natural Language Databases (NLDBs)

Natural language databases (Thorne et al., 2021a,b) model large collections of facts stored in plain text as the storage media for database reasoning. In contrast to open-domain question answering, database reasoning requires making inferences over large sets of facts related to one query. Conventional open-domain question-answering methods need to encode all relevant facts, possibly in the thousands, perform discrete reasoning to get the most related facts, and then decode a sequence of tokens representing the answer to the query. Previous works have studied small synthetic settings (Weston et al., 2016b) or reasoning over a single passage (Dua et al., 2019).

Conventional databases store facts in structured forms with labeled columns and are queried with formal languages such as SQL. Much work in NLP has studied the parsing of user queries into structured representations or exposing the database through a natural language interface (Androutsopoulos et al., 1995; Zhong et al., 2017). However, in NLDBs, because *both* the stored text and queries are natural languages, NLDBs are not restricted by any predefined database schema allowing the addition of new topics without defining tables or columns, reducing maintenance overheads.

NLDBs are studied using the WikiNLDB dataset (Thorne et al., 2021a), which contains databases varying in size (from 25 to 1000 facts) and question-answer pairs. An example is provided in Figure 2. In WikiNLDB, four different types of queries require different reasoning processes (specifically, counting, min/max, argmin/argmax, and set-based answers) and over single entities and short multi-hop chains (referred to as *joins*).

2.2 Virtual Knowledge Graphs (VKGs)

Our proposed solution is to perform retrieval by modeling the set of facts as a VKG: a knowledge graph representation where pairs of entities and the relation between them is embedded: $(m_{e_1}, m_{e_2}, \vec{r}_{(e_1,e_2)})$. VKG representations have been used for retrieval in QA, but their usage and constructions vary by application. **DrKIT** (Dhingra et al., 2020) and **TOME** (de Jong et al., 2021) used the entity representation as a memory bank for fixed-length multi-hop retrieval. **OPQL** (Sun et al., 2021) constructs a key-value memory with VKG for the fixed length of multi-hop retrieval and multi-hop slot filling task. The *key* in OPQL is the concatenation of the target entity embedding and the relation vector, and the remaining entity embedding becomes the *value* of the memory. **VKGDR** (Seonwoo et al., 2022) uses VKG for zero-shot domain-specific retrieval and calculates the relevance score of queries and documents by multiplying the relation vectors. In contrast to previous work in VKG-based retrieval, which uses a subset of the VKG for a fixed number of hops, we use the whole VKG representation to perform variable-length multi-hop retrieval.

3 Methods

Our multi-hop fact retriever **VKGFR** comprises two key steps: first, facts and queries are embedded into VKGs (Section 3.1, Figure 3); second, multi-hop retrieval is performed over the embedded VKG (Section 3.2, Figure 4). In contrast to SSG (Thorne et al., 2021a), the embeddings of facts are immutable and can be pre-indexed, yielding faster retrieval. For inference, VKG embeddings of new facts or queries can be embedded on demand.

3.1 Building the VKG

Entity Encoder We extract the entity spans from the text with a predefined entity vocabulary built over the Wikipedia entities. All possible pairs of extracted entities become part of the VKG. We use a pre-trained language model to compute the contextualized embeddings of those entities. We experiment with various models (Karpukhin et al., 2020; de Jong et al., 2022; Devlin et al., 2019) and use the best-performing model, *DensePhrase*.

Relation Encoder The relation encoder computes a relation vector between a pair of entities (Seonwoo et al., 2022; Sun et al., 2021; Baldini Soares et al., 2019). Consistent with previous approaches, the input to the relation encoder is a sentence with two entities masked and a special relation token inserted behind each masked token (e.g. "[ENT] [R1] is a [ENT] [R2] who lives in L.A."). The masking makes the model learn the relation representation based on the context of the entities rather than the textual representation itself. For the two relation tokens, the relation vector is computed by concatenation and linear projection:

$$\vec{r}_{e_1,e_2} = W^{\intercal}[h_{r_1}; h_{r_2}] \quad (1)$$

Hyper parameter described on section 8

The relation encoder is trained with supervision that relations containing the same entity pairs are located in a similar vector space. The relation vectors that consist of the same entity pairs are regarded as positive samples. Below is the cross-entropy training loss for the relation encoder:

$$L_{rel\_enc} = \mathrm{CE}(\sigma(\vec{r}^{\intercal}_{e_1,e_2}\vec{r}_{e_i,e_j}), \mathbb{I}_{(e_1=e_i,e_2=e_j)}) \quad (2)$$

Following Sun et al. (2021), we pre-train the relation encoder with Wikidata and fine-tune it on the respective target datasets (WikiNLDB, MetaQA).

VKG for WikiNLDB As described above, we build VKG embeddings for the facts and queries in WikiNLDB. For the facts, we extract the entity span

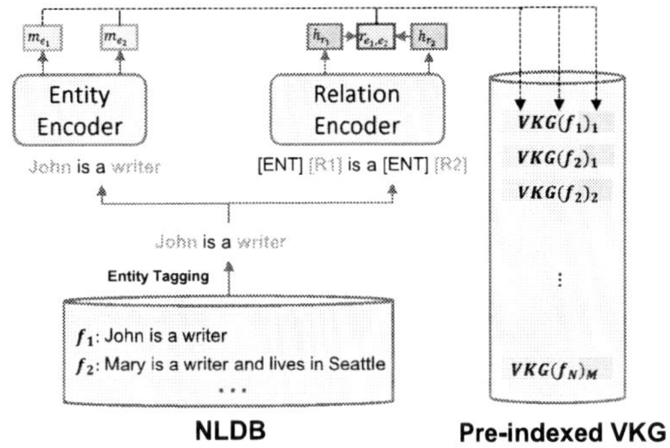

Figure 3: Illustration of our VKG construction method. Each encoder independently builds the vectorized representation of facts. The concatenation of the entity and relation embeddings becomes our VKG representations of the text. For the f_2, there are two entity pairs (Mary-writer, Mary-Seattle) so the corresponding VKG representation is indexed as two different triplets $(VKG(f_2)_1, VKG(f_2)_2)$.

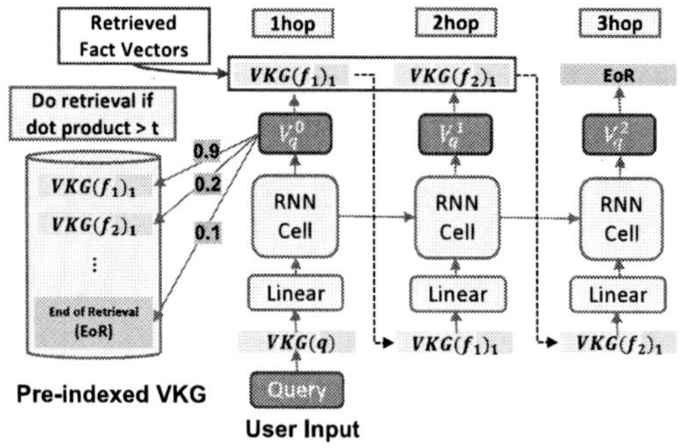

Figure 4: Illustration of VKGFR's multi-hop inference procedure. The query is encoded with an RNN, and the retrieved fact (f_1) becomes the input for the next hop. This multi-hop reasoning process is repeated until the model predicts the special END vector, indicating sufficient information was returned.

(e_i, e_j) based on the Wikipedia entity vocabulary $\mathcal{E}$ and embed them with pretrained models (m_{e_i}, m_{e_j}) and calculate a relation vector $r_{(e_i,e_j)}$ for each pair. As in Figure 2, facts can contain many entity pairs, so there can be multiple mention-relation-mention triplets of the same fact. The VKG representations for fact f that have n entity pairs are denoted as follows:

$$vkg(f) = \{[m_{e_i}; m_{e_j}; r_{e_i,e_j}]_k\}_{k=1}^{n}, \quad \forall i \; e_i \in \mathcal{E} \tag{3}$$

For queries, we mask the entity and add the special relation token at the end of the sentence to compute the relation vector (e.g. "How many people study at [ENT][R1]? [ENT][R2]"). If there are multiple entities in the query, we average the VKG representation per each entity and take the average because the query is a single unit used for comparison, so it is more beneficial to include all entity pair relations in the query. The following is VKG representation for query q that has n entities:

$$vkg(q) = \frac{1}{n}\sum_{k=1}^{n}[m_{e_i}; m_{e_j}; r_{e_i,e_j}]_k, \; \forall i \; e_i \in \mathcal{E} \tag{4}$$

3.2 Multi-hop Retriever

Figure 4 depicts the comprehensive inference mechanism of VKGFR. VKGFR retrieves relevant facts by searching over a pre-indexed fact VKG with the given query VKG. For each retrieval step, VKGFR applies a linear layer to project the fact (W_f) and query (W_q) VKG embeddings. Then, to encode the multi-hop aspect of retrieval, we apply an RNN layer to transform the vector (Equation 5), considering the retrieval history.

$$V_q^0, h^0 = RNN(W_q^{\intercal} vkg(q), 0) \in \mathbb{R}^D \tag{5}$$

Using the query vector, the fact that the relation probability is over the threshold (τ) is returned ($vkg(f_t)$ = *retrieve*(V_q^t,τ)). For each retrieval hop, the retrieved fact vector becomes the input of the next step (Equation 6)

$$V_q^{t+1}, h^{t+1} = RNN(W_f^{\intercal} vkg(f_t), h^t) \in \mathbb{R}^D \tag{6}$$

The retrieved facts are further processed by VKGFR, repeating this retrieval step until a special End-of-retrieval (EoR) vector is retrieved.

Training We optimize the cross entropy loss between the inner products of fact, query vectors, and the ground truth (*gt*) label that is 1 if the fact is correct for the query and 0 otherwise.

$$L_{retreiver} = \text{CE}(\sigma(V_{f_i}^{\intercal} V_q^t), \mathbb{I}_{f_i \in gt(q)}) \tag{7}$$

Retrieval The relevance probability between the query and fact is estimated by computing the inner product of the query and fact vectors. If this probability exceeds a hyper-parameterized threshold $\tau = 0.5$, the fact is retrieved. To model multi-set multi-hop retrieval for WikiNLDB, the retrieval process branches if more than one fact is retrieved. Each branch is independently decoded until EoR is predicted.

4 Experiments on WikiNLDB

4.1 Experimental Setup

Data The WikiNLDB dataset consists of databases between 25 and 1000 facts. The size of the database defines the upper bound of the number of candidates for retrieval. Following the original paper (Thorne et al., 2021a), we use the training data from the database size 25 and train a single model which was tested for all sizes.

VKG Embedding For the entity encoder, we use the publicly available BERT-base size DensePhrase checkpoint[1]. For the relation encoder, we pretrained the BERT-large with the Wikidata and finetuned this on WikiNLDB.

[1] https://github.com/princeton-nlp/DensePhrases

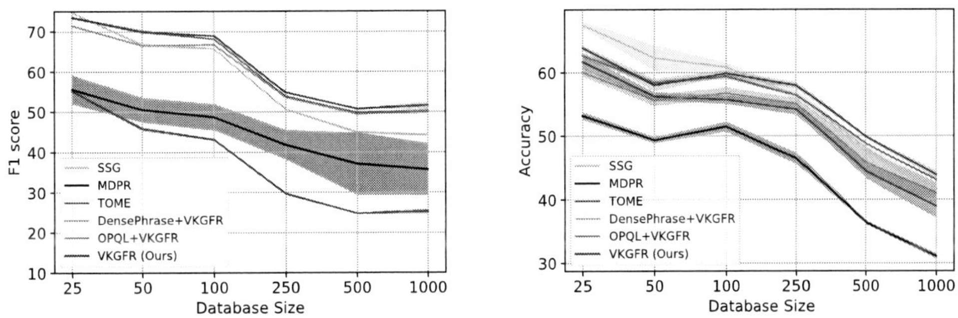

(a) Retriever performance

(b) Reader performance

Figure 5: Retriever and reader performance of models on all database sizes

Retriever VKGFR is trained with the pre-indexed VKGs. We use one RNN layer for multi-hop retrieval, chosen empirically. We sample hard negative facts that share the same entity or same relation with the ground truth facts for training. We set the sample ratio as 1:10 and the threshold as 0.5 based on empirical performance on the validation set.

Full Pipeline (With Reader) The contributions in this paper focus on the retrieval side of a two-part architecture. For completeness, we experiment with the reader component. We use the pre-existing NeuralSPJ model from Thorne et al. (2021a). This model is an encoder-decoder transformer based on the T5 architecture that generates a machine-readable version of a natural language fact given a query if the fact is relevant or no output otherwise. Following previous approach, we trained this model using the gold passages from WikiNLDB and sampled false-positive facts from our retriever for resilience. To train the model to predict no output for false-positive retrieved facts, we sample false positives from our retrieved facts.

For evaluation, we report precision, recall, and F1 score for the retriever and answer exact-match from the reader. To evaluate variance, we run each experiment with three seeds and average the results. Appendix 8 describes the hyperparameters.

4.2 Retrieval Baselines

SSG (Thorne et al., 2021a) is a SentenceBERT-based multi-hop retriever, using an inner-product-based search mechanism with branching for multi-hop retrieval. **TOME** (de Jong et al., 2022) uses predefined mention encoding for multi-hop retrieval. This shows the best performance on the fact verification task. We fine-tune TOME for WikiNLDBs. **MDPR** (Xiong et al., 2021) uses dense representation for multi-hop retrieval, iteratively encoding the questions using the question encoder. To apply MDPR to the WikiNLDB dataset, the number of candidates retrieved for every reasoning step needs to be set, and we set the number as the maximum reasoning steps of the NLDB training data (Asai et al., 2020). **DensePhrase** (Lee et al., 2021) is the text retrieval model we use for entity embedding, and we experiment with only the DensePhrase embedding on our model to figure out the effect of *our* relation embedding. **OPQL** (Sun et al., 2021) memory uses VKG for multi-hop reasoning, but their VKG representations consist of only the relation vector and target entity embedding, so we compare our VKG building method to the OPQL memory. To enable variable lengths of multi-hop reasoning on DensePhrase and OPQL, we add VKGFR over the pre-indexed DensePhrase and OPQL embedding.

4.3 Ablation Study

To verify our VKG encoding method, we conduct an ablation study with the following types of entity embedding: 1) DensePhrase (Lee et al., 2021, DP) records the dense representation of passages, which can be a single entity. 2) Mention Encoder (de Jong et al., 2022, ME) encodes dense vector representations of every entity mention in a text, which is built on the transformer architecture, and the entity span is projected to the fixed-sized vector space. 3) The average value of BERT (Devlin et al., 2019) hidden embedding between the entity span used as an entity representation. We build VKG triplets based on different embedding models and trained VKGFR over those representations with the same hyperparameter. 4) We compare the VKGFR model structure between the *RNN* and *Linear* layer.

5 Results on WikiNLDB

5.1 Overall Results on Whole Databases

Figure 5 describes the overall performance of the retriever and reader for all sizes.

Retriever Performance For retrieval performance, VKGFR shows the best or comparable F1 score on all database sizes. SSG performs best on the smallest database size (25 facts), but as the database size increases, the performance drastically drops. VKGFR is consistently better than DensePhrase and OPQL, which means that our VKG-building methods are effective in improving retrieval. Compared to other retrieval baselines, MDPR shows low performance with high variance, indicating that the fixed number of candidates had a negative impact on performance. TOME shows the lowest performance, implying that the mention encoding strategy of TOME is not effective on this dataset.

Reader Performance VKGFR shows the best performance on large database sizes (>100), but the SSG is better on smaller database sizes. DensePhrase, TOME, and OPQL showed consistently lower performance than VKGFR on all database sizes. MDPR showed much lower performance for the reader even though it showed a better retrieval score than the TOME, caused by noise from the fixed number of retrieval candidates.

5.2 Results for Different Types of Queries

WikiNLDB consists of four different types of queries: min/max, set, count, and boolean. We analyze results from the models with different types of queries on the largest database size (1000 facts).

Retriever Performance We report retrieval results for all models in Table 1. VKGFR shows the highest F1 score on most query types, min/max, set, and count. In comparison to the SSG, VKGFR showed better precision which leads better F1 score but the recall score of SSG is higher than VKGFR. TOME and MDPR showed the lowest precision but comparable recall scores. All models' performance of the boolean query is very low because 94% of boolean queries have 0-2 positive facts, making it hard to conduct accurate retrieval on a large size of database.

Reader Performance We report the corresponding reader accuracy in Table 2. Because of the

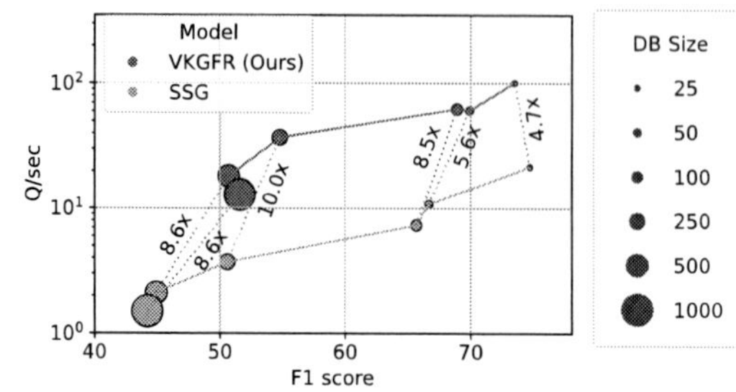

Figure 6: Inference speed and the retrieval performance of SSG (orange circles) and VKGFR (blue circles) on different sizes of the WikiNLDB test set. The x-axis represents the retrieval F1 score, and the y-axis represents the inference speed. The size of the circles indicates the database sizes. The numbers on the circles indicate the ratio of q/sec between two models on the same DB size.

higher variation in reader performance, we report the standard deviations in the table. Compared to the SSG, VKGFR shows better answer accuracy, indicating that our more precise retriever leads to performance improvements on the reader. In comparison to the OPQL and DensePhrase, VKGFR shows better total accuracy. The answer candidates of the boolean query are easier than the other queries, so the accuracy is much higher for all models, even TOME, compared to other question types. The count query exhibits the lowest accuracy compared to the others due to its requirement of accurately predicting every positive sample.

5.3 Computational Efficiency

We measure the number of queries that each retriever can process in a second (Q/sec); the inference speed is measured by one Quadro RTX A6000 48GB GPU. We plot the speed-accuracy trade-off with our model and the SSG baseline in Figure 6. The speed of all models includes the time required for query embedding. VKGFR showed at least 8.9 times faster inference speed than the SSG on all database sizes and a higher F1 score on DB size larger than 25, which is more representative of real-world applications. Table 3 shows the retrieval speed of each model on the largest database size (1000 facts). VKGFR models can conduct efficient retrieval with the simple model structure compared to the other transformer-based models. To perform inference on WikiNLDB on TOME, MDPR, and SSG, a new query vector must be encoded for each reasoning step. For example, based on the SSG, 440 BERT encodings are required per query in DB

Model	Min/Max P	Min/Max R	Min/Max F	Set P	Set R	Set F	Count P	Count R	Count F	Bool P	Bool R	Bool F	Total P	Total R	Total F
TOME	17.5	72.5	28.2	15.1	77.5	25.2	14.8	80.5	25.0	2.6	90.9	5.0	15.1	77.2	25.3
MDPR	25.8	72.4	37.7	23.2	77.9	35.3	22.5	79.9	34.9	15.8	77.9	26.2	23.5	76.2	35.7
SSG	35.0	88.3	50.1	27.7	84.7	41.7	26.8	84.6	40.6	19.2	82.4	31.1	29.8	85.9	44.2
VKGFR (Ours)	44.3	70.5	**54.4**	37.8	76.3	**50.5**	39.3	76.9	**52.0**	17.5	82.8	28.9	39.4	74.6	**51.6**
w/ OPQL embedding	44.0	68.5	53.6	35.2	75.6	48.0	36.5	75.6	49.2	17.7	84.0	29.2	37.9	73.3	50.0
w/ DensePhrase embedding	41.6	68.8	51.8	37.3	72.8	49.3	39.8	74.0	51.7	19.8	83.0	**32.0**	38.5	72.2	50.2

Table 1: Precision, Recall, F1 score and retrieval speed of each retriever on the database size 1000. VKGFR shows the highest F1 score on Min/Max, Set, and Count type queries.

Model	Min/Max (std)	Set (std)	Count (std)	Bool (std)	Tot (std)
TOME	36.68 (0.75)	54.91 (2.81)	15.69 (3.81)	**86.75** (3.71)	38.97 (1.94)
MDPR	35.67 (1.28)	41.03 (1.53)	10.83 (1.97)	56.84 (1.77)	31.01 (0.43)
SSG	43.04 (0.44)	58.03 (1.74)	15.37 (1.78)	78.21 (3.06)	41.64 (0.99)
VKGFR (Ours)	44.92 (1.03)	**60.01** (0.86)	**17.80** (0.89)	83.23 (2.18)	**43.91** (0.59)
w/ OPQL embedding	**45.61** (1.44)	57.08 (0.94)	16.86 (0.49)	82.16 (0.81)	43.10 (0.23)
w/ DensePhrase embedding	41.30 (3.59)	55.39 (0.70)	**17.80** (0.49)	79.70 (0.74)	41.04 (1.64)

Table 2: Fine-tuned reader accuracy on each retriever's result for different types of queries on the database size 1000. The standard deviation is included in this table because the std of the reader results is bigger than the retrieval results' std.

Model	Speed (Q/sec)	F1
TOME	0.19	25.29
MDPR	0.63	35.67
SSG	1.46	44.21
VKGFR (Ours)	12.83	**51.59**
w/ OPQL embedding	**13.01**	49.95
w/ DensePhrase embedding	12.45	50.22

Table 3: Represents the speed of each model on the largest database size (1000) and corresponding retrieval F1 score.

DB Size	# of DBs	Avg Size/DB	Avg Indexing Time /DB
25	621	1MB	0.3s
50	499	2MB	0.6s
100	250	4MB	1.2s
250	100	10MB	3.3s
500	50	17MB	6.1s
1000	25	26MB	12.0s

Table 4: Represents the size of pre-indexes for test dataset on each database size, and taking time for the embedding queries and facts.

size 1000 on average, but VKGFR only needs 1 BERT encoding per query.

We included the amortized time for indexing our embeddings to ensure a fair comparison. However, this indexing includes additional storage overheads. We report these storage costs in Table 4.

6 Experiments and Results on MetaQA

Experiment Setup To verify VKGFR on other tasks, we experiment with MetaQA (Zhang et al., 2018), which is a multi-hop retrieval over a predefined knowledge base built on the WikiMovies dataset. Unlike WikiNLDB, the number of hops is prefixed before the inference, so there is no end prediction for this case. The questions of MetaQA are generated from predefined templates, and corresponding answers exist on the knowledge base. We fine-tune the relation encoder with MetaQA dataset as Sun et al. (2021) and use the same training & inference configuration as 4.1. For inference, we apply a sparse filter that the retrieved knowledge base should include the topic entity of the query for increasing the accuracy (Dhingra et al., 2020; Sun et al., 2021).

Results Table 5 reports the Hit@1 results of different models on the MetaQA dataset. The VKGFR outperforms the previous approach by at least 1.7 points in every case, indicating our VKG representation contains the essential information for the question-answering task more than others. The 1-hop performance of OPQL is not mentioned in the paper, but the authors said the performance is lower than the DrKIT.

Model	1Hop	2Hop	3Hop
KVMem	-	7.0	19.5
DrQA	55.3	32.5	19.7
GRAFT-Net	82.5	36.2	40.2
PullNet	84.4	81.0	78.2
DrKIT	84.4	86.0	87.6
OPQL	-	88.5	87.1
VKGFR	**86.1**	**93.7**	**92.1**

Table 5: Hit@1 results on MetaQA dataset. Each result is from the original paper.

7 Related Works

Building a semi-structured representation from textual sources has been an important direction in handling reasoning queries (Asai et al., 2020; Sun et al., 2019; Dhingra et al., 2020). This is because reasoning tasks often require entity matching, and previous dense retrieval methods are insufficient for entity representation learning. For this reason, many studies have focused on entity-matching-based retrieval methods (Sun et al., 2018, 2019; Cao et al., 2019). These studies find supporting facts by iteratively matching entities that appeared in a given question and documents, similar to human information-seeking processes. Furthermore, contextualized entity embedding methods have been proposed. These methods are specifically designed for entity representation and capture more fine-grained semantic meanings of entities (Lee et al., 2021; de Jong et al., 2021).

Inspired by previous entity-matching-based approaches, some studies propose to use relations between entities as well as entity vectors (Dhingra et al., 2020; Sun et al., 2021; Seonwoo et al., 2022). These approaches use a relation encoder to encode the semantic meaning of the relation of entities, then construct a graph consisting of entity vectors and their relation vectors. Dhingra et al. (2020) proposes a virtual knowledge base, which consists of trainable entity vectors. Sun et al. (2021) further develops this approach to use the relation between entities and propose a virtual knowledge graph (VKG), which consists of entity and relation vectors. Seonwoo et al. (2022) adopts the VKG to the domain-specific document retrieval with insufficient training data. Unlike the previous approach, our methods target variable length of multi-hop database reasoning and show the best performance.

8 Conclusions

In this paper, we propose **VKGFR** enable multi-hop retrieval with faster speed and high performance over the WikiNLDB dataset. Our multi-hop retrieval mechanism does not require re-embedding of facts, resulting in fewer queries to an encoder model and allowing it to take advantage of pre-indexed fact representations. VKGFR retrieves upon that pre-indexed VKG representation which is highly contributing to the faster inference speed. On other tasks, VKGFR shows the best performance on the general knowledge-base multi-hop QA dataset, MetaQA. This research demonstrates the applicability of VKG text representation in the task of multi-hop database reasoning.

Limitations

VKGFR retrieves the knowledge base that consists of explicit entities and relations. If the knowledge base becomes more complex, with no explicit entities and relations in the sentence, new VKG encoding methods will be required for good performance.

References

Ion Androutsopoulos, Graeme D Ritchie, and Peter Thanisch. 1995. Natural language interfaces to databases–an introduction. *Natural language engineering*, 1(1):29–81.

Akari Asai, Kazuma Hashimoto, Hannaneh Hajishirzi, Richard Socher, and Caiming Xiong. 2020. Learning to retrieve reasoning paths over wikipedia graph for question answering. In *8th International Conference on Learning Representations, ICLR 2020, Addis Ababa, Ethiopia, April 26-30, 2020*. OpenReview.net.

Livio Baldini Soares, Nicholas FitzGerald, Jeffrey Ling, and Tom Kwiatkowski. 2019. Matching the blanks: Distributional similarity for relation learning. In *Proceedings of the 57th Annual Meeting of the Association for Computational Linguistics*, pages 2895–

2905, Florence, Italy. Association for Computational Linguistics.

Yu Cao, Meng Fang, and Dacheng Tao. 2019. BAG: Bi-directional attention entity graph convolutional network for multi-hop reasoning question answering. In *Proceedings of the 2019 Conference of the North American Chapter of the Association for Computational Linguistics: Human Language Technologies, Volume 1 (Long and Short Papers)*, pages 357–362, Minneapolis, Minnesota. Association for Computational Linguistics.

Michiel de Jong, Yury Zemlyanskiy, Nicholas FitzGerald, Fei Sha, and William Cohen. 2021. Mention memory: incorporating textual knowledge into transformers through entity mention attention. *ArXiv preprint*, abs/2110.06176.

Michiel de Jong, Yury Zemlyanskiy, Nicholas FitzGerald, Fei Sha, and William W. Cohen. 2022. Mention memory: incorporating textual knowledge into transformers through entity mention attention. In *International Conference on Learning Representations*.

Jacob Devlin, Ming-Wei Chang, Kenton Lee, and Kristina Toutanova. 2019. BERT: Pre-training of deep bidirectional transformers for language understanding. In *Proceedings of the 2019 Conference of the North American Chapter of the Association for Computational Linguistics: Human Language Technologies, Volume 1 (Long and Short Papers)*, pages 4171–4186, Minneapolis, Minnesota. Association for Computational Linguistics.

Bhuwan Dhingra, Manzil Zaheer, Vidhisha Balachandran, Graham Neubig, Ruslan Salakhutdinov, and William W. Cohen. 2020. Differentiable reasoning over a virtual knowledge base. In *8th International Conference on Learning Representations, ICLR 2020, Addis Ababa, Ethiopia, April 26-30, 2020*. OpenReview.net.

Dheeru Dua, Yizhong Wang, Pradeep Dasigi, Gabriel Stanovsky, Sameer Singh, and Matt Gardner. 2019. DROP: A reading comprehension benchmark requiring discrete reasoning over paragraphs. In *Proceedings of the 2019 Conference of the North American Chapter of the Association for Computational Linguistics: Human Language Technologies, Volume 1 (Long and Short Papers)*, pages 2368–2378, Minneapolis, Minnesota. Association for Computational Linguistics.

Vladimir Karpukhin, Barlas Oguz, Sewon Min, Patrick Lewis, Ledell Wu, Sergey Edunov, Danqi Chen, and Wen-tau Yih. 2020. Dense passage retrieval for open-domain question answering. In *Proceedings of the 2020 Conference on Empirical Methods in Natural Language Processing (EMNLP)*, pages 6769–6781, Online. Association for Computational Linguistics.

Jinhyuk Lee, Mujeen Sung, Jaewoo Kang, and Danqi Chen. 2021. Learning dense representations of phrases at scale. In *Proceedings of the 59th Annual Meeting of the Association for Computational Linguistics and the 11th International Joint Conference on Natural Language Processing (Volume 1: Long Papers)*, pages 6634–6647, Online. Association for Computational Linguistics.

Ilya Loshchilov and Frank Hutter. Decoupled weight decay regularization. In *International Conference on Learning Representations*.

Fabio Petroni, Aleksandra Piktus, Angela Fan, Patrick Lewis, Majid Yazdani, Nicola De Cao, James Thorne, Yacine Jernite, Vladimir Karpukhin, Jean Maillard, Vassilis Plachouras, Tim Rocktäschel, and Sebastian Riedel. 2021. KILT: a benchmark for knowledge intensive language tasks. In *Proceedings of the 2021 Conference of the North American Chapter of the Association for Computational Linguistics: Human Language Technologies*, pages 2523–2544, Online. Association for Computational Linguistics.

Nils Reimers and Iryna Gurevych. 2019. Sentence-BERT: Sentence embeddings using Siamese BERT-networks. In *Proceedings of the 2019 Conference on Empirical Methods in Natural Language Processing and the 9th International Joint Conference on Natural Language Processing (EMNLP-IJCNLP)*, pages 3982–3992, Hong Kong, China. Association for Computational Linguistics.

Yeon Seonwoo, Seunghyun Yoon, Franck Dernoncourt, Trung Bui, and Alice Oh. 2022. Virtual knowledge graph construction for zero-shot domain-specific document retrieval. In *Proceedings of the 29th International Conference on Computational Linguistics*, pages 1169–1178, Gyeongju, Republic of Korea. International Committee on Computational Linguistics.

Haitian Sun, Tania Bedrax-Weiss, and William Cohen. 2019. PullNet: Open domain question answering with iterative retrieval on knowledge bases and text. In *Proceedings of the 2019 Conference on Empirical Methods in Natural Language Processing and the 9th International Joint Conference on Natural Language Processing (EMNLP-IJCNLP)*, pages 2380–2390, Hong Kong, China. Association for Computational Linguistics.

Haitian Sun, Bhuwan Dhingra, Manzil Zaheer, Kathryn Mazaitis, Ruslan Salakhutdinov, and William Cohen. 2018. Open domain question answering using early fusion of knowledge bases and text. In *Proceedings of the 2018 Conference on Empirical Methods in Natural Language Processing*, pages 4231–4242, Brussels, Belgium. Association for Computational Linguistics.

Haitian Sun, Patrick Verga, Bhuwan Dhingra, Ruslan Salakhutdinov, and William W. Cohen. 2021. Reasoning over virtual knowledge bases with open predicate relations. In *Proceedings of the 38th International Conference on Machine Learning, ICML 2021, 18-24 July 2021, Virtual Event*, volume 139 of *Proceedings of Machine Learning Research*, pages 9966–9977. PMLR.

James Thorne, Majid Yazdani, Marzieh Saeidi, Fabrizio Silvestri, Sebastian Riedel, and Alon Halevy. 2021a. Database reasoning over text. In *Proceedings of the 59th Annual Meeting of the Association for Computational Linguistics and the 11th International Joint Conference on Natural Language Processing (Volume 1: Long Papers)*, pages 3091–3104, Online. Association for Computational Linguistics.

James Thorne, Majid Yazdani, Marzieh Saeidi, Fabrizio Silvestri, Sebastian Riedel, and Alon Halevy. 2021b. From natural language processing to neural databases. In *Proceedings of the VLDB Endowment*, volume 14, pages 1033–1039. VLDB Endowment.

Ashish Vaswani, Noam Shazeer, Niki Parmar, Jakob Uszkoreit, Llion Jones, Aidan N Gomez, Łukasz Kaiser, and Illia Polosukhin. 2017. Attention is all you need. *Advances in neural information processing systems*, 30.

Quan Wang, Zhendong Mao, Bin Wang, and Li Guo. 2017. Knowledge graph embedding: A survey of approaches and applications. *IEEE Transactions on Knowledge and Data Engineering*, 29(12):2724–2743.

Jason Weston, Antoine Bordes, Sumit Chopra, and Tomás Mikolov. 2016a. Towards ai-complete question answering: A set of prerequisite toy tasks. In *4th International Conference on Learning Representations, ICLR 2016, San Juan, Puerto Rico, May 2-4, 2016, Conference Track Proceedings*.

Jason Weston, Antoine Bordes, Sumit Chopra, and Tomás Mikolov. 2016b. Towards ai-complete question answering: A set of prerequisite toy tasks. In *4th International Conference on Learning Representations, ICLR 2016, San Juan, Puerto Rico, May 2-4, 2016, Conference Track Proceedings*.

Thomas Wolf, Lysandre Debut, Victor Sanh, Julien Chaumond, Clement Delangue, Anthony Moi, Pierric Cistac, Tim Rault, Rémi Louf, Morgan Funtowicz, Joe Davison, Sam Shleifer, Patrick von Platen, Clara Ma, Yacine Jernite, Julien Plu, Canwen Xu, Teven Le Scao, Sylvain Gugger, Mariama Drame, Quentin Lhoest, and Alexander M. Rush. 2020. Transformers: State-of-the-art natural language processing. In *Proceedings of the 2020 Conference on Empirical Methods in Natural Language Processing: System Demonstrations*, pages 38–45, Online. Association for Computational Linguistics.

Wenhan Xiong, Xiang Lorraine Li, Srini Iyer, Jingfei Du, Patrick S. H. Lewis, William Yang Wang, Yashar Mehdad, Scott Yih, Sebastian Riedel, Douwe Kiela, and Barlas Oguz. 2021. Answering complex open-domain questions with multi-hop dense retrieval. In *9th International Conference on Learning Representations, ICLR 2021, Virtual Event, Austria, May 3-7, 2021*. OpenReview.net.

Yuyu Zhang, Hanjun Dai, Zornitsa Kozareva, Alexander J. Smola, and Le Song. 2018. Variational reasoning for question answering with knowledge graph. In *Proceedings of the Thirty-Second AAAI Conference on Artificial Intelligence, (AAAI-18), the 30th innovative Applications of Artificial Intelligence (IAAI-18), and the 8th AAAI Symposium on Educational Advances in Artificial Intelligence (EAAI-18), New Orleans, Louisiana, USA, February 2-7, 2018*, pages 6069–6076. AAAI Press.

Victor Zhong, Caiming Xiong, and Richard Socher. 2017. Seq2sql: Generating structured queries from natural language using reinforcement learning. *CoRR*, abs/1709.00103.

A Hyperparameters

We use the AdamW optimizer (Loshchilov and Hutter) with a warmup ratio of 0.1 in all our experiments, and use four Quadro RTX A6000 48GB GPUs for model training. Table 6 represents our training hyper-parameters. The relation encoder and NeuralSPJ are based on the bert-large and T5 respectively. We trained our model based on the hugging face transformers(Wolf et al., 2020). For the hyperparameters for relation encoder and NeuralSPJ, we followed the original paper. For the VKGFR, we experiement with different learning rate (5e-4, 1e-4) and choosed the best performing one. For the layer number, we experimented with 1,2,4,8 and choosed the best-performing one.

B Model Parameter Size

Table 7 represents the number of parameters of baseline models.

C Dataset

The WikiNLDB Data is available on GitHub[2] and we used the pre-splited train, valid and test data. The MetaQA dataset can also be found on GitHub[3], and we followed a similar methodology as WikiNLDB when working with it.

[2]https://github.com/facebookresearch/NeuralDB

[3]https://github.com/yuyuz/MetaQA

Model	Hyperparmeter	Value
Relation Encoder	Learning rate	2e-5
	Number of epochs (fine-tuning)	2
	Number of epochs (pre-tuning)	3
	Batch size per device	24
	Relation vector size	1024
VKGFR	Learning rate	5e-4
	Hidden dimension of linear layer	4096 * 512
	Layer number of rnn	1
	Dropout rate	0.2
	Number of epochs	20
	Batch size for device	16396
NeuralSPJ (Reader)	Learning rate	1e-4
	Number of epochs	3
	Batch size for device	8

Table 6: Hyperparameters of pre-training and fine-tuning the relation encoder

Model	Number of parameters
TOME	53,057,920
MDPR	125,238,274
SSG	66,362,880
VKGFR (Ours)	6,297,088

Table 7: Represents the number of parameters of baseline models

Zero- and Few-Shots Knowledge Graph Triplet Extraction with Large Language Models

Andrea Papaluca[1], Daniel Krefl[2], Sergio J. Rodríguez Méndez[1], Artem Lensky[3,4], Hanna Suominen[1,5,6]

[1]School of Computing, The Australian National University, Canberra, ACT, Australia, [2]Independent,
[3]School of Engineering and Technology, The University of New South Wales, ACT, Australia,
[4]School of Biomedical Engineering, The University of Sydney, NSW, Australia,
[5]School of Medicine and Psychology, The Australian National University, Canberra, ACT, Australia,
[6]Department of Computing, University of Turku, Turku, Finland

Correspondence: andrea.papaluca@anu.edu.au

Abstract

In this work, we tested the Triplet Extraction (TE) capabilities of a variety of Large Language Models (LLMs) of different sizes in the Zero- and Few-Shots settings. In detail, we proposed a pipeline that dynamically gathers contextual information from a Knowledge Base (KB), both in the form of context triplets and of (sentence, triplets) pairs as examples, and provides it to the LLM through a prompt. The additional context allowed the LLMs to be competitive with all the older fully trained baselines based on the Bidirectional Long Short-Term Memory (BiLSTM) Network architecture. We further conducted a detailed analysis of the quality of the gathered KB context, finding it to be strongly correlated with the final TE performance of the model. In contrast, the size of the model appeared to only logarithmically improve the TE capabilities of the LLMs. We release the code on GitHub [1] for reproducibility.

1 Introduction

The task of Triplet Extraction (TE) (Nayak et al., 2021) is of fundamental importance for Natural Language Processing (NLP). This is because the core meaning of a sentence is usually carried by a set of $(subject, predicate, object)$ triplets. Therefore, the capability to identify such triplets is a key ingredient for being able to understand the sentence.

Currently, the State-Of-The-Art (SOTA) for TE is achieved by models that approach the TE task in an *end-to-end* fashion (Zheng et al., 2017; Zeng et al., 2018; Fu et al., 2019; Zeng et al., 2019; Tang et al., 2022). That is, they are trained to perform all the TE sub-tasks, namely, Named Entity Recognition (NER (Yadav and Bethard, 2018)), Entity Linking (EL (Alam et al., 2022)), and Relation Extraction (RE (Detroja et al., 2023)), together. These SOTA models follow the classic NLP paradigm, *i.e.*, they are trained by supervision on specific TE datasets. However, this dependence on labeled data restricts their generality and, therefore, limits the applicability of such models to the real world.

While several labeled datasets for the TE task are publicly available (Riedel et al., 2010; Gardent et al., 2017), these cover only part of the spectrum of possible entities and relations. This means that a supervised model trained on these public data will be restricted to the closed set of entities and relations seen during training, implying that it may lack generalization capabilities. Producing a tailored dataset for training a model for particular applications, is, however, in general expensive (Johnson et al., 2018).

For this reason, the recent language understanding and reasoning capabilities demonstrated by Large Language Models (LLMs), such as the Generative Pre-trained Transformer 4 (GPT-4) (OpenAI, 2023), LLM Meta AI (LLaMA) (Touvron et al., 2023), and Falcon (Penedo et al., 2023) to name a few, have led researchers (Chia et al., 2022; Kim et al., 2023; Wadhwa et al., 2023; Wei et al., 2023b; Zhu et al., 2023) to investigate whether they represent a viable option to overcome the limitations imposed by supervised models for TE. In detail, the new approach being that at inference time the LLMs are prompted to extract the triplets contained in a sentence, while being provided with only a few labeled examples (or no example at all in the Zero-Shot setting). This LLM approach largely limits the amount of data needed to perform the task, and, in particular, lifts the restriction of adhering to a predefined closed set of relations. However, the investigations so far indicated that the Zero and Few-Shots performance of the LLMs appears to be often underwhelming compared to the classic fully trained NLP models (Wadhwa et al., 2023; Wei et al., 2023b; Zhu et al., 2023).

In order to enhance the abilities of LLMs in the

[1]`https://github.com/BrunoLiegiBastonLiegi/KG-TE-with-LLMs`

Proceedings of the 1st Workshop on Knowledge Graphs and Large Language Models (KaLLM 2024), pages 12–23
August 15, 2024 ©2024 Association for Computational Linguistics

TE task, we propose in this work to aid them with the addition of a Knowledge Base (KB). We demonstrate that augmenting LLMs with KB information, *i.e.*, dynamically gathering contextual information from the KB, largely improves their TE capabilities, thereby making them more competitive with classic NLP baselines. In particular, we show that when the retrieved information is presented to the LLMs in the form of complete TE examples relevant to the input sentence, their performance gets closer to the fully trained SOTA models.

2 Related Work

Classical *end-to-end* fully supervised models currently hold the best performance in the TE task. Starting from the older baseline, Zheng et al. (2017), which also introduced the revised version of the WebNLG dataset for Natural Language Generation (NLG) that is commonly used, several other architectures based on the bidirectional Recurrent Neural Networks (RNNs) (Zeng et al., 2018; Fu et al., 2019; Zeng et al., 2019) have steadily improved the SOTA over the years. More recently, Transformer-based models achieved a big leap forward in performance, with the recent UniRel model being the current SOTA (Tang et al., 2022) in the datasets we consider. A further class of fully supervised models, such as Huguet Cabot and Navigli (2021) and Josifoski et al. (2022), treats the TE problem as a *sequence-to-sequence* generation task, which is more similar to the LLM approach adopted here, but still requires some training or finetuning.

With the advent of LLMs, Chia et al. (2022) and Kim et al. (2023) tested the use of such models for those TE cases where the availability of examples to train on is low. The first work proposed to use a LLM to generate training examples to finetune a *Relation Extractor* model to recognize relations for which labels were not available. The latter work, instead, suggested using relation templates of the form *⟨X⟩ relation ⟨Y⟩* and finetune a LLM to fill out *⟨X⟩* and *⟨Y⟩* with the entities appearing in the sentence. Wadhwa et al. (2023),Wei et al. (2023b), and Zhu et al. (2023) investigated the general TE task in both Zero- and Few-Shots settings. These studies proposed different approaches based on LLM prompting. The first work tested the Few-Shots performance of GPT-3 (Brown et al., 2020a) and Text-to-Text Transfer Transformer (T5) (Raffel et al., 2023) under the inclusion of manually-crafted and dataset-dependent contextual information in the prompt. The second work proposed to perform TE by sequentially prompting ChatGPT in two stages: asking to individuate the possible relation types first and then extracting the entities participating in each relation. The procedure demonstrated better results than a one-stage approach where the model is prompted to extract the triplet directly. Finally, the third work, evaluated GPT-3 (Brown et al., 2020b) and GPT-4 (OpenAI, 2023) on some standard benchmarks in the Zero- and One-Shot settings. However, classical fine-tuned models proved to be superior in the majority of the cases.

In our study, we similarly test the Zero- and Few-Shots capabilities of LLMs in two standard TE datasets that have not been covered by these previous works. In contrast to Wadhwa et al. (2023) that manually crafted static dataset-specific context to be fed to the LLM, we propose here to dynamically gather contextual information useful for extracting the triplets from a KB. This makes our approach more flexible and less data-dependent, as the KB does not require any manual operation and can be easily switched depending on the need. Also, in contrast to other works, we investigate a wide range of Language Models with varying sizes. This allows us to provide an in-depth analysis of the scaling of the performance, both, from the perspective of the model chosen, and the quality of the contextual KB information included in the prompt.

3 The Pipeline

In this section, we provide a detailed illustration of the pipeline used to test the TE capabilities of LLMs.

3.1 Task Formulation

Given a sentence composed of tokens $(t_1, t_2, \cdots, t_N)$, the TE task consists of identifying all the relations expressed in it and extracting them in the form of triplets (s, p, o). Here, $s = (t_i, \cdots, t_{i+n_s})$ and $o = (t_k, \cdots, t_{k+n_o})$ represent a subject and an object of length n_s and n_o tokens, and p is the predicate. Usually, the task is related to a specific KB, *i.e.*, a graph of the form $\mathcal{G} = (\mathcal{V}, \mathcal{E})$, composed of entities $e \in V$ as vertices and relations $r \in \mathcal{E}$ as directed edges. Therefore, s and o of the sentence correspond to vertices $e_s, e_o \in \mathcal{V}$. The predicate p is mapped to a relation included in the closed set of possible edge types of the KB.

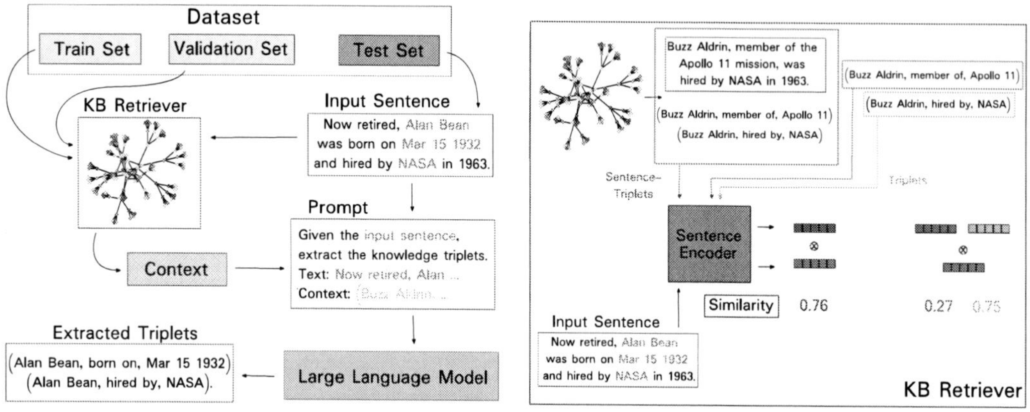

Figure 1: The TE pipeline. Left: illustration of the pipeline. A KB is constructed from the training and validation splits of a given dataset. For each test sentence, the relevant contextual information is retrieved from the KB and included in the prompt for a LLM-based TE. Right: summary of information retrieval from the KB. Either the sentence-triplets pairs or the single triplets alone are encoded by a sentence encoder and compared to the encoding of the input sentence by cosine similarity.

3.2 LLMs as Triplet Generators

In order to perform TE, we can prompt LLMs to generate, for a given input sentence, a sequence of tokens corresponding to the set of entity-relation triplets $\left\{(e_s^i, r_p^i, e_o^i)\right\}_{i=1}^{n}$. As demonstrated by Wadhwa et al. (2023), Wei et al. (2023b), and Zhu et al. (2023), LLMs are, in principle, able to extract the knowledge triplets contained in a text without a need for task-specific training, under a suitable choice of prompt. In general, successful LLM prompts follow a fixed schema that provides a detailed explanation of what the task consists of, a clear indication of the sentence to process, and some hints or examples for the desired result.

In this work, we tested the use of three different prompts: a simple baseline and two slight variations of it. However, preliminary testing in TE showed no significant difference in the F1 scores among them. Therefore, we opted for using only the base prompt reported in Figure 2 in the main experiments. The details of the prompts tested and their results can be found in Appendix A.3.

3.3 KB-aided Triplet Extraction

In order to support LLMs in the TE task, we propose the pipeline illustrated in Figure 1. The pipeline augments the LLM with external KB information. In detail, for each input sentence, relevant context information contained in the KB is retrieved and attached to the LLM prompt described above. The context-enriched prompt is then fed to the LLM for the knowledge triplet generation.

We prepare the information coming from the KB in two different forms: either as simple context triplets

$$T_c = \left\{(e_s^i, r_p^i, e_o^i)\right\}_{i=1}^{N_{KB}} \in \mathcal{G}\,, \tag{1}$$

or as sentence-triplets pairs

$$E_c = \left\{(S_c^i, T_c^i)\right\}_{i=1}^{N_{KB}}\,. \tag{2}$$

The latter provides factual examples of triplets to be extracted for specific sentences. Note that we indicate with N_{KB} the number of triplets, respectively,

Triplet Extraction Prompt

Some text is provided below. Extract up to {max_triplets} knowledge triplets in the form (subject, predicate, object) from the text.

Examples:

Text: Abilene, Texas is in the United States.
Triplets:
(abilene texas, country, united states)

Text: The United States includes the ethnic group of African Americans and is the birthplace of Abrahm A Ribicoff who is married to Casey Ribicoff.
Triplets:
(abrahm a. ribicoff, spouse, casey ribicoff)
(abrahm a. ribicoff, birth places, united states)
(united states, ethnic group, african americans)

Text: {text}
Triplets:

Figure 2: The base prompt we experimented with. At inference time the $\{text\}$ and $\{max\_triplets\}$ variables are substituted with the sentence to process, respectively, the maximum number of triplets found in a sentence in the corresponding dataset.

sentence-triplets pairs retrieved from the KB. In the first case, augmentation is achieved by simply attaching the retrieved triplets T_c as an additional "Context Triplets" argument to the base prompt reported in Figure 2. For the second approach, instead, we substitute the two static examples provided in the base prompt, with the input relevant examples E_c retrieved from the KB.

The relevant context information to build the T_c triplets set for each input sentence is retrieved as follows. Given the KB, we isolate all the triplets $(e_s^i, r_p^i, e_o^i) \in \mathcal{G}$ contained therein, and store them in a node based vector store index (Liu, 2022). In detail, each node of this index corresponds to one and only one of the triplets and stores the embedding obtained by running a small-scale sentence encoder, MiniLM (Wang et al., 2020), on the corresponding $(subject, predicate, object)$ string. In the first approximation, this should be enough to provide a meaningful embedding for each triplet. During inference (*i.e.*, TE), we first encode the input sentence using the MiniLM. This is followed by comparing the obtained sentence embedding with all the triplet embeddings contained in the index to retrieve the top N_{KB} most similar triplets to the input sentence. Out of this N_{KB}-dimensional sample, we further select the first two triplets for each relation type present in the sample. This is done to obtain a more diverse set of context triplets with a more homogeneous distribution over the relations. In some cases, indeed, the risk of obtaining a highly biased distribution towards a specific relation type exists, which is sub-optimal for those sentences that contain several different relationships.

Note that a similar procedure can be followed to prepare the E_c examples set. However, in this case, the focus will be shifted to the example sentences we wish to include. Namely, each node of the vector store index is going to consist both of the example sentence and the KB triplets to be extracted from it. Then, the embedding vector is obtained by running the sentence encoder on either, the example sentence alone, or the sentence and triplets combined. As before, at inference time the top N_{KB} most similar (sentence, triplets) pairs to the input sentence are retrieved and included in the prompt as Few-Shots examples.

4 Experiments

In this section, we first provide details about the datasets and models we tested. This is followed by the presentation of the main results for the TE task.

	Train	Validation	Test	Relations	Max	Avg
WebNLG	5,019	500	703	171	7	2.29
NYT	56,195	5,000	5,000	24	22	1.72

Table 1: Statistics of the WebNLG and NYT datasets. The number of training, validation, and testing sentences is reported, together with the number of relations types in the dataset and the maximum and average number of triplets contained in a sentence.

	Parameters [B]	Context
GPT-2 (Radford et al., 2019)	0.1 | 1.5	1,024
Falcon (Penedo et al., 2023)	7 | 40	2,048
LLaMA (Touvron et al., 2023)	13 | 65	2,048

Table 2: The number of parameters (in billions [B]) and context window size of the selected LLMs.

4.1 Datasets and Models

In order to test the TE capabilities of a selected set of LLMs (see Table 2 for their comparison), we experimented with two standard benchmarks for the TE task: the aforementioned WebNLG (Gardent et al., 2017) and the New York Times (NYT) (Riedel et al., 2010) dataset (see Table 1 for their basic statistics). The former was initially proposed as a benchmark for the NLG task, but has been successively adapted to the TE task and included in the WebNLG challenge (Castro Ferreira et al., 2020). As the revision provided by Zheng et al. (2017) appears to be the most widely used in the literature, we decided to run our tests on that particular version of WebNLG. The NYT benchmark is a dataset created by distant supervision, aligning more than 1.8 million articles from the NYT newspaper with the Freebase KB. For each dataset, we used the training and validation splits to build the corresponding KB following the procedure outlined in Section 3.3.

We selected the LLMs reported in Table 2 for testing. We ran locally all the models in their 8-bit quantized version provided by the HuggingFace (Wolf et al., 2020) library. We tested the use of OpenAI models through their provided API as well. However, as their results were often inconsistent and given the limited access and control we had over them, we decided to exclude these models from the main report. All the experiments regarding them can be found in Appendix A.1. The temperature was set to $\tau = 0.1$ for all the experiments. We experimented with higher temperatures but observed that they were detrimental to the TE

Model	WebNLG	NYT
NovelTagging (Zheng et al., 2017)	0.283	0.420
CopyRE (Zeng et al., 2018),	0.371	0.587
GraphRel (Fu et al., 2019)	0.429	0.619
OrderCopyRE (Zeng et al., 2019)	0.616	0.721
UniRel (Tang et al., 2022)	**0.947**	**0.937**

Table 3: Micro-averaged F1 of some finetuned models selected from the literature.

Model		WebNLG		NYT	
		0-Shot	2-Shots	0-Shot	2-Shots
GPT-2	base	0.000	0.006	0.000	0.000
	xl	0.000	0.037	0.000	0.000
Falcon	7b	0.000	0.066	0.000	0.002
	40b	0.021	0.158	0.000	0.007
LLaMA	13b	0.006	0.129	0.000	0.002
	65b	**0.041**	**0.219**	0.000	**0.017**

Table 4: Zero and 2-Shots micro-averaged F1 performance of the LLMs tested with the prompt of Figure 2 and without any context coming from the KB.

performance of the model. For Falcon and LLaMA LLMs, we also explored their *instructed* counterparts, *i.e.*, models that were fine-tuned for chat applications, either through Reinforcement Learning with Human Feedback (RLHF) (Christiano et al., 2023) or supervision from other LLMs (Taori et al., 2023). However, as the instructed models always performed on par, or worse, in our tests, we decided to present the base variants.

We made use of the LlamaIndex (Liu, 2022), LangChain (Chase, 2022) and HuggingFace transformers (Wolf et al., 2020) python libraries for the implementation of the pipeline.

4.2 Zero- and 2-Shots without the KB

As a baseline, we test the Zero- and 2-Shots capabilities of the LLMs without any additional information supplemented from a KB. As described in Section 3, we prompt the LLM with the base prompt of Figure 2 to extract all the triplets for a sentence in the form (subject, predicate, object). In particular, for the 2-Shots settings, two standard examples are included in the prompt but not changed over the different sentences (*c.f.* Figure 2).

In general, the LLMs queried by the base prompt do not seem capable of performing well in the TE task (Table 4). The two static examples included in the 2-Shots setting help to clarify the task and improve substantially the performance over the Zero-Shot. However, all models struggle to achieve the performance of the classical base-

Model		WebNLG		NYT	
		0.5-Shot	5-Shots	0.5-Shot	5-Shots
GPT-2	base	0.249	0.430	0.175	0.375
	xl	0.297	0.517	0.193	0.448
Falcon	7b	0.381	0.567	**0.250**	0.519
	40b	0.345	0.615	0.226	0.547
LLaMA	13b	0.374	0.609	0.247	0.582
	65b	0.377	**0.677**	0.243	**0.647**

Table 5: 0.5 and 5-Shots micro-averaged F1 performance of the LLMs tested with the prompt of Figure 2 augmented with $N_{KB} = 5$ triplets, respectively, sentence-triplets pairs retrieved from the KB.

line NLP models (Table 3). The sole exception is the LLaMA 65B model that achieves an F1 score close to the one obtained by Zheng et al. (2017) in the WebNLG dataset with 2-Shots. In particular, the NYT benchmark appears to be challenging for LLMs as they have difficulties even reaching a mere 1% F1 score. This discrepancy in performance between the datasets could potentially be explained as follows: In contrast to the WebNLG dataset, which features more linear and simple sentences, in NYT articles quite complex structures, with several subordinate clauses and implicit relations, are frequent. In particular, the triplet labels of the NYT dataset often cover only a subset of the actual relations found in the sentence. Therefore, without training examples available, LLMs cannot infer which relations are and are not supposed to be extracted.

4.3 Zero-shot with KB Triplets (0.5-Shots)

If we supplement the LLMs with context triplets retrieved from the KB, as described in Section 3.3 and illustrated in Figure 1, the performance of the LLM in the TE task increases substantially (see Table 5). We refer to this setting where only a set of context triplets, but no example sentence, is provided to the model as 0.5-Shots. The additional triplets hint at which relations and entities the LLM should expect, but they do not give any indication of which sentence pattern they could arise from.

In this case, the smallest model we tested, namely GPT-2 *base*, is competitive with the LLaMA 65B model without context triplets, both, for the WebNLG and the NYT dataset. Furthermore, the bigger models (Falcon, LLaMa) perform better or on par with some of the classical NLP baselines for the WebNLG dataset given in Table 3.

Even so for the NYT dataset a large improvement is obtained under the addition of context triplets, all the LLMs are not able to reach scores competitive with the classical NLP models. The reason behind this might be related to the lower capability of the KB retriever to gather relevant context for NYT (*c.f.* Figure 3) discussed below and to the specific difficulties associated with the NYT dataset discussed in the previous section.

In general, it is interesting to observe that performance with the addition of the context triplets appears to be less dependent on the particular LLM used in case of 0.5-Shot setting. Quite remarkably, the small GPT-2 *xl* is able to retain most of the performance of the larger models. This is particularly evident for the NYT dataset, where all the LLMs are not able to perform better than a 25% F1 threshold. This could be seen as a symptom of the TE accuracy being mainly driven by the added context triplets in this case. Indeed, we also tested this KB triplets augmentation combined with the inclusion of the two static examples used in Section 4.2, but no significant differences were observed.

4.4 Few Shots with KB Sentence-Triplets Pairs

To further aid LLMs in the TE task, we experiment with inclusion in the prompt of input-specific (sentence, triplets) example pairs retrieved from the KB, as detailed in Section 3.3. Such updated prompts should provide a much stronger signal to the LLM as they not only suggest which entities and relations the LLM should expect, but also which kind of patterns in the sentence correspond to a specific relation. In particular, as it will be discussed in Section 4.5, the measured train-test overlapping seems to be large for both datasets (*c.f.* Figure 3) and, therefore, the updated prompts are likely to include examples of similar sentences. Therefore, performance improvements are expected, and in fact, looking at Table 5, we see that including 5 of these examples in the prompt makes the LLM competitive with most of the classical baselines reported in Table 3 (except the most recent SOTA from Tang et al. (2022)).

Interestingly, the performance gap between the two datasets narrowed under the updated prompt. In particular, the NYT corpus seems to have become far easier now for the LLMs. As discussed in Section 4.2, this dataset consists of sentences with a much more complex structure and more implicit relations. Therefore, having available examples of similarly constructed sentences might have helped the models to more easily identify the correct triplets.

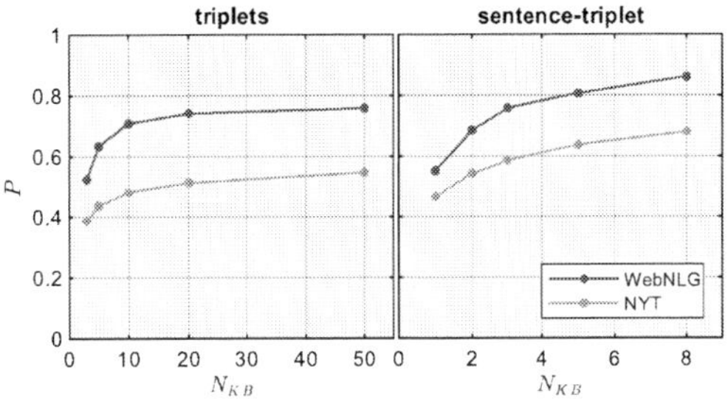

Figure 3: Probability that the correct triplet is present inside the retrieved KB context consisting of (left) triplets alone or (right) sentence-triplet example pairs, plotted against the amount of context gathered, N_{KB}.

4.5 Quality of the KB Context

To evaluate the effectiveness of the KB retriever and the quality of the included KB context, we plot in Figure 3 the probability of finding the correct triplets with increasing N_{KB}, *i.e.*, the solution to the TE task, inside the gathered KB context. Namely, for each test sentence contained in the two datasets, we looped over every labeled triplet and counted the number of times it was contained inside the context provided by the retriever. We repeated this procedure for different values of N_{KB}.

Figure 3(left) suggests that $N_{KB} \sim 10 - 20$ retrieved triplets almost maximize the probability of retrieving a useful context already, as, beyond that, the improvement is only marginal. However, as few as five triplets worked the best in our tests. Probably, a greater number of context triplets retrieved leads to a marginally increased likelihood of including relevant information, but at the cost of a larger dilution. Conversely, as illustrated by Figure 3(right), for the sentence-triplets augmentation convergence is not reached with $N_{KB} = 8$ yet. However, in our experiments, the final TE performance only marginally improved going from 5 to 8 sentence-triplets examples included. Still, it is interesting to note that LLM performance increases with N_{KB} in this case, providing further evidence that the examples composed of sentence-triplets pairs are much more informative. Adding several of them does not lead to a dilution of useful information, but rather contributes to widening the spectrum of examples the LLM can take "inspiration" from.

In general, the probability of providing the correct triplet to the LLM through the context appears

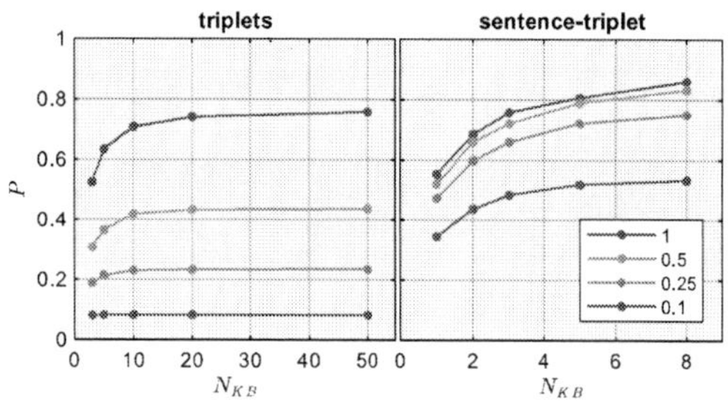

Figure 4: Probability that the correct triplet is present among the retrieved KB context for the WebNLG dataset, as in Figure 3, but with different scaled-down versions of the original KB.

to be large: greater than 50% in the majority of the cases, and even approaching the 70 $\sim$ 80% for the WebNLG dataset. This is symptomatic of substantial overlap that exists between the training, validation, and test splits for both datasets, to the point that even a stochastic model, that randomly sampled the triplets out of the KB context retrieved, was able achieve performance competitive with many of the LLMs and baselines of Table 3 in some cases (see Appendix A.2 for more details).

4.6 Ablation Study

To further investigate the impact of the additional knowledge retrieved from the KB, we revisit in this section the performance of one of our best performing LLMs, LLaMA-65b. In detail, we construct a scaled-down version of the KB via randomly sampling from the original training and validation splits, keeping only a fraction of the original sentences and triplets. For this reduced KB, the probability of having the correct triplet answer already within the retrieved information is reduced (*c.f.* Figure 4). This allows us to evaluate how the accuracy of the model is impacted by the quality of the retrieved data.

We decided to conduct this test on the WebNLG dataset. As $P(N_{KB})$ for the full-scale KB has been larger than for the NYT dataset, *c.f.* Figure 3, a wider range of values to be explored is allowed. Nonetheless, a preliminary test on the NYT dataset yielded similar results. In Figure 5a we report the variation of the final F1 score obtained by LLaMA-65b with prompts augmented by $N_{KB} = 5$ triplets and sentence-triplets pairs gathered from a KB of different scales $S = 0,\ 0.1,\ 0.25,\ 0.5,\ 1$. Here, the scale refers to the fraction of left-over data from the original KB. Note that $S = 0$ corresponds to the original prompt without any additional information from the KB. The F1 score is plotted against the probability $P_S(N_{KB} = 5)$ of having the correct triplet inside the retrieved data with $N_{KB} = 5$ for the different KB sizes. This corresponds to the probability curves of Figure 4 evaluated at $N_{KB} = 5$. We observe that the performance degrades as the probability $P_S(N_{KB})$ shrinks with decreasing S, as expected. In particular, the relation appears to be linear: $\text{F1}_{triplets} \sim 0.25 \cdot P_s(N_{KB} = 5) + 0.21$. $F1_{sentence-triplets} \sim 0.55 \cdot P_s(N_{KB} = 5) + 0.21$. with measured determination coefficients $r^2 = 0.98$ and $r^2 = 0.96$, respectively. This suggests that there is a strong correlation between the TE capabilities of the model and the quality of the retrieved data.

Furthermore, we investigated how the final TE performance scales with the size of the model. In Figure 5b, the F1 score is plotted against the number of parameters N_{par} in log scale for all the models we tested. The plot includes the results obtained for both the WebNLG and NYT datasets, for all settings considered. We observe that for each of the three settings, the models' performance grows linearly in log scale with respect to their sizes. The scaling in the number of parameters N_{par} in log scale can be approximated by

$$F1_{norm} \sim m \cdot \log N_{par}. \tag{3}$$

The slope parameters of the linear fit for WebNLG are $m = 0.0456, 0.0304$, and 0.0871 for, respectively, 2-Shot, 0.5-Shot(KB), 5-Shots(KB) settings, and for the NYT the corresponding parameters are $m = 0.0028, 0.0257$ and 0.0906. The determination coefficients for the WebLNG and NYT datasets are, respectively, $r^2 = 0.67$, 0.62, and 0.97, and $r^2 = 0.18$, 0.7 and 0.90. Interestingly, the F1 score increase with the size of the model is steeper for the few-shots prompt (*c.f.* Figure 5b right). This suggests that larger models might be more capable in making use of several examples included inside of the prompt.

Therefore, the $F1$ score and thus the TE accuracy appears to scale linearly with the size of the KB (*c.f.* Figure 5a), but only logarithmically with the size of the model (*c.f.* Figure 5b). This suggests that it could be better to invest resources to improve the quality of the KB and its associated information retriever, rather than in training larger models.

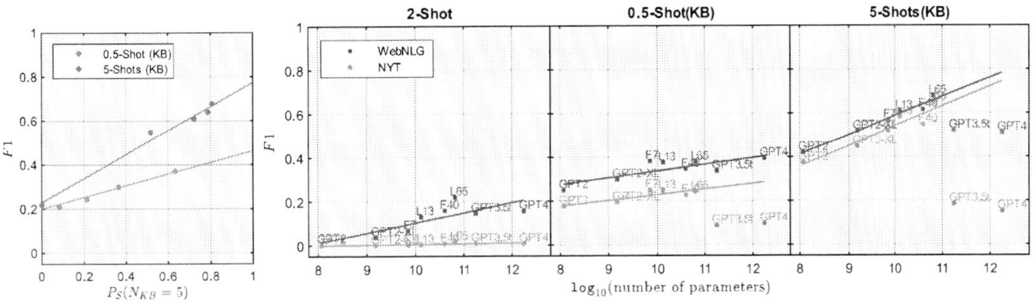

(a) KB scaling

(b) LLM scaling

Figure 5: (Left) Triplets (orange) and sentence-triplets (green) KB augmented performance of the LLaMA-65b model with different scaled-down versions of the KB built for the WebNLG, $S = 0, 0.1, 0.25, 0.5, 1$. The F1 score is plotted against the probability of retrieving the correct triplet with $N_{KB} = 5$ for each S (namely $P(N_{KB} = 5)$ for each curve of Figure 4). (Right) $F1$ score obtained by the tested models, plotted against their corresponding log of number of parameters, for WebNLG (blue) and NYT (orange) in the three settings: 2-shots, 0.5-shots with KB triplets ($N_{KB} = 5$), and 5-shots with KB sentence-triplets pairs ($N_{KB} = 5$). The outliers (GPT-4 and GPT-3.5 turbo) are shown in green.

5 Conclusion

In this work, a pipeline for Zero- and Few-Shots TE from sentences was presented and tested for various LLMs. We showed that the inclusion of KB information into the LLMs prompting can substantially improve the TE performance. In particular, small models were often able to outperform their bigger siblings without access to the additional KB information. Furthermore, with the information from the KB organized as sentence-triplets pair examples relevant to the input sentence, the accuracy of the LLMs improved further. In this setting, the larger LLMs were getting closer to the classical SOTA models and outperformed most of the older baselines. However, even for the largest models, TE remains a challenging task without any finetuning. LLMs were still no match for SOTA classical finetuned models in the two standard benchmark datasets we tested as part of our work, in agreement with Wadhwa et al. (2023); Wei et al. (2023b); Zhu et al. (2023).

Moreover, the performed investigation of the quality of the retrieved KB context showed that the solution to the TE task was often contained inside it already. This first indicated that a large overlapping between the train, validation and tests sets exists for both WebNLG and NYT, leading us to reconsider their generality for benchmarking TE capabilities and suggesting that a revision with better test isolation might be helpful. Secondly, it demonstrated that, while LLMs are capable of correctly individuating the relevant information in the context, they do not shine, yet, in re-elaborating such information, generalizing and making use of it for different examples. Indeed, the investigation of the impact of the quality of the retrieved KB context, showed as the performance of the LLaMA-65b model linearly decreased with the probability of finding the solution of the task within the context already, indicating that the intrinsic incompleteness of KBs might represent a big limiting factor of this approach. Concurrently, we found that the TE performance improved only approximately logarithmically with the size of the model. This suggests that improving the quality of the KB and the associated information retriever might be more effective than increasing the modeling power of the LLM for TE.

Acknowledgements

Andrea Papaluca was supported by an Australian Government Research Training Program International Scholarship. Artem Lensky was partially supported by the Commonwealth Department of Defence, Defence Science and Technology Group.

References

Mehwish Alam, Davide Buscaldi, Michael Cochez, Francesco Osborne, Diego Reforgiato Recupero, Harald Sack, Özge Sevgili, Artem Shelmanov, Mikhail Arkhipov, Alexander Panchenko, Chris Biemann, Mehwish Alam, Davide Buscaldi, Michael Cochez, Francesco Osborne, Diego Refogiato Recupero, and Harald Sack. 2022. Neural entity linking: A survey of models based on deep learning. *Semant. Web*, 13(3):527–570.

Tom B. Brown, Benjamin Mann, Nick Ryder, Melanie Subbiah, Jared Kaplan, Prafulla Dhariwal, Arvind Neelakantan, Pranav Shyam, Girish Sastry, Amanda Askell, Sandhini Agarwal, Ariel Herbert-Voss, Gretchen Krueger, Tom Henighan, Rewon Child, Aditya Ramesh, Daniel M. Ziegler, Jeffrey Wu, Clemens Winter, Christopher Hesse, Mark Chen, Eric Sigler, Mateusz Litwin, Scott Gray, Benjamin Chess, Jack Clark, Christopher Berner, Sam McCandlish, Alec Radford, Ilya Sutskever, and Dario Amodei. 2020a. Language models are few-shot learners. *Preprint*, arXiv:2005.14165.

Tom B. Brown, Benjamin Mann, Nick Ryder, Melanie Subbiah, Jared Kaplan, Prafulla Dhariwal, Arvind Neelakantan, Pranav Shyam, Girish Sastry, Amanda Askell, Sandhini Agarwal, Ariel Herbert-Voss, Gretchen Krueger, Tom Henighan, Rewon Child, Aditya Ramesh, Daniel M. Ziegler, Jeffrey Wu, Clemens Winter, Christopher Hesse, Mark Chen, Eric Sigler, Mateusz Litwin, Scott Gray, Benjamin Chess, Jack Clark, Christopher Berner, Sam McCandlish, Alec Radford, Ilya Sutskever, and Dario Amodei. 2020b. Language models are few-shot learners. *Preprint*, arXiv:2005.14165.

Thiago Castro Ferreira, Claire Gardent, Nikolai Ilinykh, Chris van der Lee, Simon Mille, Diego Moussallem, and Anastasia Shimorina. 2020. The 2020 bilingual, bi-directional WebNLG+ shared task: Overview and evaluation results (WebNLG+ 2020). In *Proceedings of the 3rd International Workshop on Natural Language Generation from the Semantic Web (WebNLG+)*, pages 55–76, Dublin, Ireland (Virtual). Association for Computational Linguistics.

Harrison Chase. 2022. Langchain.

Yew Ken Chia, Lidong Bing, Soujanya Poria, and Luo Si. 2022. RelationPrompt: Leveraging prompts to generate synthetic data for zero-shot relation triplet extraction. In *Findings of the Association for Computational Linguistics: ACL 2022*, pages 45–57, Dublin, Ireland. Association for Computational Linguistics.

Paul Christiano, Jan Leike, Tom B. Brown, Miljan Martic, Shane Legg, and Dario Amodei. 2023. Deep reinforcement learning from human preferences. *Preprint*, arXiv:1706.03741.

Kartik Detroja, C.K. Bhensdadia, and Brijesh S. Bhatt. 2023. A survey on relation extraction. *Intelligent Systems with Applications*, 19:200244.

Tsu-Jui Fu, Peng-Hsuan Li, and Wei-Yun Ma. 2019. GraphRel: Modeling text as relational graphs for joint entity and relation extraction. In *Proceedings of the 57th Annual Meeting of the Association for Computational Linguistics*, pages 1409–1418, Florence, Italy. Association for Computational Linguistics.

Claire Gardent, Anastasia Shimorina, Shashi Narayan, and Laura Perez-Beltrachini. 2017. Creating training corpora for NLG micro-planners. In *Proceedings of the 55th Annual Meeting of the Association for Computational Linguistics (Volume 1: Long Papers)*, pages 179–188, Vancouver, Canada. Association for Computational Linguistics.

Pere-Lluís Huguet Cabot and Roberto Navigli. 2021. REBEL: Relation extraction by end-to-end language generation. In *Findings of the Association for Computational Linguistics: EMNLP 2021*, pages 2370–2381, Punta Cana, Dominican Republic. Association for Computational Linguistics.

Mark Johnson, Peter Anderson, Mark Dras, and Mark Steedman. 2018. Predicting accuracy on large datasets from smaller pilot data. In *Proceedings of the 56th Annual Meeting of the Association for Computational Linguistics (Volume 2: Short Papers)*, pages 450–455, Melbourne, Australia. Association for Computational Linguistics.

Martin Josifoski, Nicola De Cao, Maxime Peyrard, Fabio Petroni, and Robert West. 2022. GenIE: Generative information extraction. In *Proceedings of the 2022 Conference of the North American Chapter of the Association for Computational Linguistics: Human Language Technologies*, pages 4626–4643, Seattle, United States. Association for Computational Linguistics.

Bosung Kim, Hayate Iso, Nikita Bhutani, Estevam Hruschka, Ndapa Nakashole, and Tom Mitchell. 2023. Zero-shot triplet extraction by template infilling. *Preprint*, arXiv:2212.10708.

Jerry Liu. 2022. LlamaIndex.

Tapas Nayak, Navonil Majumder, Pawan Goyal, and Soujanya Poria. 2021. Deep neural approaches to relation triplets extraction: a comprehensive survey. *Cognitive Computation*, 13(5):1215–1232.

OpenAI. 2023. Gpt-4 technical report. *Preprint*, arXiv:2303.08774.

Guilherme Penedo, Quentin Malartic, Daniel Hesslow, Ruxandra Cojocaru, Alessandro Cappelli, Hamza Alobeidli, Baptiste Pannier, Ebtesam Almazrouei, and Julien Launay. 2023. The refinedweb dataset for falcon llm: Outperforming curated corpora with web data, and web data only. *Preprint*, arXiv:2306.01116.

Alec Radford, Jeff Wu, Rewon Child, David Luan, Dario Amodei, and Ilya Sutskever. 2019. Language models are unsupervised multitask learners.

Colin Raffel, Noam Shazeer, Adam Roberts, Katherine Lee, Sharan Narang, Michael Matena, Yanqi Zhou, Wei Li, and Peter J. Liu. 2023. Exploring the limits of transfer learning with a unified text-to-text transformer. *Preprint*, arXiv:1910.10683.

Sebastian Riedel, Limin Yao, and Andrew McCallum. 2010. Modeling relations and their mentions without labeled text. In *Machine Learning and Knowledge Discovery in Databases*, pages 148–163, Berlin, Heidelberg. Springer Berlin Heidelberg.

Wei Tang, Benfeng Xu, Yuyue Zhao, Zhendong Mao, Yifeng Liu, Yong Liao, and Haiyong Xie. 2022. UniRel: Unified representation and interaction for joint relational triple extraction. In *Proceedings of the 2022 Conference on Empirical Methods in Natural Language Processing*, pages 7087–7099, Abu Dhabi, United Arab Emirates. Association for Computational Linguistics.

Rohan Taori, Ishaan Gulrajani, Tianyi Zhang, Yann Dubois, Xuechen Li, Carlos Guestrin, Percy Liang, and Tatsunori B. Hashimoto. 2023. Stanford alpaca: An instruction-following llama model. `https://github.com/tatsu-lab/stanford_alpaca`.

Hugo Touvron, Thibaut Lavril, Gautier Izacard, Xavier Martinet, Marie-Anne Lachaux, Timothée Lacroix, Baptiste Rozière, Naman Goyal, Eric Hambro, Faisal Azhar, Aurelien Rodriguez, Armand Joulin, Edouard Grave, and Guillaume Lample. 2023. Llama: Open and efficient foundation language models. *Preprint*, arXiv:2302.13971.

Somin Wadhwa, Silvio Amir, and Byron C. Wallace. 2023. Revisiting relation extraction in the era of large language models. *Proceedings of the conference. Association for Computational Linguistics. Meeting*, 2023:15566–15589.

Wenhui Wang, Furu Wei, Li Dong, Hangbo Bao, Nan Yang, and Ming Zhou. 2020. Minilm: Deep self-attention distillation for task-agnostic compression of pre-trained transformers. *Preprint*, arXiv:2002.10957.

Jason Wei, Xuezhi Wang, Dale Schuurmans, Maarten Bosma, Brian Ichter, Fei Xia, Ed Chi, Quoc Le, and Denny Zhou. 2023a. Chain-of-thought prompting elicits reasoning in large language models. *Preprint*, arXiv:2201.11903.

Xiang Wei, Xingyu Cui, Ning Cheng, Xiaobin Wang, Xin Zhang, Shen Huang, Pengjun Xie, Jinan Xu, Yufeng Chen, Meishan Zhang, Yong Jiang, and Wenjuan Han. 2023b. Zero-shot information extraction via chatting with chatgpt. *Preprint*, arXiv:2302.10205.

Thomas Wolf, Lysandre Debut, Victor Sanh, Julien Chaumond, Clement Delangue, Anthony Moi, Pierric Cistac, Tim Rault, Rémi Louf, Morgan Funtowicz, Joe Davison, Sam Shleifer, Patrick von Platen, Clara Ma, Yacine Jernite, Julien Plu, Canwen Xu, Teven Le Scao, Sylvain Gugger, Mariama Drame, Quentin Lhoest, and Alexander M. Rush. 2020. Transformers: State-of-the-art natural language processing. In *Proceedings of the 2020 Conference on Empirical Methods in Natural Language Processing: System Demonstrations*, pages 38–45, Online. Association for Computational Linguistics.

Vikas Yadav and Steven Bethard. 2018. A survey on recent advances in named entity recognition from deep learning models. In *Proceedings of the 27th International Conference on Computational Linguistics*, pages 2145–2158, Santa Fe, New Mexico, USA. Association for Computational Linguistics.

Xiangrong Zeng, Shizhu He, Daojian Zeng, Kang Liu, Shengping Liu, and Jun Zhao. 2019. Learning the extraction order of multiple relational facts in a sentence with reinforcement learning. In *Proceedings of the 2019 Conference on Empirical Methods in Natural Language Processing and the 9th International Joint Conference on Natural Language Processing (EMNLP-IJCNLP)*, pages 367–377, Hong Kong, China. Association for Computational Linguistics.

Xiangrong Zeng, Daojian Zeng, Shizhu He, Kang Liu, and Jun Zhao. 2018. Extracting relational facts by an end-to-end neural model with copy mechanism. In *Proceedings of the 56th Annual Meeting of the Association for Computational Linguistics (Volume 1: Long Papers)*, pages 506–514, Melbourne, Australia. Association for Computational Linguistics.

Suncong Zheng, Feng Wang, Hongyun Bao, Yuexing Hao, Peng Zhou, and Bo Xu. 2017. Joint extraction of entities and relations based on a novel tagging scheme. In *Proceedings of the 55th Annual Meeting of the Association for Computational Linguistics (Volume 1: Long Papers)*, pages 1227–1236, Vancouver, Canada. Association for Computational Linguistics.

Yuqi Zhu, Xiaohan Wang, Jing Chen, Shuofei Qiao, Yixin Ou, Yunzhi Yao, Shumin Deng, Huajun Chen, and Ningyu Zhang. 2023. Llms for knowledge graph construction and reasoning: Recent capabilities and future opportunities. *Preprint*, arXiv:2305.13168.

A Appendix

A.1 OpenAI Models results

We report here the results obtained by the OpenAI models listed in Table 6. We ran them remotely through the OpenAI API and always setting a temperature $T = 0.1$. We were not able to find any information regarding the parameter precision they used. Note that the GPT-3.5 and GPT-4 are instructed models. For some experiments we also tested the use of *text-davinci-002*, which is a non-instructed model based on GPT-3 and, apparently, the only base variant OpenAI provides through their API.

	Parameters [B]	Context
text-davinci-002 (Brown et al., 2020b)	175*	2,048
GPT-3.5 (Brown et al., 2020b)	175*	4,096
GPT-4 (OpenAI, 2023)	1,760*	8,192

Table 6: The number of parameters (in billions [B]) and context window size of the OpenAI LLMs. We indicate by * the numbers that are not officially confirmed.

Tables 7 and 8 report the results obtained by the OpenAI models on the WebNLG and NYT datasets in all the different settings. The comparison with the other models, *c.f.* Tables 4 and 5, shows them to be comparable to the Falcon 40B model in the majority of the cases. However, they recorded very underwhelming results on the NYT dataset both, in the 0.5-Shots and Few-Shots settings. Our manual inspection of the triplets they provided as an answer suggested that they were less keen to adhere to the entities and relations appearing in the provided KB context, often paraphrasing or reformulating them in a more prolix form that lowered the accuracy. This might be a consequence of the instructed training they had gone through, as discussed in Section 4.1. In contrast, the results provided by the non-instructed *text-davinci-002* model were more in line with all the other LLMs.

A.2 Random Model

In order to better understand the results obtained by the KB-augmented LLMs, we considered the following simple random TE model: first, we randomly select the number of triplets $n \in [1, max\_triplets]$ to extract, with $max\_triplets$ indicating the maximum number of triplets contained in a sentence of the dataset. Then, we uniformly sample n triplets out of the retrieved KB context. Surprisingly, the random model is very competitive with the KB-augmented LLM for small N_{KB} on the WebNLG dataset (see Figure 6), and similar results were observed for the NYT dataset. This can be explained by the hand of Figure 3. In detail, we infer from the figure that the KB-augmented prompt has a large probability of containing the correct triplets to extract already, therefore, even randomly selecting a subset of them yields a relatively high accuracy. This provides further confirmation that the TE performance is largely driven by the KB retriever.

However, the performance of the random model decreases polynomially with N_{KB}, as the probability of randomly sampling the correct triplets

Model		WebNLG		NYT	
		0-Shot	2-Shots	0-Shot	2-Shots
OpenAI	GPT-3.5	0.000	0.144	0.000	**0.008**
	GPT-4	**0.007**	**0.156**	0.000	0.007

Table 7: Zero and 2-Shots micro-averaged F1 performance of the LLMs tested with the prompt of Figure 2 and without any context coming from the KB.

Model		WebNLG		NYT	
		0.5-Shot	5-Shots	0.5-Shot	5-Shots
OpenAI	*text-davinci-002*	**0.403**	0.491	**0.144**	**0.418**
	GPT-3.5	0.336	**0.520**	0.088	0.184
	GPT-4	0.394	0.510	0.096	0.151

Table 8: 0.5 and 5-Shots micro-averaged F1 performance of the OpenAI LLMs tested with the prompt of Figure 2 augmented with $N_{KB} = 5$ triplets, respectively, sentence-triplets pairs retrieved from the KB.

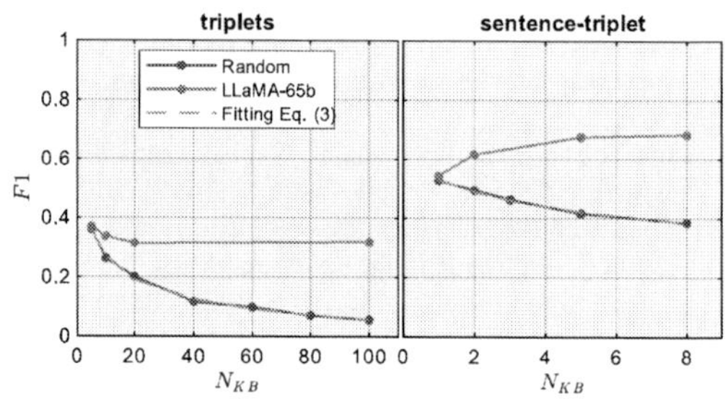

Figure 6: Degradation of the random model performance with the increase of the context information included, N_{KB}. The LLaMA-65b, instead, is able to retain most of its performance when more triplets are added (left panel), and sees a significant F1 rise with an increasing number of sentence-triplets pairs (right panel). For reference, we also report the fit of (4) as a dashed orange line.

follows the empirical scaling relation

$$F1_{rand}(N_{KB}) \sim \left(\frac{P(N_{KB})}{N_{KB}}\right)^n, \quad (4)$$

with n number of triplets to extract and $P(N_{KB})$ probability of retrieving the correct triplet from the KB (Figure 3).

In contrast, the LLM is able to retain much of its original performance for a larger number of triplets provided (*c.f.* Figure 6(left)) or even improve under the inclusion of more sentence-triplets examples (*c.f.* Figure 6(right)).

A.3 Prompts

Here we report all the TE prompts that we tested. Figures 7 and 8 report two variations of the base prompt of Figure 2. The first one implements a Chain-of-Thought (Wei et al., 2023a) approach where multi-step reasoning is enforced. The second tries to provide the LLM with more information about the task, describing in more detail the role of each one of the core components of TE. In Table 9 the three prompts of Figures 2, 7, and 8 are compared for the WebNLG and NYT datasets

Chain-of-Thought Prompt

```
Some text is provided below. Procede step by step:
- Identify a predicate expressed in the text
- Identify the subject of that predicate
- Identify the object of that predicate
- Extract the corresponding (subject, predicate, object)
  knowledge triplet
- Repeat until all predicates contained in the text have been extracted,
  but no more than {max_triplets} times
-----------------------------------------------------------------
Text: {text}
Triplets:
```

Figure 7: Prompt implementing the Chain-of-Thoughts approach (Wei et al., 2023a).

Documented Prompt

```
Some text is provided below. The text might contain one or more
predicates expressing a relation between a subject and an object.
The subject is the entity that takes or undergo the action expressed by
the predicate.
The object is the entity which is the factual object of the action.
The information provided by each predicate can be summarized as a
knowledge triplet of the form (subject, predicate, object).
Extract all the information contained in the text in the form of
knowledge triplets. Extract no more than {max_triplets} knowledge
triplets.
-----------------------------------------------------------------
Text: {text}
Triplets:
```

Figure 8: Prompt providing more details about the core components of the TE task, namely, including definitions of subject, object, predicate, and triplet.

under the use of two different LLMs, GPT-2 *xl*, and LLaMA 65B. The three prompts yield similar micro-averaged F1 scores, with small deviations.

Figure 9 reports the prompt that we used in the 0.5-Shots setting. The prompt consists of a simple adaptation of the base prompt of Figure 2 to accommodate for the additional triplets retrieved from the KB.

	Prompt	WebNLG	NYT
GPT-2 xl	*base*	0.037	0.0002
	documented	0.034	0.0003
	chain-of-thought	0.039	0.0004
		0.002	0.0001
LLaMA-65b	*base*	0.219	0.017
	documented	0.213	0.012
	chain-of-thought	0.219	0.015
		0.003	0.002

Table 9: Comparison of the 2-Shots TE micro-averaged F1 performance with the three different prompts of Figures 2, 7, and 8. The standard deviation of the performance across the three prompts is reported below each column.

0.5-Shots Prompt

```
Some text and some context triplets in the form
(subject, predicate, object) are provided below.
Firstly, select the context triplets that are relevant to the input text.
Then, extract up to {max_triplets} knowledge triplets in the form
(subject, predicate, object) contained in the text taking inspiration
from the context triplets selected.
-----------------------------------------------------------------
Text: {text}
Context Triplets:
{context_triplets}
Triplets:
```

Figure 9: Adaptation of the base prompt found in Figure 2 to the 0.5-Shots setting. An additional $\{context\_triplets\}$ argument is included to accommodate for the KB triplets retrieved from the KB.

Analysis of LLM's "Spurious" Correct Answers Using Evidence Information of Multi-hop QA Datasets

Ai Ishii[1], Naoya Inoue[2,1], Hisami Suzuki[1], Satoshi Sekine[1]
[1]RIKEN AIP, Tokyo, Japan,
[2]Japan Advanced Institute of Science and Technology, Ishikawa, Japan
ai.ishii@riken.jp, naoya-i@jaist.ac.jp, hisami.suzuki@a.riken.jp, satoshi.sekine@riken.jp

Abstract

Recent LLMs show an impressive accuracy on one of the hallmark tasks of language understanding, namely Question Answering (QA). However, it is not clear if the correct answers provided by LLMs are actually grounded on the correct knowledge related to the question. In this paper, we use multi-hop QA datasets to evaluate the accuracy of the knowledge LLMs use to answer questions, and show that as much as 31% of the correct answers by the LLMs are in fact spurious, i.e., the knowledge LLMs used to ground the answer is wrong while the answer is correct. We present an analysis of these spurious correct answers by GPT-4 using three datasets in two languages, while suggesting future pathways to correct the grounding information using existing external knowledge bases.

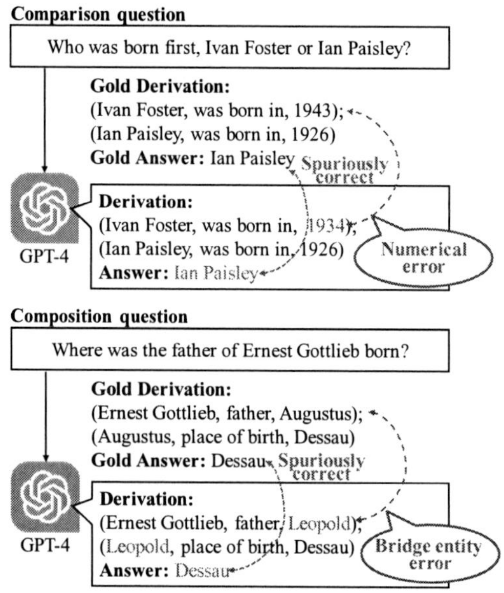

Figure 1: Examples of spurious correct answers. Red text indicates where the model (GPT-4) makes mistakes, blue text indicates where the model's answer is correct. See Appendix A for other types of errors.

1 Introduction

Question Answering (QA) is one of the hallmark tasks that evaluate language understanding capabilities of NLP systems. We are currently witnessing the flourishment of highly capable large language models (LLMs) that solve this complex task, requiring both knowledge and inference skills, with an impressive accuracy (Bang et al., 2023). On the other hand, it has been shown that LLMs can generate content that contradicts facts (Bang et al., 2023; Ji et al., 2023), and several verification results have been reported regarding the evaluation of LLMs' internal knowledge and whether LLMs can provide answers based on facts (Wang et al., 2023; Manakul et al., 2023; Lin et al., 2022; Zheng et al., 2023; Pezeshkpour, 2023).

At this point, it is not clear exactly to what extent such LLMs possess the knowledge needed to solve QA problems and how accurately they perform inference to leverage that knowledge. How often do LLMs rely on "hallucinated" knowledge during inference? Can these hallucinations be remedied by structured knowledge bases (KBs) carefully crafted by humans? Previous studies have reported that correct answers are often obtained despite errors in the reasoning path that LLMs output to solve QA (Bao et al., 2024; Sprague et al., 2024; Nguyen et al., 2024; Ishii et al., 2024). Ishii et al. (2024) shows the specific error patterns by question type in such cases and the possibility of complementing errors with KBs using JEMHopQA dataset[1], which has evidence information in the form of triples, but their analysis is limited to one dataset in Japanese.

In this paper, we focus on investigating how such "spurious" correct answers by LLMs occur more deeply in other datasets and languages. We use three datasets from two languages – HotPotQA (Yang et al., 2018) with $\mathcal{R}^4\mathcal{C}$ (Inoue et al.,

[1]https://github.com/aiishii/JEMHopQA

Proceedings of the 1st Workshop on Knowledge Graphs and Large Language Models (KaLLM 2024), pages 24–34
August 15, 2024

	HotPot	2Wiki	JEMHop
#Avg. question	16.50	11.87	30.71
#Avg. answer	3.42	2.30	4.32
#Avg. derivations	2.50 (3.00)	2.37 (2.42)	2.04 (2.07)

Table 1: Question and answer lengths and number of derivation triples of each dataset. The #Avg. question and #Avg. answer in HotPot and 2Wiki are the average number of tokens, that in JEMHop is the average number of characters, and the number in parentheses in #Avg. derivations is the average number of derivations in each original dataset.

Question type	HotPot	2Wiki	JEMHop
Comparison	19%	27%	61%
Composition	80%	55%	39%
Bridge-comparison	1%	18%	0%

Table 2: Distribution of question types.

2020) and 2WikiMultiHopQA (Ho et al., 2020) for English, and JEMHopQA for Japanese. These three datasets present the task of outputting the knowledge (derivation) that serves as the evidence for the answer in the form of derivation triples (as in Fig. 1), so they can be used directly to measure the spuriousness of correct answers in QA. In addition, we investigate the extent to which gold derivation triples in each dataset are covered by existing KBs, suggesting that hallucinatory knowledge can be corrected by combining LLMs with such KBs.

2 Analysis Method

2.1 Datasets

In this analysis, we use questions, answers, and supporting evidence from widely used HotPotQA, 2WikiMultiHopQA, and JEMHopQA, which are Wikipedia-based multi-hop QA datasets. We use $\mathcal{R}^4\mathcal{C}$ for derivation triples of HotPotQA, and randomly extract 100 instances from the development set as **HotPot**. We randomly extract 100 instances from the 2WikiMultiHopQA development set as **2Wiki** and use all 120 instances from the JEMHopQA development set as **JEMHop**. Table 1 summarizes the details of these datasets, where the average number of derivation triples are roughly the same across them.

In these datasets, questions comprise of three different types[2]: (i) Comparison questions, where the two derivation triples have the same relation, as in at the top of Fig. 1; (ii) Composition questions, where two derivation triples share a "bridge" entity, as in the example at the bottom of Fig. 1 where "Augustus" serves as the bridge; (iii) Bridge-comparison, which combines a composition with a comparison, where a comparison is made after finding the bridge entity, e.g., "Which film has the director who is older, Aardram or Land and Freedom?". The distribution of these three types of questions is shown in Table 2.

As Ishii et al. (2024) reports that comparison questions (numerical comparisons in particular) are more susceptible to spurious correct answers, we created additional datasets that include the samples of such questions in our study. The number of numerical comparison questions differs considerably across our dataset (HotPot: 4%, 2Wiki: 17%, JEMHop: 28%), so we created focused datasets consisting only of numerical comparisons by taking 30 samples from the development set of the datasets, resulting in **HotPot_NC**, **2Wiki_NC**, and **JEMHop_NC**. We also extracted 30 multi-hop QA instances that compare numerical values from DROP (Dua et al., 2019), a widely used QA dataset that requires mathematical operations, and use them as the analysis set **DROP_NC**.

The supporting evidence in each dataset is in the form of triples representing a semi-structured relationship (e.g., "date of birth") between a subject entity ("Ivan Foster") and an object entity ("1943"), as shown in Fig. 1. The questions are those that require multi-hop reasoning, and each question-answer pair is accompanied by two or more derivation steps. The task of evaluating LLMs using each dataset is, given a question Q, (i) to predict the answer A, and (ii) to generate a derivation D that justifies A.

2.2 Evaluation Metrics

Answers For HotPot and 2Wiki, we use exact match (EM) and partial match, F_1 score measuring the average overlap between gold and predicted answers. For JEMHop, we use similarity match (SM) score based on the Levenshtein distance.

Derivations To account for differences in the structure of the triples and to measure semantic matches, the authors manually evaluated derivation triplets. Even if predicted derivation has a different surface form from the gold derivation, it is consid-

[2]Although 2WikiMultiHopQA has an "Inference" type, we consider it a subtype of composition in this paper.

	Answer EM / F_1 or SM (%)		
	HotPot	**2Wiki**	**JEMHop**
Zero-shot	38.7/45.3	23.7/28.8	51.7/52.5
5-shot	39.7/49.9	34.3/39.8	56.1/57.8
CoT 5-shot	**41.5/50.9**	**48.3/56.4**	**62.8/64.5**
Comparison	71.1/78.9	86.4/86.4	81.3/81.3
Composition	35.0/44.9	22.4/36.4	34.0/38.3
Brg-comparison	0.0/0.0	70.4/72.2	-/-

Table 3: Results of GPT-4 with different prompts.

ered correct if the information contained is correct, in the form of a triple, and sufficient to answer the question.

Note that each dataset provides evaluation scripts for both answers and derivation triples, but we use these scripts to evaluate answers only and rely on human evaluation for derivation triples.

2.3 Evaluation Setup Using GPT-4

We use `gpt-4-0613` model via OpenAI API with the prompt for the Chain-of-Thought (CoT) (Wei et al., 2022) 5-shot setting as a method of eliciting the derivation triples that the model uses to infer. More specifically, the CoT 5-shot prompt consists of an instruction to provide a CoT reasoning path, along with 5 few-shot samples. To ensure that the setting of the CoT 5-shot prompt to output the inference path at the same time as the answer does not affect the accuracy of the answer, we also use zero-shot (ask a question only) and non-CoT 5-shot (include 5 random samples from the training set) prompts (see examples in Appendix B).

Based on the results of preliminary experiments, we use temperature parameters of 0.1, 0.2, and 0.0 for HotPot, 2Wiki, and JEMHop, respectively. The maximum token limit is set to 32 for the zero-shot and 5-shot prompts, and to 256 for the CoT prompt. Due to the sampling-based decoding of GPT-4 API, we run each experiment three times and report the average of all runs.

3 Results and Discussion

3.1 How well can GPT-4 answer multi-hop questions correctly?

In Table 3, the first three rows show the results for the answers in the zero-shot, 5-shot, and CoT 5-shot settings for each dataset. In all datasets, the 5-shot setting performed better than the zero-shot setting, and the CoT 5-shot setting achieved the highest accuracy. These results confirm that the CoT 5-shot prompt setting, which outputs the derivation triples simultaneously with the answer, does not affect the accuracy of the answers.

The last two rows show that composition questions are significantly harder to answer correctly than comparison questions in all datasets. A major factor for this large difference is suspected to be that in comparison questions, the two subject entities are explicitly mentioned in the question and the answers tend to be binary (choosing one of the two entities), while in composition question, a bridge entity is implicit and must be identified, and the answers for these questions tend not to be binary (an entity as an answer). Bridge-comparison questions fell in the middle as this tasks for a binary answer while needing to identify a bridge entity.

3.2 When do spurious correct answers occur?

Table 4. shows the performance of GPT-4, where we present the results in a matrix along both answer correctness and derivation triple correctness. Cases where the derivation triples were considered correct even though they differed from the gold derivation triples in this evaluation are described in detail in Appendix C. We found that only 0-1% cases had an error in inference (Answer is F and Derivation is T); the remaining cases had errors in derivation (i.e., hallucination). As shown in the table, spurious correct answers (Answer is T and Derivation is F) comprise 18% of all cases (which is 31% of the correctly answered cases) in 2Wiki and 15.8% (which is 25% of the correctly answered cases) in JEMHopQA, showing that they occur also quite frequently in English. More than 90% of these spurious correct answers occur in comparison questions and bridge-comparison; they occur less frequently in HotPot because there are fewer comparison questions.

The question type that generated spurious correct answers most frequently (38% on 2Wiki and 68% on JEMHop) was questions comparing numerical values or dates (see detail in Appendix A). Therefore, we also manually classified the correctness of the derived triples and answers for the numerical comparison questions, adding the evaluation of HotPot_NC, 2Wiki_NC, JEMHop_NC and DROP_NC (see in §2.1) in the CoT 5-shot setting[4].

[3]Note that this classification table does not include the formatting errors that occurred in two cases in JEMHop and one case in HotPot_NC as derivation triple errors, so the total does not add up to 100%.

[4]As DROP lacks evidence information, few-shot examples

		Derivation Triples					
		HotPot		2Wiki		JEMHop	
		T	F	T	F	T	F
Answer	T	50.0%	**8.0%**	39.0%	**18.0%**	47.5%	**15.8%**
	F	1.0%	41.0%	0.0%	43.0%	0.8%	34.1%

Table 4: Classification of right (T) and wrong (F) of answers and derived triples[3].

		Derivation Triples							
		HotPot_NC		2Wiki_NC		JEMHop_NC		DROP_NC	
		T	F	T	F	T	F	T	F
Answer	T	73.3%	**16.7%**	40.0%	**46.7%**	50.0%	**36.7%**	46.7%	**36.7%**
	F	0.0%	6.7%	0.0%	13.3%	0.0%	13.3%	0.0%	16.7%

Table 5: Classification of right (T) and wrong (F) of answers and derived triples of numerical comparison questions[3].

The results are in Table 5.

In this table, we find that as much as 36-46% of the answers were spuriously correct in 3 of the 4 datasets – with the exception of HotPot_NC, where the rate of spurious correct answers remained lower at 16.7%. While it was not obvious to us why HotPot_NC behaved differently, we could see why spurious correctness happens often in numerical comparison: they occur when the relative order of numbers or dates are not affected even when there is an error in derivation triples. This is also observed when we analyzed the results of bridge comparison questions in 2Wiki – out of 14 correct answers of this type, 10 were in fact spurious in the same manner as the numerical comparison questions: there was an error in the identification of bridge entity (identifying a wrong person), but the relative order of the dates required for the answer was unaffected. In order for the answers to be spuriously correct in this way, the error margin for the numbers/dates in the grounding knowledge must be small enough so as not to impact the relative order. Exactly how "wrong" or "close" GPT-4 is when it comes to the numerical aspect of the grounding information deserves further investigation; we leave this for future work.

3.3 Can External KBs Remedy Spurious Correct Answers?

GPT-4 "hallucinated" wrong derivation triples in 50-60% in each dataset as a whole. We investigated whether this knowledge hallucination can be fixed by using external KBs.

For this, we used two existing KBs on Wikipedia, namely Wikidata (Vrandečić and Krötzsch, 2014) and Shinra[5] (Sekine et al., 2019). The latter extracts attribute-value pairs from Japanese Wikipedia articles and structures them according to the ENE (Sekine, 2008) categories in Sekine et al. (2020); this is used for JEMHopQA only as it is in Japanese. Also, in 2Wiki, all hallucinated derivation triples can be found by Wikidata as the questions of 2Wiki-MultihopQA derive from the knowledge triples in Wikidata. Therefore, we studied the extent to which gold derivation triples in each dataset are covered by external KBs for HotPot and JEMHop only. Knowledge representation in these KBs is compatible with the derivation triples used in our task, allowing for a straightforward application.

In Table 6, the first three columns show the coverage of derivation triples of each dataset for GPT-4, Wikidata, and GPT-4 combined with Wikidata. We assume that the derivation triples generated by GPT-4 in answering the questions are GPT-4's internal knowledge and estimate GPT-4's coverage by calculating how well GPT-4's internal knowledge covers the gold derivation triples in each dataset. As a multi-hop question requires two or more triples to answer, a partial coverage statistic is also given. We see that GPT-4 provides complete evidence for 51% and 48% of HotPot and JEMHop questions respectively, but if combined with Wikidata, it can cover up to 59% and 63% respectively. The last three columns show the coverage of derivation triples of Shinra, GPT-4 combined Shinra and GPT-4 combined with both KBs. GPT-4 and both KBs seem to complement each other well: GPT-4 combined with both KBs achieves 81.7% of coverage, up by

of CoT-5shot are created using the same data as 2Wiki.

[5]http://shinra-project.info/

Dataset	Coverage	GPT-4	Wikidata (W)	GPT-4+W	Shinra (S)	GPT-4+S	GPT-4+W+S
HotPot ($\mathcal{R}^4\mathcal{C}$)	Full	51.0%	31.0%	59.0%	-	-	-
	Partial	17.0%	51.0%	41.0%	-	-	-
	None	32.0%	18.0%	0.0%	-	-	-
JEMHop	Full	48.3%	29.2%	63.3%	50.0%	78.3%	81.7%
	Partial	23.3%	28.3%	26.7%	29.2%	15.0%	13.3%
	None	28.3%	42.5%	10.0%	20.8%	7.5%	5.0%

Table 6: Coverage of derivation steps in the test set by existing KBs and GPT-4.

31% as compared with GPT-4 alone (48.3%). This indicates that a further improvement in multi-hop QA task is possible by combining LLM with existing KBs, a fruitful direction for future research.

4 Conclusions

In this paper, we presented the evaluation of GPT-4 on multi-hop QA in three datasets in English and Japanese, focusing on how the answers are/are not grounded on the knowledge internal to the model. The results show that almost all of the incorrect answers are due to knowledge hallucination, and that even when the answer is correct, up to 31% of them (40% in numerical comparison questions) are in fact spurious. We also showed that the knowledge GPT-4 uses for grounding is complementary with external KBs, indicating a future direction of integrating them for solving multi-hop questions. Our analysis is based on the assumption that the derivation triples generated by the LLM are reasoning of the LLM, but we hope to clarify whether this assumption is correct in the future.

Acknowledgements

This work was supported by JSPS KAKENHI Grant Number JP20269633 and 19K20332. The authors would like to thank the anonymous reviewers for their insightful feedback.

References

Yejin Bang, Samuel Cahyawijaya, Nayeon Lee, Wenliang Dai, Dan Su, Bryan Wilie, Holy Lovenia, Ziwei Ji, Tiezheng Yu, Willy Chung, Quyet V. Do, Yan Xu, and Pascale Fung. 2023. A multitask, multilingual, multimodal evaluation of ChatGPT on reasoning, hallucination, and interactivity. In *Proceedings of the 13th International Joint Conference on Natural Language Processing and the 3rd Conference of the Asia-Pacific Chapter of the Association for Computational Linguistics (Volume 1: Long Papers)*, pages 675–718, Nusa Dua, Bali. Association for Computational Linguistics.

Guangsheng Bao, Hongbo Zhang, Linyi Yang, Cunxiang Wang, and Yue Zhang. 2024. Llms with chain-of-thought are non-causal reasoners. *Preprint*, arXiv:2402.16048.

Dheeru Dua, Yizhong Wang, Pradeep Dasigi, Gabriel Stanovsky, Sameer Singh, and Matt Gardner. 2019. DROP: A reading comprehension benchmark requiring discrete reasoning over paragraphs. In *Proceedings of the 2019 Conference of the North American Chapter of the Association for Computational Linguistics: Human Language Technologies, Volume 1 (Long and Short Papers)*, pages 2368–2378, Minneapolis, Minnesota. Association for Computational Linguistics.

Xanh Ho, Anh-Khoa Duong Nguyen, Saku Sugawara, and Akiko Aizawa. 2020. Constructing a multi-hop QA dataset for comprehensive evaluation of reasoning steps. In *Proceedings of the 28th International Conference on Computational Linguistics*, pages 6609–6625, Barcelona, Spain (Online). International Committee on Computational Linguistics.

Naoya Inoue, Pontus Stenetorp, and Kentaro Inui. 2020. R4C: A benchmark for evaluating RC systems to get the right answer for the right reason. In *Proceedings of the 58th Annual Meeting of the Association for Computational Linguistics*, pages 6740–6750, Online. Association for Computational Linguistics.

Ai Ishii, Naoya Inoue, Hisami Suzuki, and Satoshi Sekine. 2024. JEMHopQA: Dataset for Japanese explainable multi-hop question answering. In *Proceedings of the 2024 Joint International Conference on Computational Linguistics, Language Resources and Evaluation (LREC-COLING 2024)*, pages 9515–9525, Torino, Italia. ELRA and ICCL.

Ziwei Ji, Nayeon Lee, Rita Frieske, Tiezheng Yu, Dan Su, Yan Xu, Etsuko Ishii, Ye Jin Bang, Andrea Madotto, and Pascale Fung. 2023. Survey of hallucination in natural language generation. *ACM Comput. Surv.*, 55(12).

Stephanie Lin, Jacob Hilton, and Owain Evans. 2022. TruthfulQA: Measuring how models mimic human falsehoods. In *Proceedings of the 60th Annual Meeting of the Association for Computational Linguistics (Volume 1: Long Papers)*, pages 3214–3252, Dublin, Ireland. Association for Computational Linguistics.

Potsawee Manakul, Adian Liusie, and Mark Gales. 2023. SelfCheckGPT: Zero-resource black-box hallucination detection for generative large language models. In *Proceedings of the 2023 Conference on Empirical Methods in Natural Language Processing*, pages 9004–9017, Singapore. Association for Computational Linguistics.

Minh-Vuong Nguyen, Linhao Luo, Fatemeh Shiri, Dinh Phung, Yuan-Fang Li, Thuy-Trang Vu, and Gholamreza Haffari. 2024. Direct evaluation of chain-of-thought in multi-hop reasoning with knowledge graphs. *Preprint*, arXiv:2402.11199.

Pouya Pezeshkpour. 2023. Measuring and modifying factual knowledge in large language models. *arXiv preprint arXiv:2306.06264*.

Satoshi Sekine. 2008. Extended named entity ontology with attribute information. In *Proceedings of the Sixth International Conference on Language Resources and Evaluation (LREC'08)*, Marrakech, Morocco. European Language Resources Association (ELRA).

Satoshi Sekine, Maya Ando, Akio Kobayashi, and Aska Sumida. 2020. Updated Extended Named Entity Definitions and Japanese Wikipedia Classification Data 2019. In *Proceedings of the 26th Conference on Natural Language Processing in Japan (NLP 2020)*.

Satoshi Sekine, Akio Kobayashi, and Kouta Nakayama. 2019. Shinra: Structuring wikipedia by collaborative contribution. In *Conference on Automated Knowledge Base Construction*.

Zayne Rea Sprague, Xi Ye, Kaj Bostrom, Swarat Chaudhuri, and Greg Durrett. 2024. MuSR: Testing the limits of chain-of-thought with multistep soft reasoning. In *The Twelfth International Conference on Learning Representations*.

Denny Vrandečić and Markus Krötzsch. 2014. Wikidata: A free collaborative knowledgebase. *Commun. ACM*, 57(10):78–85.

Cunxiang Wang, Sirui Cheng, Zhikun Xu, Bowen Ding, Yidong Wang, and Yue Zhang. 2023. Evaluating open question answering evaluation. *CoRR*, abs/2305.12421.

Jason Wei, Xuezhi Wang, Dale Schuurmans, Maarten Bosma, Fei Xia, Ed Chi, Quoc V Le, Denny Zhou, et al. 2022. Chain-of-thought prompting elicits reasoning in large language models. *Advances in Neural Information Processing Systems*, 35:24824–24837.

Zhilin Yang, Peng Qi, Saizheng Zhang, Yoshua Bengio, William Cohen, Ruslan Salakhutdinov, and Christopher D. Manning. 2018. HotpotQA: A dataset for diverse, explainable multi-hop question answering. In *Proceedings of the 2018 Conference on Empirical Methods in Natural Language Processing*, pages 2369–2380, Brussels, Belgium. Association for Computational Linguistics.

Shen Zheng, Jie Huang, and Kevin Chen-Chuan Chang. 2023. Why does chatgpt fall short in answering questions faithfully? *arXiv preprint arXiv:2304.10513*.

A Detailed Types of Spurious Correct Answers

Table 7 shows the percentage of spurious correct answers by question type in each dataset. They mainly appeared in comparison and bridge-comparison questions, with numerical comparison being the most frequent (38% in 2Wiki comparison , 50% in 2Wiki bridge-comparison, 68% in JEMHop).

Spurious correct answers of comparison questions. Table 8 shows examples of spurious correct answers in comparison questions. In "numerical comparison", the relative order of dates (e.g., "1212" vs "1248") or values (e.g., "1.5" vs "2.0") in GPT-4's derivations matched the gold, despite incorrect date or values. In "shared predicate", the answer condition (e.g., whether authors are the same in both entities) was unaffected, despite different authors ("Meka Tanaka" vs "Oreko Tachibana") in GPT-4's and gold derivations.

Spurious correct answers of composition questions. Table 9 shows examples where the answer was correct despite incorrect bridge entities. In one case, different princes were from the same family and birthplace. In others, the bridge entity was unspecified or non-existent, suggesting the model knew the answer in advance. For example, GPT-4 correctly answered "World War II" for when a facility was established, despite using a non-existent bridge entity.

Spurious correct answers of brige-comparison questions. Table 10 shows examples in "numerical comparison" and "shared predicate" types. The answer was unaffected despite wrong bridge entities, as the relative order of dates (e.g., "1936" vs "1956") or conditions like directors' countries remained unchanged.

B Example of Prompts for GPT-4

The following are examples of the three types of prompts we used in our experiments:

	HotPot	2Wiki	JEMHop
Comparison			
Numerical comparison	16.7%	38.9%	68.4%
Entity selection	16.7%	0.0%	10.5%
Shared predicate	0.0%	0.0%	15.8%
Composition			
Entity or value answer	66.7%	5.6%	5.3%
Bridge-comparison			
Numerical comparison	0.0%	50.0%	-
Shared predicate	0.0%	5.6%	-

Table 7: Types of spurious correct answers by question type. Each percentage is the number of spurious correct answer cases in HoPot (6 cases), 2Wiki (18 cases) and JEMHop (19 cases).

1. **Zero-shot**: ask a question only, as in:

   > Output your answers to the following questions.
   > Answers should be brief noun phrases or "yes/no" answers.:
   > Which film came out first, 3 Dots or Dying God? =>

2. **5-shot**: include 5 random samples from the training set as few-shot examples, as in:

   > Output your answers to the following questions, referring to the examples.
   > Answers should be brief noun phrases or "yes/no" answers.:
   > When was the director of film Antarjali Jatra born? => 24 July 1950
   > Who died later, Bob Dispirito or John Wilton? => Bob Dispirito
   > (...3 more examples)
   > Which film came out first, 3 Dots or Dying God? =>

3. **Chain-of-Thought (CoT) 5-shot**: add an instruction to provide a CoT reasoning path, along with 5 few-shot samples.

   > Output your answers and rationale to the following questions in the form of examples.
   > Answers should be brief noun phrases or "yes/no" answers.:
   > When was the director of film Antarjali Jatra born? => (Antarjali Jatra, director, Goutam Ghose);(Goutam Ghose, date of birth, 24 July 1950) => 24 July 1950
   > Who died later, Bob Dispirito or John Wilton? => (Bob DiSpirito, date of death, December 21, 2015);(John Wilton, date of death, 10 May 1981) => Bob Dispirito
   > (...3 more examples)
   > Which film came out first, 3 Dots or Dying God? =>

C Detailed Manual Evaluation of Derivations

In the manual evaluation of the derivations output by GPT-4, even if the derivations did not exactly match the gold derivations, they were considered correct if they were in the form of triples and provided sufficient information to derive the answer from the question. The specific cases considered correct are as follows:

i Differences in wording (tense, synonymous verbs or nouns, presence or absence of modifiers).

ii Differences in granularity of information (geographic, temporal, etc. units).

iii Differences in type of information.

iv Differences in the amount of information contained in a triple (cases where multiple triples of information in the gold are combined into one in the pred (GPT-4 output) and vice versa).

v Differences in how triples are formed (the subject and object of the triple are opposite, or part of the object of the gold triple is included in the relation of the pred triple, etc.).

Examples for each pattern are shown in Table 11.

Question Type	Example
Numerical comparison	**Question:** Which occured first, the Battle of Las Navas de Tolosa or king Fernando III gave a new fuero to the city? **Gold derivation:** ("Battle of Las Navas de Tolosa", "start time", "July 16, 1212"); ("Giving of new fuero by Fernando III", "start time", "1219") **Gold answer:** Battle of Las Navas de Tolosa **GPT-4's derivation:** ("Battle of Las Navas de Tolosa", "start time", "July 16, 1212"); ("Giving of new fuero by Fernando III", "start time", "1248") **GPT-4's answer:** Battle of Las Navas de Tolosa
Numerical comparison	**Question:** Which start has a higher absolute magnitude, A-type star or B9-type star? **Gold derivation:** ("A-type star", "absolute magnitude", "0.2") ; ("B9-type star", "absolute magnitude", "0.4") **Gold answer:** B9-type **GPT-4's derivation:** ("A-type star", "absolute magnitude", "1.5") ; ("B9-type star", "absolute magnitude", "2.0") **GPT-4's answer:** B9-type star
Shared predicate	**Question:** Are Ai Yazawa the author of both "A" and "Promise Cinderella"? **Gold derivation:** ("A", "author", "Ai Yazawa") ; ("Promise Cinderella", "author", "Oreko Tachibana") **Gold answer:** No **GPT-4's derivation:** ("A", "author", "Ai Yazawa") ; ("Promise Cinderella", "author", "Meka Tanaka") **GPT-4's answer:** No

Table 8: Examples of spurious correct answers in comparison questions. Red text indicates where there was an error in the derivation, blue text indicates that the answer is correct.

Error type	Example
Bridge entity is wrong	**Question:** Where was the father of Ernest Gottlieb, Prince Of Anhalt-Plötzkau born? **Gold derivation:** ("Ernest Gottlieb, Prince of Anhalt-Plötzkau", "father", "Augustus, Prince of Anhalt-Plötzkau"); ("Augustus, Prince of Anhalt-Plötzkau", "place of birth", "Dessau") **Gold answer:** Dessau **GPT-4's derivation:** ("Ernest Gottlieb, Prince of Anhalt-Plötzkau", "father", "Leopold, Duke of Anhalt-Dessau"); ("Leopold, Duke of Anhalt-Dessau", "place of birth", "Dessau") **GPT-4's answer:** Dessau
Bridge entity is not identified	**Question:** A 1946 musical comedy starred a British actor who lived in what country throughout his adult life? **Gold derivation:** ("Two Sisters from Boston", "is", "a 1946 musical comedy film"); ("Two Sisters from Boston", "stars", "Peter Lawford"); ("Peter Lawford", "is", "a British actor"); ("Peter Lawford", "lived throughout adult life in", "the United States") **Gold answer:** United States **GPT-4's derivation:** ("A 1946 musical comedy", "starred", "a British actor"); ("The British actor", "lived in, "the United States throughout his adult life") **GPT-4's answer:** The United States
Bridge entity is fictitious	**Question:** The facility where Hideki Tojo died and died was established after what war? **Gold derivation:** ("Hideki Tojo", "Place of death", "Sugamo Prison"); ("Sugamo Prison", "War that led to its establishment", "World War II") **Gold answer:** World War II **GPT-4's derivation:** ("Hideki Tojo","facility where he died and died", "Suginami Ward Hirozawa Hospital"); ("Suginami Ward Hirozawa Hospital","when established","post-World War II") **GPT-4's answer:** World War II

Table 9: Examples of spurious correct answers in composition questions. Red text indicates where there was an error in the derivation, blue text indicates that the answer is correct.

<table>
<tr><th>Question Type</th><th>Example</th></tr>
<tr><td>Numerical comparison</td><td>Question:
Which film has the director who is older, Aardram or Land And Freedom?

Gold derivation:
("Aardram", "director", "Suresh Unnithan");
("Suresh Unnithan", "date of birth", "30 July 1956");
("Land and Freedom", "director", "Ken Loach");
("Ken Loach", "date of birth", "17 June 1936")
Gold answer:
Land And Freedom

GPT-4's derivation:
("Aardram", "director", "Sibi Malayil") ;
("Sibi Malayil", "date of birth", "2 May 1956") ;
("Land And Freedom", "director", "Ken Loach") ;
("Ken Loach", "date of birth", "17 June 1936")
GPT-4's answer:
Land And Freedom</td></tr>
<tr><td>Shared predicate</td><td>Question:
Are the directors of films Penelope (1966 Film) and Sioux Blood both from the same country?

Gold derivation:
("Penelope (1966 film") ,"director", "Arthur Hiller") ;
("Arthur Hiller", "country of citizenship", "Canadian") ;
("Sioux Blood", "director", "John Waters") ;
("John Waters (director born 1893") ,"country of citizenship", "American")
Gold answer:
No

GPT-4's derivation:
("Penelope", "director", "Arthur Hiller") ;
("Arthur Hiller", "country of birth", "Canada") ;
("Sioux Blood", "director", "John Ford") ;
("John Ford", "country of birth", "United States")
GPT-4's answer:
No</td></tr>
</table>

Table 10: Examples of spurious correct answers in bridge-comparison questions. Red text indicates where there was an error in the derivation, blue text indicates that the answer is correct.

Pattern	Derivation examples: gold	Derivation examples: pred
(i) wording	(Kingdom of the Isles, covered a total land area of, over 8300 km2) (Michaël Llodra, gained victory over, Juan Martín del Potro)	(The Isles, covers, a total land area of over 8300 km2) (Michaël Llodra, defeated, Juan Martín del Potro)
(ii) granularity	(Great Neck School District, is in, the town of North Hempstead, Nassau County, New York, United States) (Disney Magazine, is published quarterly from, December 1965 to April 2005) (Dirk Nowitzki, was born, June 19, 1978)	(Great Neck School District, is located in, Great Neck, New York); (Disney Magazine, ceased publication in,2005) (Dirk Nowitzki, was born in, 1978)
(iii) type	(Shinjo-city, city tree, Cherry tree) (Avengers: Infinity War, previous film, Avengers: Age of Ultron)	(Shinjo-city, city tree, exist) (Avengers: Infinity War, position of the work, third film in the Avengers series)
(iv) information per one triple	(Modest Mouse, was formed in, Issaquah); (Issaquah, is in, Washington) (Finish What Ya Started, features Sammy Hagar, on a rhythm guitar)	(Modest Mouse, formed in, Issaquah, Washington) ("Finish What Ya Started", is a song from, OU812); (OU812, features, Sammy Hagar); (Sammy Hagar,plays,guitar)
(v) form	(Lantern Waste, is the place where, Lucy Pevensie and Mr. Tumnus meet) (The Spiderwick Chronicles (film), follows the adventures on a family as they discover, magical creatures)	(Lucy Pevensie and Mr. Tumnus, meet at, Lantern Waste) (The Spiderwick Chronicles, is about, a New England family who discover magical creatures around their estate)

Table 11: Examples of derivatives that were considered correct.

Application of Generative AI as an Enterprise Wikibase Knowledge Graph Q&A System

René de Ávila Mendes and **Dimas Jackson de Oliveira** and **Victor Hugo Fiuza Garcia**
Mackenzie Presbyterian Institute
GERTI - Department of Technology and Innovation
Rua da Consolação, 930 - São Paulo - SP - Brazil
rene.mendes@mackenzie.br dimas.oliveira@terceiros.mackenzie.br victor.garcia@mackenzie.br

Abstract

Generative AI and Large Language Models are increasingly used in business contexts. One application involves natural language conversations contextualized by company data, which can be accomplished by Enterprise Knowledge Graphs, standardized representations of data. This paper outlines an architecture for implementation of an Enterprise Knowledge Graph using open-source Wikibase software. Additionally, it is presented a Knowledge Graph Q&A System powered by Generative AI.

1 Introduction

Knowledge Graphs (KG) are semantic networks that represent information in a graph structure, with entities as nodes and relationships as edges (Heist et al., 2020), built from diverse data to integrate and organize knowledge (Paulheim, 2016). They can be applied in areas such as the labor market (Popping, 2003), education methods (cao, 2023), and medicine (Vidal Rolim et al., 2021), and are valued in Artificial Intelligence (AI) for their clarity and flexibility (Shen et al., 2022). An example is the combination of KG with AI technologies, such as Microsoft's Azure OpenAI, which further enhances their potential by facilitating the integration and analysis of large volumes of data more efficiently and accurately (Sarica et al., 2020).

In this context, the use of Wikibase to create KG offers significant advantages. Wikibase allows the integration of heterogeneous data, flexible data schema modeling, and collaborative knowledge curation, enabling the construction of comprehensive and up-to-date graphs for applications such as recommendation, analysis, and research (Sarica et al., 2020). In Brazil, KG have driven advancements in areas such as smart cities and healthcare (Vidal Rolim et al., 2021; bel, 2023). Despite the challenges, research is exploring their potential, such as the Brazilian Legislation and Brazilian History KG (de Paiva and Rademaker, 2024; Navas-Loro et al., 2022).

Large Language Models (LLMs) are reshaping the way humans interact with machines, specially through Generative AI applications. Known for their immense scale and intricate architecture, LLMs have transformed the field of natural language processing. These models undergo rigorous stages, including data gathering, preprocessing, model selection, training, and fine-tuning, all aimed at achieving peak performance (Linkon et al., 2024). Presently, experts are exploring the Gen AI capacity to redefine a company's valuation and improving its cost structure, which can fully impact several business in the future (Scappaticci, 2023). Although the progress in these models is promising, they do come with limitations. Large language models struggle to expand or modify their memory, lack transparency in their predictions, and may even generate "hallucinations." However, models that blend training data with company data (retrieval-based) can mitigate some of these challenges (Lewis et al., 2020a). This technique is called Retrieval-Augmented Generation (RAG) and allows expansion of knowledge, as well as inspection and interpretation of accessed information (Lewis et al., 2020b).

Mackenzie Presbyterian Institute (IPM) maintains one of the oldest institutions of education in Brazil, founded in 1870. Its structure encompasses a University, with campuses in 6 Brazilian cities and with about 37,000 students enrolled, a School with about 9,000 students enrolled, and two Hospitals, which together provide more than 2.3 million health care encounters and procedures in 2022 (Mackenzie Presbyterian Institute, 2022).

In a corporate context such as IPM, data integration was being addressed with the use of datawarehouses and datalakes, trying to offer a 360-degree view of the customer and allow the board to have an integrated view of the company. However, the

Proceedings of the 1st Workshop on Knowledge Graphs and Large Language Models (KaLLM 2024), pages 35–42
August 15, 2024

growing understanding of student interactions, patients and the various services offered by IPM seems to be naturally represented by a graph and well documented through business glossaries and ontologies, suggesting that Knowledge Graphs can offer a more complete and integrated experience of IPM data (Martin et al., 2021; Blumauer and Nagy, 2020).

The possibility of integrating Large Language Models (LLM) with Knowledge Graphs (KG) opened a new horizon for offering data to IPM end users: the possibility of asking questions about the integrated data and being answered in natural language. But how complex would it be to implement this solution for IPM? And what would be the results of the interaction of an LLM with IPM data? These are some of the questions we need to answer.

In this article we will detail a RAG Q&A system that accesses data from an Enterprise Knowledge Graph based on Wikibase, created to integrate company data. For the experiments, the graph was loaded with synthetically generated students and patients data, thus preserving the identity and privacy of both patients and students.

This article is structured as follows: Section 2 depicts the entire solution of the Knowledge Graph, including its ontologies, its data, and its architecture; Section 3 discuss the tests and results obtained when adopting LLM to build the Q&A system; Section 4 concludes the article and presents contributions, limitations, and future improvement opportunities.

2 Knowledge Graph

The KG that is being built for our company can be defined as an Enterprise Knowledge Graph (EKG), as it is restricted to corporate use and is applied to commercial use cases. The objectives for building a KG in our context include: gain insights into students' relationships with courses, teachers, subjects and content, as well as patients' relationships with treatments, medications and medical procedures; integrate data from different sources; build the foundation of what will become a semantic data catalog, and build the foundation that supports data analysis.

An important concern for our company was to provision an EKG that could demonstrate its data integration potential in the shortest possible time and in a performant manner, or, as in the words of Blumauer and Nagy (2020), *"deliver the right data in the right format in a timely and high-performance manner"*. In this sense, Wikibase proved to be more advantageous compared to classic RDF KG solutions, as it offers out-of-the-box services (Diefenbach et al., 2021). In just a few days of work, we had a fully operational sandbox environment provisioned on Docker containers, including a SPARQL endpoint, a full-text search solution for concepts and attributes, and a graphical interface for SPARQL queries. The fact that Wikibase is a solution for Open Knowledge Graphs (OKG) is still a concern for us because Wikidata does not allow restricting data access according to user groups and, in a corporate environment, users should only access data relating to their activities. At least intuitively this concern can be addressed by using extensions (Kapica, 2023) or even developing one.

In the next sections we will discuss the KG components, including the ontologies, data and technologies adopted in its construction.

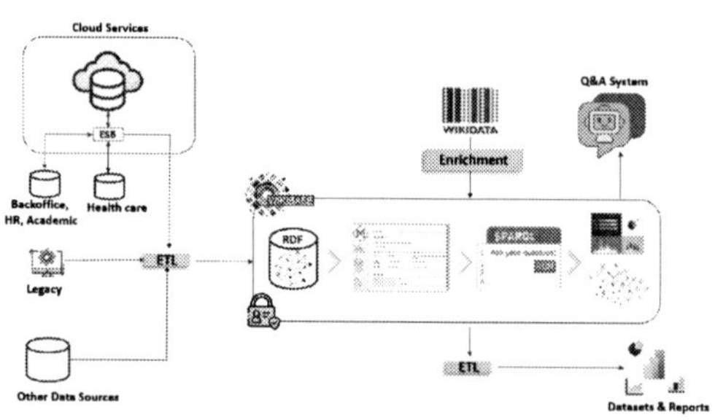

Figure 1: System architecture, highlighting the data sources, the Wikibase components, the enrichment interface, the outputs of datasets and reports and the interface with Q&A system.

2.1 Technologies

The Figure 1 shows the system architecture. Instances of concepts defined in ontologies (Subsection 2.2) are extracted from internal data sources through ETL workflows and loaded into the KG with the support of both OpenRefine[1] and QuickStaments[2] tools. For natural language processing tests synthetically generated data were loaded into KG (Subsection 2.3).

Once loaded to the KG, instances of concepts, called "items" in Wikibase, are available to be

[1]https://openrefine.org

[2]https://www.wikidata.org/wiki/Help:QuickStatements

queried by a SPARQL endpoint or by a data visualization interface called Query Service. Items can be edited or even enriched through data loads from Wikidata[3] or even through references to items defined in Wikidata. The concepts defined in the KG make up a data glossary, and instances of these concepts can be offered to data consumers through datasets or reports fed directly into Microsoft Power BI workspaces, or as a data source for the intelligent natural language processing system (Subsection 3.1).

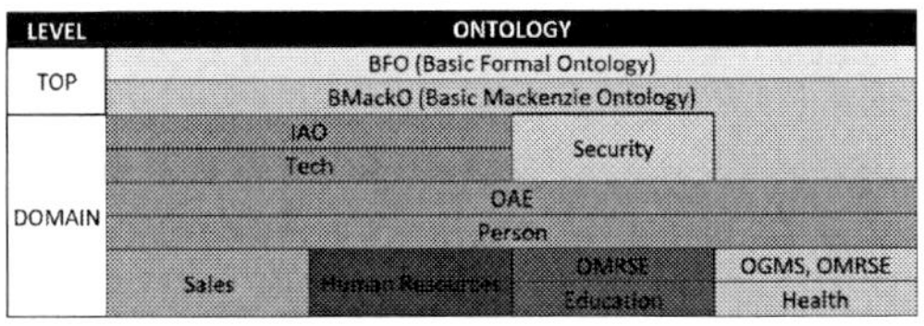

Figure 2: Ontology definition levels, organized by top and domain levels.

2.2 Ontologies

The concepts used in the KG were defined in ontologies, which are formal representations of terms in a given domain (Hogan et al., 2021). In ontologies, concepts are defined through classes, which are collections of objects, and the characteristics of concepts are represented by attributes. Interactions between classes are represented by special types of attributes: relations. Individuals in an ontology are represented as instances (Sack and Alam, 2020).

The definition of the concepts used in the KG was based on the Basic Formal Ontology (BFO) (Smith et al., 2020), an ontology that defines general terms common to all knowledge domains, that is, a top-level ontology. Under the BFO is the Basic Mackenzie Ontology (BMackO), a proprietary top-level ontology dedicated to the definition of terms and attributes common to all other ontologies adopted by IPM. The concepts relating to the domains covered by the KG were defined in either proprietary or public ontologies, the latter located using the Ontobee (Xiang et al., 2011) tool. All domain ontologies adopted in the KG (Tech, Security, Person, Sales, Human Resources, Education and Health), extend the BFO ontology. The complete hierarchy of ontologies adopted in KG is depicted in Figure 2.

The Tech and Security ontologies aim to define the concepts and properties that must be applied to all other domain ontologies. For example, in the Security ontology, the attributes "is personally identifiable information" and "is sensitive information" were defined. These two attributes are applicable to attributes of ontologies that are below the Security ontology (Figure 2). The proprietary ontologies Tech, Person, Education, and Health extend the following publicly shared ontologies: Information Artifact Ontology (IAO) (Ruttenberg et al., 2022), Ontology for General Medical Science (OGMS) (Zheng et al., 2009), Ontology for Modeling and Representation of Social Entities (OMRSE) (Brochhausen et al., 2024) and Ontology of Adverse Events (OAE) (Smith et al., 2022).

2.3 Gen AI Synthetic Data Creation

In Section 3 we will present a Knowledge Graph Q&A System that we built to allow natural language quering. Since this app is a prototype, we choose the free version of Gemini Pro 1.0 as the best option to run tests. With the aim of avoiding the leakage of sensible information, we connected the LLM only to a development knowledge base, filled with synthetic data. To generate high quality synthetic data similar to real data we used GPT-3 providing the fields and data types. An example of prompt used can be found in the Appendix B. We generated academic and customer/lead data, similar to data retrieved in our Customer Relationship Management (CRM) system.

3 Large Language Models

We will also discuss the tests and results obtained when adopting LLM to build a KG questions and answers system.

3.1 Knowledge Graph Q&A System

With the KG implementation, we looked for an intelligent natural language processing system that could understand and respond to user queries in a conversational manner. The goal was to improve the accessibility of information stored in the private Wikibase instance repository, making it easier for users to retrieve relevant data through natural language interactions even for stakeholders who do not dominate SPARQL query language.

To build the Knowledge Graph Q&A system, we started from the preliminary work on the GitHub repository Langchain Wikibase (Ziff, 2024), with proposes the use of a Langchain autonomous Reasoning-Action (or Re-Act for short) Agent to

[3]https://www.wikidata.org

retrieve Wikidata information via API and answer questions. Re-Act Agents can reason about what kind of tools must be called and how to handle the tool output. In this case, the tools provided to the Re-Act agent was python functions to get properties and items information from Wikidata API. The agent looks for properties PID and items QID from Wikidata (Wikimedia Foundation, 2009–) then convert the user input question into a SPARQL query and run it in Wikidata SPARQL endpoint. The agent also generate an human readable answer from the SPARQL query result. The original repository was a simple python script to be run via CLI passing the question as argument.

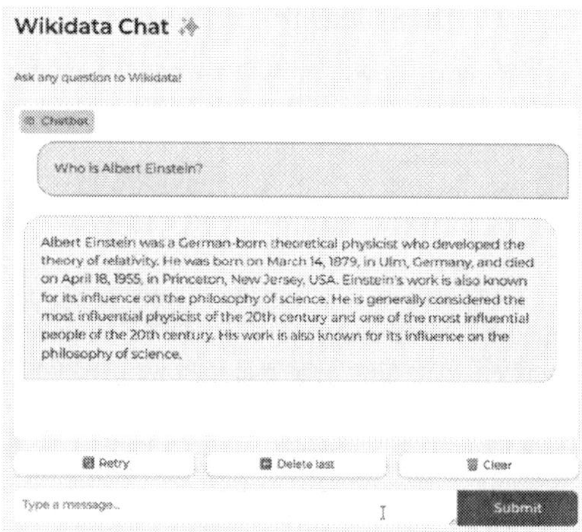

Figure 3: The user interface developed to the generative AI powered chat, built with Gradio.

We contributed to the GitHub repository Langchain Wikibase (Ziff, 2024) adding a chain tool to retrieve all properties of a given item from Wikidata rest API, enriching the Re-Act Agent app. Also, we developed a python module to wrap up the tools and customized some Lang Chain packages to use with local Wikibase instances instead of Wikidata. Furthermore, we improved the prompts and make use of the chain to properly answer descriptive questions such that "Who is Student A?" or "What is Pernambuco Federal University?" using the tool that we implemented. The application was originally designed to run over Open AI GPT models, we also enabled connection to other language models like Google Gemini 1.0 Pro and the open source model Mixtral 8 × 7B from Mistral AI (Jiang et al., 2024). Moreover, we developed a simple chatbot user interface by the Python library Gradio, which can be seen in Figure 3. All this development and improvements was already committed and merged to the original GitHub repository (Ziff, 2024).

The generative AI chatbot powered by Gemini 1.0 Pro was connected to the OKG database Wikidata and to our EKG database developed over a Wikibase (Wikimedia Deutschland, 2012–) instance. The same structure was used through both cases, reasoning about the question, running queries over the SPARQL endpoint and translating it into human readable answers. The chatbot was tested using three kinds of questions: type 1) descriptive questions e.g. "Who is Albert Einstein?", "What is Google's industry?", "What is Google?"; type 2) questions that links a property to an item e.g. "What is the Google inception?", "List 10 subsidiaries of Google.","What are the geographic coordinates of Mount Everest?"; and type 3) questions involving calculations e.g. "What is the average GDP *per capita* of the Africa continent countries?", "What is the sum of the population of USA, Canada and Mexico?", "What is the sum of the number of countries in South America and North America?".

The percentage of correct answered questions for each type can be found in Figure 4. The criteria used to determine if the Re-Act Agent correctly answered a question was human evaluation, comparing the generated answer with data available in Wikidata or our EKG and the generated SPARQL queries with human written queries. To monitor the app and inspect costs we used the developer framework Langsmith, which allows an end-to-end track of the LLM-powered application lifecycle. Appendix A shows the reasoning process of the Langchain Re-Act Agent to answer a question, using Python functions as tools to interact with the KG.

4 Conclusion

Even at the prototype stage, the Knowledge Graph Q&A System demonstrated a good hit rate, specially in simple questions. As illustrated in Figure 4, the Re-Act agent performed significantly better with type 1 questions when connected to our private Knowledge Graph, yielding 31% more correct answers. This improvement can be attributed to our Enterprise Knowledge Graph (EKG) being restricted to subjects of interest for our company, as opposed to Wikidata, which covers a wide range of topics. The discrepancy shown in Figure 4 between

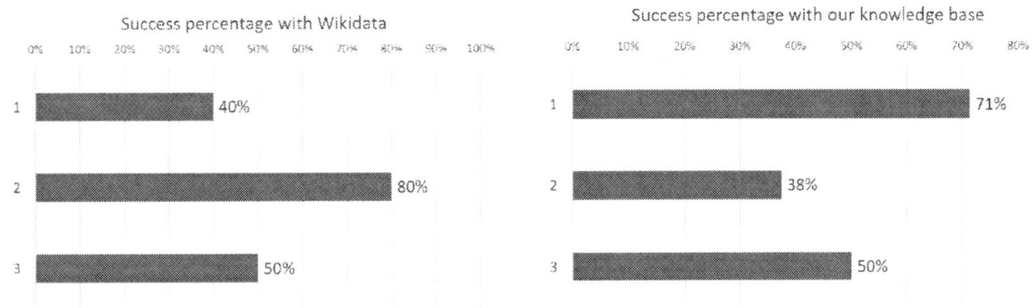

Figure 4: Comparison of KG Q&A System connected to Wikidata and our EKG. The type 1 are descriptive questions, type 2 questions that links an item to a property and type 3 questions involving calculations.

local EKG and Wikidata for type 2 questions are possibly due to training data about the Wikidata, since several PIDs and QIDs are known by Gemini 1.0 pro. Occasionally, the answers generated by the Re-Act agent connected to our private EKG contain some Wikidata properties, resulting in empty results from our SPARQL endpoint. Using a more robust LLM like Gemini 1.5 pro or GPT-4 and fine tuning the model to better generate SPARQL may fix this problem and improve the success rate. When deploying the chatbot to production, this will be our approach. Also, when using premium LLM versions, the providers guarantee that no private data are used to train models, making them suitable to a production version.

On privacy, an opportunity to improve the KG is the segregation of access to items based on the authenticated user's profile, and the reproduction of this segregation of access for the SPARQL queries submitted to the SPARQL endpoint and to the Wikibase Query Service (WDQS).

The results obtained so far have been favorable to the adoption of KGs as a solution for data integration and LLM for the construction of a search and response interface in natural language for IPM's corporate data. While adopting an Open Knowledge Graph solution like Wikibase in an enterprise environment presents the challenge of segregating data access, the gains from Wikidata Query Service's out-of-the-box data visualization options and simplicity of horizontal scaling of Wikibase's docker swarm implementation are self-demonstrable.

Acknowledgments

We would like to thank the Mackenzie Presbyterian Institute and the Department of Technology and Innovation for supporting the development of KG and the publication of this article. We would like to thank professor Donald Ziff for starting the project that originated our Q&A system.

References

2023. *Exploration on the application of knowledge graph in modern chinese teaching*. 2023 International Seminar on Computer Science and Engineering Technology (SCSET). IEEE.

2023. *Inovação de serviços em cidades inteligentes: Interação de pessoas não-especialistas com knowledge graphs*.

Andreas Blumauer and Helmut Nagy. 2020. *The knowledge graph cookbook: Recipes that work*. edition mono/monochrom.

Mathias Brochhausen, William Hogan, Amanda Hicks, Shariq Tariq, and Swetha Garimalla. 2024. Ontology for modeling and representation of social entities. Accessed: May 15, 2024.

Valeria de Paiva and Alexandre Rademaker. 2024. Towards a brazilian history knowledge graph.

Dennis Diefenbach, Max De Wilde, and Samantha Alipio. 2021. Wikibase as an infrastructure for knowledge graphs: The eu knowledge graph. In *The Semantic Web–ISWC 2021: 20th International Semantic Web Conference, ISWC 2021, Virtual Event, October 24–28, 2021, Proceedings 20*, pages 631–647. Springer.

Nicolas Heist, S Hertling, Daniel Ringler, and Heiko Paulheim. 2020. Knowledge graphs on the web - an overview. *ArXiv*, abs/2003.00719.

Aidan Hogan, Eva Blomqvist, Michael Cochez, Claudia d'Amato, Gerard de Melo, Claudio Gutiérrez, Sabrina Kirrane, José Emilio Labra Gayo, Roberto Navigli, Sebastian Neumaier, Axel-Cyrille Ngonga Ngomo, Axel Polleres, Sabbir M. Rashid, Anisa Rula, Lukas Schmelzeisen, Juan F. Sequeda,

Steffen Staab, and Antoine Zimmermann. 2021. *Knowledge Graphs*. Number 22 in Synthesis Lectures on Data, Semantics, and Knowledge. Springer.

Albert Q. Jiang, Alexandre Sablayrolles, Antoine Roux, Arthur Mensch, Blanche Savary, Chris Bamford, Devendra Singh Chaplot, Diego de las Casas, Emma Bou Hanna, Florian Bressand, Gianna Lengyel, Guillaume Bour, Guillaume Lample, Lélio Renard Lavaud, Lucile Saulnier, Marie-Anne Lachaux, Pierre Stock, Sandeep Subramanian, Sophia Yang, Szymon Antoniak, Teven Le Scao, Théophile Gervet, Thibaut Lavril, Thomas Wang, Timothée Lacroix, and William El Sayed. 2024. Mixtral of experts. *Preprint*, arXiv:2401.04088.

Aleš Kapica. 2023. Extension access control. Accessed: May 16, 2024.

Patrick Lewis, Ethan Perez, Aleksandra Piktus, Fabio Petroni, Vladimir Karpukhin, Naman Goyal, Heinrich Küttler, Mike Lewis, Wen-tau Yih, Tim Rocktäschel, Sebastian Riedel, and Douwe Kiela. 2020a. Retrieval-augmented generation for knowledge-intensive nlp tasks. In *Advances in Neural Information Processing Systems*, volume 33, pages 9459–9474. Curran Associates, Inc.

Patrick S. H. Lewis, Ethan Perez, Aleksandra Piktus, Fabio Petroni, Vladimir Karpukhin, Naman Goyal, Heinrich Küttler, Mike Lewis, Wen-tau Yih, Tim Rocktäschel, Sebastian Riedel, and Douwe Kiela. 2020b. Retrieval-augmented generation for knowledge-intensive NLP tasks. *CoRR*, abs/2005.11401.

Ahmed Ali Linkon, Mujiba Shaima, Md Shohail Uddin Sarker, Norun Nabi, Md Nasir Uddin Rana, Sandip Kumar Ghosh, Mohammad Anisur Rahman, Hammed Esa, Faiaz Rahat Chowdhury, et al. 2024. Advancements and applications of generative artificial intelligence and large language models on business management: A comprehensive review. *Journal of Computer Science and Technology Studies*, 6(1):225–232.

Mackenzie Presbyterian Institute. 2022. Instituto presbiteriano mackenzie - relatório anual - institucional & sustentabilidade 2022. Accessed: May 15, 2024.

Sean Martin, Ben Szekely, and Dean Allemang. 2021. *The Rise of the Knowledge Graph: Toward Modern Data Integration and the Data Fabric Architecture*. O'Reilly Media, Incorporated.

María Navas-Loro, Carlos Badenes-Olmedo, Manolis Koubarakis, Luis Redondo, Sabrina Kirrane, Nandana Mihindukulasooriya, Ken Satoh, and Maribel Acosta, editors. 2022. *Building and analyzing the brazilian legal knowledge graph*, volume 3257. CEUR-WS.org.

Heiko Paulheim. 2016. Knowledge graph refinement: A survey of approaches and evaluation methods. *Semantic Web*, 8:489–508.

Roel Popping. 2003. Knowledge graphs and network text analysis. *Social Science Information*, 42:106 – 91.

Alan Ruttenberg, Barry Smith, Bjoern Peters, Carlo Torniai, Chris Mungall, Chris Stoeckert, Holger Stenzhorn, James A. Overton, James Malone, Jennifer Fostel, Jie Zheng, Larisa Soldatova, Lawrence Hunter, Mathias Brochhausen, Melanie Courtot, Philippe Rocca-Serra, David Osumi-Sutherland, William Hogan, Adam Goldstein, Albert Goldfain, Christian A. Boelling, Darren Natale, Gwen Frishkoff, Jonathan Rees, Matt Brush, Michel Dumontier, Paolo Ciccarese, Pat Hayes, Randy Dipert, Ron Rudnicki, Satya Sahoo, Sivaram Arabandi, Werner Ceusters, William Duncan, Yongqun He, and Clint Dowland. 2022. Information artifact ontology. Accessed: May 15, 2024.

Harald Sack and Mehwish Alam. 2020. Knowledge graphs 2020.

Serhad Sarica, Jianxi Luo, and Kristin L Wood. 2020. Technet: Technology semantic network based on patent data. *Expert Systems with Applications*, 142:112995.

Chiara Silveira Scappaticci. 2023. *Artificial intelligence: how can Gen-AI tools support the current business models of the firms and add value?* Ph.D. thesis.

Tong Shen, Fu Zhang, and Jingwei Cheng. 2022. A comprehensive overview of knowledge graph completion. *Knowledge-Based Systems*, 255:109597.

Barry Smith, Alan Ruttenberg, and John Beverley. 2020. Basic formal ontology. Accessed: May 15, 2024.

Barry Smith, Jiangan Xie, Yu Lin, Abra Guo, Bingjian Yang, Desikan Jagannathan, Edison Ong, Kelly Yang, Kevin Mo, Liwei Wang, Meiu Wong, Noemi Garg, Qingping Liu, Rebecca Racz, Shelley Zhang, Sirarat Sarntivijai, Sydni Joubran, Yongqun He, Zuoshuang Xiang, Ling Wan, David Ameriguian, Jessica DeGuise, Jiangan Xie, and Qiuyue Yang. 2022. Ontology of adverse events. Accessed: May 15, 2024.

Tulio Vidal Rolim, Caio Viktor S. Avila, Narciso Arruda, José Wellington F. da Silva, José Gilvan R. Maia, Mauro Oliveira, Luiz Odorico M. Andrade, and Vânia M. P. Vidal. 2021. *Um Enfoque Incremental para Construção do Grafo de Conhecimento do SUS*, pages 327–342. Tecnologia da Informação e Comunicação: Pesquisas em Inovações Tecnológicas. Editora Científica Digital.

Wikimedia Deutschland. 2012–. Wikibase. Accessed: May 15, 2024.

Wikimedia Foundation. 2009–. Wikidata. Accessed: May 15, 2024.

Zuoshuang Xiang, Chris Mungall, Alan Ruttenberg, and Yongqun He. 2011. Ontobee: A linked data server and browser for ontology terms. In *ICBO*.

Jie Zheng, Lindsay Cowell, Barry Smith, Alan Ruttenberg, Albert Goldfain, Werner Ceusters, Anand Kumar, Bill Hogan, Cornelius Rosse, Daniel Merico, Richard Scheuermann, Sivaram Arabandi, and Brian Aevermann. 2009. Ontology for general medical science. Accessed: May 15, 2024.

Donald Ziff. 2024. GitHub - donaldziff/langchain-wikibase — github.com. https://github.com/donaldziff/langchain-wikibase. [Accessed 14-05-2024].

A Langchain Agent-Chain Reasoning and Answering

Example of the reasoning process of the Knowledge Graph Q&A System to consult graph, generate SPARQL and answer a question:

Question: What is the population of the city of São Paulo?

Answer:

1. Find the Q item for "city of São Paulo" using the getQItem tool
   Action: getQItem
   Action Input: city of São Paulo
   Q174

2. Find P properties for "population" using the getProperty tool
   Action: getProperty
   Action Input: population
   P1082

3. Generate the simplest possible SPARQL query and check its validity with the checkSparql tool
   Action: checkSparql
   Action Input:

```
SELECT ?population WHERE {
   wd:Q174 wdt:P1082 ?population.
}
```

Query is valid

4. Run the SPARQL query using the runSparql tool and retrieve the result
   Action: runSparql
   Action Input:

```
SELECT ?population WHERE {
   wd:Q174 wdt:P1082 ?population.
}
```

result:


```
{
    'head': {
        'vars': ['population']
    },
    'results': {
        'bindings': [{
            'population': {
                'datatype':
'http://www.w3.org/2001/XMLSchema#decimal',
                'type': 'literal',
                'value': '11451245'
            }
        }]
    }
}
```


5. Summarize JSON results in natural language to generate a human-readable response

Final Answer:
The population of the city of São Paulo is approximately 11,451,245 inhabitants.

B Generating Synthetic Data through LLM

This is an example of prompt used to generate student synthetic data, similar to data from the academic Data Warehouse:

```
Create a table of synthetic student
data, with all fields filled in as
per the instructions below. The table
columns must be all of the options below
in </columns>:

<columns>
registration
status
isActive
person.code
person.name
person.socialName
person.contact.telephone
person.contact.branchLine
person.contact.email
person.contact.businessEmail
person.contact.businessTelephone
person.contact.businessBranchLine
entity.code
entity.name
subsidiary.code
subsidiary.name
educationLevel.code
educationLevel.name
school.code
school.name
courses.code
```

course.name
sourceSystem
</columns>

registration is a 7-digit identifier for each student and the person code is a 5-digit string. The status must be one of the options below between </status>:

<status>
'Inactive'
'Active'
'Canceled'
</status>
The isActive field can be true or false The entity.code must be '1' for all lines The entity.name must be 'Entity A' for all rows The subsidiary.code and subsidiary.name must be one of the options below between </sub>

<sub>
1,Subsidiary A
2,Subsidiary B
3,Subsidiary C
</sub>
The educationLevel.code and educationLevel.name must be one of the options below between </edu>:

<edu>
10,High School
11,Undergraduate
12,Post Graduation
</edu>
The school.code and school.name must be one of the options below between </sch>:

<sch>
20,School A
21,School B
22,School C
</sch>
course.code and course.name must be one of the options below between </course>

<course>
A0010,Program A
A0020,Program B
A0030,Program C
</course>

sourceSystem must be 'System A' on all lines. In each example, the code and name are separated by a comma, always in the same order. Adjust the choice of courses, school and teaching level according to similarity. Generate the table in CSV format. Don't generate code, write the table rows. The table must have 200 rows, do not stop until you complete the table. Do not repeat people's names. Fill in all fields and lines with values as per the instructions above. Follow all the rules.

KGAST: From Knowledge Graphs to Annotated Synthetic Texts

Nakanyseth Vuth and **Gilles Sérasset** and **Didier Schwab**
Univ. Grenoble Alpes, CNRS, Grenoble INP, LIG
38000 Grenoble
France
first.last@univ-grenoble-alpes.fr

Abstract

In recent years, the use of synthetic data, either as a complement or a substitute for original data, has emerged as a solution to challenges such as data scarcity and security risks. This paper is an initial attempt to automatically generate such data for Information Extraction tasks. We accomplished this by developing a novel synthetic data generation framework called **KGAST**, which leverages Knowledge Graphs and Large Language Models. In our preliminary study, we conducted simple experiments to generate synthetic versions of two datasets—a French security defense dataset and an English general domain dataset, after which we evaluated them both intrinsically and extrinsically. The results indicated that synthetic data can effectively complement original data, improving the performance of models on classes with limited training samples. This highlights **KGAST**'s potential as a tool for generating synthetic data for Information Extraction tasks.

1 Introduction

Information Extraction (IE) models serve as crucial components across various domains, enabling us to make informed decisions based on complex data. However, the effectiveness of these models is dependent on the availability and quality of training data. In this context, we encounter two critical challenges: *1) Data Scarcity*: Frequently, despite having complex modeling techniques, researchers deal with datasets that are either insufficient in size or entirely unavailable. Without a sufficient number of labeled examples, IE models struggle to generalize effectively, compromising their predictive capabilities. *2) Privacy and Compliance Concerns*: In an era of heightened data privacy regulations, organizations must navigate the balance between model performance and safeguarding sensitive information. Certain datasets whether due to privacy risks or legal constraints cannot be openly shared, which further complicates training effective IE models. To address these issues, researchers often resort to manual data augmentation. This labor-intensive process involves collecting additional data points and meticulously annotating them. While effective, it is time-consuming and resource-intensive, making it less feasible for small organizations operating on limited budgets. Numerous studies have explored the expansion of training data by introducing additional synthetic data (Kobayashi, 2018; Wei and Zou, 2019; Zhang et al., 2020). These studies presented straightforward strategies, such as substituting certain words with their equivalent terms. These equivalents can be retrieved from external sources like WordNet (Miller, 1995), DBnary (Sérasset, 2015), or they can be calculated using word embedding models such as Word2Vec (Mikolov et al., 2013), FastText (Bojanowski et al., 2016), and Glove (Pennington et al., 2014). Although these techniques can indeed augment the initial training dataset, they fail to generate adequate diversity for the models to generalize effectively in subsequent tasks, owing to the minimal semantic variations from the original data. Back-translation is another recognized technique for augmenting the initial training data. With Machine Translation models (Xie et al., 2017; Fabbri et al., 2020), paraphrases of each sentence can be obtained through the back-translation process. While back-translation effectively amplifies the dataset size twofold, it introduces a notable challenge in terms of annotation. The text derived from back-translation diverges from the original annotation. Thus, either careful manual annotation or sophisticated annotation algorithms are required to update the annotations in alignment with the back-translated text, ensuring the precision of the dataset.

To address these issues of low data diversity and misalignment of the original annotation, we propose a novel synthetic data generation

Proceedings of the 1st Workshop on Knowledge Graphs and Large Language Models (KaLLM 2024), pages 43–55
August 15, 2024

framework called **KGAST**. This framework leverages **K**nowledge **G**raph to automatically generate **A**nnotated **S**ynthetic **T**exts that can be used for training IE models. In this study, we sought to answer questions similar to the ones raised in this paper (Claveau et al., 2021):

- Can synthetic data serve as supplementary data to improve the performance of classes with limited training samples?
- Can synthetic data be a viable alternative to gold standard data?

2 Related Works

2.1 Data Augmentation

Given the resource-intensive nature of manual data creation and annotation, a variety of data augmentation strategies have been employed to address the issue of data scarcity. One of the well-known approaches is the rule-based (Kobayashi, 2018; Wei and Zou, 2019; Zhang et al., 2020) word replacement. This method requires a heuristic for selecting and replacing words within a sentence. On the other hand, some research has approached this at sentence level by leveraging dependency tree (Coulombe, 2018; Dehouck and Gómez-Rodríguez, 2020). For example: "John did the math exercises." is replaced with "The math exercise was done by John". The data augmented through these methods often conveys information very similar to the original, thereby limiting semantic diversity. Back-translation (Xie et al., 2017; Fabbri et al., 2020) is another method to augment the original dataset. This straightforward technique involves translating text from the original language to another language, and then translating it back to the original language to produce a new version. However, this method presents its own challenges, as labels from the original text may no longer align with the new text due to changes in syntax or semantics.

2.2 Distant Supervision

Automatically generating new supervised data is a compelling alternative to manual annotation, especially when creating large-scale datasets for natural language processing tasks. One such approach is Distant Supervision (Roller et al., 2015; Deng and Sun, 2019), which leverages existing knowledge bases to construct and label new training samples. The core assumption of this method is that if two entities share a relation in the knowledge base, any sentence containing those two entities might express that relation. However, the automated annotation process introduces errors such as incorrectly assumed entity types or the relations between entity pairs.

2.3 In context Learning

In-context learning (ICL) has recently emerged as a new paradigm in the field of natural language processing. This approach allows Large Language Models (LLMs) to make predictions based solely on contexts that are augmented with a select number of examples. Often, ICL aids in refining the output of an LLM, enhancing the accuracy of the output even in the absence of fine-tuning. With ICL, the performance achieved by LLMs can rival that of previous supervised learning methods (Brown et al., 2020; Shin et al., 2021; Wan et al., 2023). This can be achieved by carefully crafting clear instructional prompts along with high-quality task-specific k-shot examples (Zhao et al., 2021; Liu et al., 2022).

3 Method

3.1 Overview

Our proposed methodology is built upon two primary elements: LLMs and ICL. Contrary to previous research that modified the original texts of the dataset, our approach involves the generation of new synthetic texts and their corresponding annotations using LLMs. A well-known reasoning prompt method, Chain-of-Thoughts (Wei et al., 2022), enables us to create complex ICL prompt templates to instruct LLM models for such tasks. The intuition behind this approach stems from the concept of distant supervision, where we make a naive assumption that if a pair of entities (e_{head}, e_{tail}) is present in both the text and the Knowledge Graph (KG), these two entities maintain the same relation as the one in the KG.

3.2 Task Formulation

We formalize the task of synthesizing annotated data as a natural language generation task. Consider a given gold text $t \in \mathcal{G}$, where $\mathcal{G} = \{t_1, \ldots, t_n\}$ represents the set of gold standard texts, $A_t = \{a_1, \ldots, a_n\}$ is the set of label annotations, $R_t = \{r_1, \ldots, r_n\}$ is the set of relations, K_t is the KG and $A_t, R_t \subseteq K_t$. The intuition is to construct a text generation prompt p by utilizing the KG as an input to get our intended output synthetic

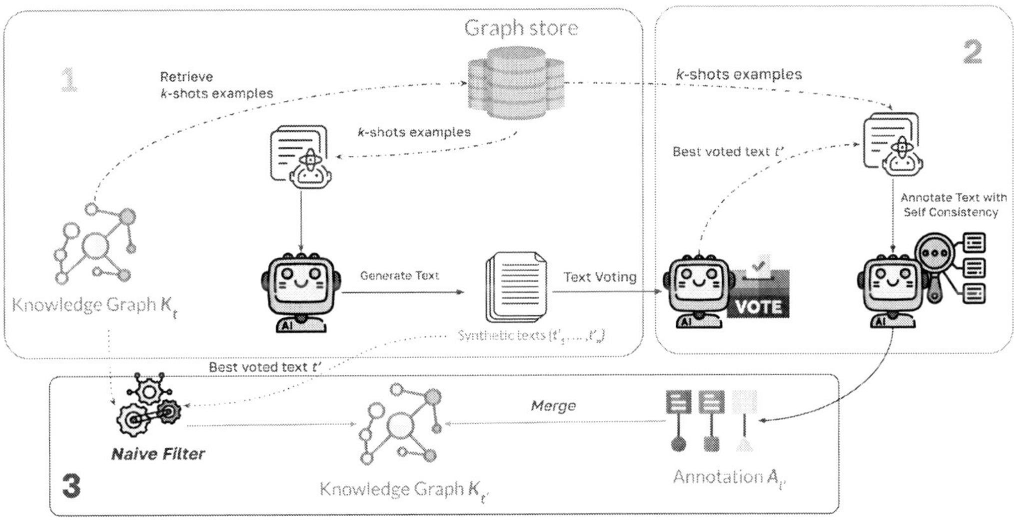

Figure 1: KGAST framework. (1) It begins by using a knowledge graph K_t as a starting point. Based on this knowledge graph, the framework retrieves a set of relevant k-shots examples to build prompt templates. We then prompt the LLM to generate a set of synthetic texts $\{t_1^{'}, \ldots, t_n^{'}\}$. (2) From these generated texts, we select the best t' through a voting prompt which will then be used as input in the annotation prompt template to prompt the model for text annotating. (3) Finally, annotations retrieved from the LLM outputs are merged with the filtered knowledge graph $K_{t'}$ to get the final annotation.

text t'. The KG K_t of a prompt p is constructed by extracting all the annotated relations R_t from the text t. Once the synthetic text t' is produced, we proceed to extract the set of label annotations $A_{t'}$ and the set of relations $R_{t'}$ by simply filtering out any triples of the KG K_t where either the head or the tail is not present in the text t'. This can be formulated as $A_{t'}, R_{t'} \subseteq K_{t'}$, where:

$$K_{t'} = \textit{naive\_filter}(K_t, t') \quad (1)$$

3.3 Prompt Construction

Our prompt template is divided into three main sections for ease of understanding.

Instruction Serves as a clear directive for the LLM, which outlines its role and task. We clearly specify the role and task for which we want to generate output. For instance, in the case of text generation:

> "You are a *creative text writer*. Write me a text using the provided Knowledge Graph. Your objective is to write a coherent text that incorporates all the given triples (head, relation, tail) of the Knowledge Graph. You have the right to make the text creative and informative, but you must make sure that the text reflects the given Knowledge Graph."

For text annotation, we draw inspiration from Tree-of-thought (Yao et al., 2023) prompting and construct the instruction as follows:

> "You are a *text annotator*. Your objectives are to: 1/ Analyze the given text in detail, 2/ Annotate possible entities based on these entity types: person(PER), location(LOC), organization(ORG), time(TIME), numbers(NUM), and miscellaneous entity names(MISC). Response with the annotation in this format: "Possible Entities: e_1 e_2,...., e_n", where e_1 to e_n are the extracted entities."

k-shots Examples Similar to the Retrieval-Augmented Generation (RAG) (Lewis et al., 2020), where all documents are embedded into latent space, we did the same for all examples retrieved from $\mathcal{G}$. We then use top-k retrieval to find examples that are close to the input KG K_t as k-shot examples for prompting.

Test Input We used KG K_t as an input in the form of a list of triples in natural language to prompt the LLM model. The structure of these input triples is as follows:

```
("Head":Type, "Relation", "Tail":Type)
```

The goal is to provide the LLM with as much information as possible so that it can generate a coherent text that corresponds to the input triples.

3.4 The Framework: KGAST

The process outlined in Section 3.2 yields both the text and its corresponding annotation. However, we identified two primary issues:

Incomplete Text Annotation Despite having annotations, we found that it is often incomplete as seen in Figure 2. The method's effectiveness is heavily reliant on the performance of the LLM used. Consequently, the likelihood of generating a text, t', that includes all the input triples of K_t is contingent on the LLM's performance for our given tasks.

Text Coherence and Validity Without a validation heuristic, the texts generated by our method may contain nonsensical phrases. This is because LLMs are known to produce hallucinations, such as incoherent texts with their input KGs, repetitive tokens, inclusion of parts of the prompt, and texts in different languages.

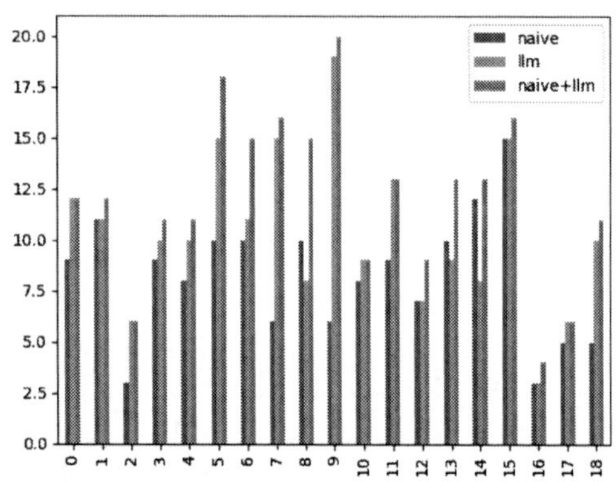

Figure 2: The graph displays entity coverage statistics for various texts. The Y-axis represents the number of entities, while the X-axis corresponds to the text.

To address these shortcomings, we integrated Self-consistency (Wang et al., 2022) into our framework, aiming to mimic real human annotation processes as closely as possible. The idea behind self-consistency is to prompt the LLM to generate a set of n outputs and select the most consistent one. For text generation, we prompted LLM to generate $n = 3$ outputs. We used the 3 output texts as input to prompt the LLM to vote $n = 5$ times, evaluating each based on creativity, coherence, and the text's capacity to include all the input triples of the KG. We then select the best text t' with the highest voting score. A similar approach is also applied for extracting annotations from text t'. We prompted the same model to generate $n = 5$ outputs and merged the most consistent annotation with a threshold of 0.5. This means that if an annotation appears in at least 50% of the n outputs, it is extracted. Subsequently, this annotation is merged with the annotation from our naive heuristic. The entire procedure is described in Figure 1.

4 Experiment Setup

4.1 Datasets

For simplicity, we will refer to gold standard data as $\mathcal{G}$ and synthetic data as $\mathcal{S}$.

DocRED (Yao et al., 2019), is a document-level relation extraction dataset constructed from Wikipedia and Wikidata. This dataset contains a total of 96 relations and 6 entity types for English general domain. Each relation is annotated along with its supporting evidence.

French Security and Defense for which we will refer as **FRSD**, is a document-level relation extraction dataset that covers the annotation for Event Extraction, Entity Recognition, Attribute Extraction, and Relation Extraction tasks for French intelligence service. FRSD contains 2,000 French documents, of which 800 are manually written and annotated by humans. It consists of 35 entity types, 20 attributes, and 49 relations.

4.2 Synthetic Data Generation

In this preliminary study of generating synthetic data, we did simple generation experiments by using the training set of $\mathcal{G}$ as a reference to generate the synthetic version $\mathcal{S}$. For DocRED, this resulted in a total of 3023 new documents along with their annotations. The LLM model used in the framework for this dataset was Zephyr-7B[1], a fine-tuned model of Mistral-7B (Jiang et al., 2023). The same approach was applied to FRSD but on 400 (train) documents. In FRSD, we observed a significant data imbalance among Event classes. With this in mind, we manually selected the top 10 event classes with the fewest samples and used their texts as a reference to generate 1200 new documents (Oversampling). We used Vigostral-7B[2], a chat-

[1]https://huggingface.co/HuggingFaceH4/zephyr-7b-beta

[2]https://huggingface.co/bofenghuang/vigostral-7b-chat

Pre-training Strategy	Events		Entities	
	F1 Macro	F1 Micro	F1 Macro	F1 Micro
No pre-training	43.28±1.32	58.58 ±1.90	66.78 ±1.59	81.81±0.33
$\mathcal{S}$ pre-training	45.17 ±0.83	58.81 ±0.46	67.45 ±1.33	81.61±0.12
$\mathcal{G}$ pre-training	43.60 ±3.46	58.56±1.95	67.72 ±2.13	81.95±0.36
$\mathcal{S} \cup \mathcal{G}$ pre-training	**45.19** ±2.07	**58.93**±0.90	**68.38** ±0.34	**82.03**±0.34

Table 1: Unified Model results for Event and Entity Extraction.

Pre-training Strategy	Attributes		Relations	
	F1 Macro	F1 Micro	F1 Macro	F1 Micro
No pre-training	**61.63**±2.15	81.87±0.52	44.53±1.45	56.74±0.78
$\mathcal{S}$ pre-training	60.05±1.97	**82.07**±0.62	43.26±1.22	55.85±0.75
$\mathcal{G}$ pre-training	55.98 ±8.18	81.33±0.73	43.25±4.78	**57.10**±0.70
$\mathcal{S} \cup \mathcal{G}$ pre-training	60.39±2.76	81.27±0.75	**46.49**±0.55	56.87±0.84

Table 2: Unified Model results for Attribute and Relation Extraction.

based model that has been fine-tuned on Mistral-7B (Jiang et al., 2023) for this dataset. Supporting evidence for each relation of $\mathcal{S}$ on both datasets was automatically extracted using a simple heuristic. This heuristic identifies the sentence index where the head or the tail entity appears and uses it as supporting evidence.

4.3 Tasks

To evaluate the effectiveness of our proposed framework, two types of evaluations were conducted:

Intrinsic Evaluation This evaluation aims to understand the accuracy of our framework's annotations. We evaluated the annotation accuracy of DocRED's synthetic documents. For Named Entity, this was done by using BERT-NER[3] as an inference model to predict the set of synthetic texts, and then comparing the output prediction with our framework's annotations. As for Relations, we used the best model of DREEAM (Ma et al., 2023) (RoBERTa)[4] as the inference model and followed the same procedure.

Extrinsic Evaluation The goal of this evaluation is to assess how $\mathcal{S}$ impacts the performance of downstream tasks. For DocRED, we used $\mathcal{S}$ to train on two tasks: Named Entity Recognition (NER), and Relation Extraction (RE). NER task was trained on the Flair framework[5] which used Bi-LSTM with flair embeddings. RE was trained using DREEAM (teacher) model, which is based on BERT with $\lambda = 0.05$. We trained a total of 5 times with different seeds, evaluated the models against the original test set, and computed the average to get the final results. For FRSD, we conducted experiments on two models: Boundary Smoothing (BS) (Zhu and Li, 2022): which is used for Event, Entity, and Attribution recognition tasks. Unified Model (UM) (Prieur et al., 2024): this model approaches the tasks jointly for NER and RE tasks. The architecture of this model includes a module for detecting entity spans and a second for predicting their interactions. In these experiments, we follow the same as the experiment conducted with DocRED and report the results in Section 5.3.

5 Experiment Results

5.1 Dataset Characteristic

A descriptive statistic of both datasets can be seen in Table 3. We observed that $\mathcal{G}$ tends to contain longer documents and possesses a greater number of unique entities and labeled tokens, indicating a higher semantic quality and more robust representation of specific objects, people, places, etc. We computed the Self-BLEU (trigram) for each dataset, revealing lower Self-BLEU scores for $\mathcal{G}$. The scores suggest that the gold datasets are more diverse and less prone to repetitive use of the same tokens/entities in the text. On the other hand, $\mathcal{S}$ can be seen to have a larger number of entity pairs (triples) due to the repetition of entities used in the texts. While this increases the raw count of entity

[3] https://huggingface.co/dslim/bert-base-NER
[4] https://github.com/YoumiMa/dreeam
[5] https://huggingface.co/flair/ner-english

pairs, it may not necessarily enhance the diversity or quality of these pairs.

In addition to the descriptive statistics of the datasets, we also studied the semantic and lexical difference between the set of gold texts t and synthetic text t' using Cosine Similarity as a measure. The sentence encoders, SimCSE[6] (for English) Camembert-large[7] (for French), were used for analyzing the semantic difference, while Bag-of-Words with TF-IDF was used for the lexical difference. Figure 3 shows the distribution of the score. Since t and t' describe the same knowledge graph K_t, despite their different writing styles, higher semantic similarity scores are expected. Lower lexical similarity scores indicate that different lexical properties and grammatical structures were used, even though both t and t' describe roughly the same K_t. A more in-depth study for producing more diverse texts needs to be done whether through parameter control, reworking the prompt template, or filtering out texts that will increase the Self-BLEU score.

	DocRED		FRSD	
	$\mathcal{G}$	$\mathcal{S}$	$\mathcal{G}$	$\mathcal{S}$
# Docs	3053	3023	400	1200
# Tokens	603468	493638	56128	184667
Toks/Doc	197.66	163.29	140.32	153.89
Sents/Doc	7.94	6.66	6.20	6.69
Sent Len	25.96	24.94	23.48	23.53
# Entity	79481	56766	11436	36825
# Triples	117712	157905	12940	41771
# Labels	147358	102558	15781	46912
Labels/Doc	48.27	33.93	39.45	39.09
Self-BLEU	0.53	0.63	0.58	0.76

Table 3: Descriptive statistics of $\mathcal{G}$ and $\mathcal{S}$ for both the DocRED and FRSD dataset. **# Labels** here represents the total number of labeled tokens in the dataset.

5.2 Intrinsic Evaluation

The performance on NER task can be observed in Table 4. We achieved high F1-scores of 0.93 and 0.92, demonstrating the effectiveness of our framework's annotation capacity. Among all the tags, we noticed that `MISC` was the only tag that scored the lowest. As for RE tasks, we considered two types of annotation accuracy: 1) Relation and 2) Evidence. We need to take into account that, originally the best DREEAM model only achieved a 67.53 F1-score on DocRED test set, thus the results reported might not be very accurate. Table 5 presents the accuracy results, showing that our naive assumption heuristic achieved a 0.63 F1-score for Relation and a 0.37 F1-score for Evidence. As $\mathcal{S}$'s evidence was solely based on a very naive heuristic, an over-prediction of the evidence is to be expected, leading to a low precision score and a high recall score.

	Precision	**Recall**	**F1-score**
B-LOC	0.95	0.98	0.96
B-MISC	0.92	0.74	0.82
B-ORG	0.91	0.89	0.90
B-PER	0.98	0.97	0.98
I-LOC	0.96	0.93	0.94
I-MISC	0.83	0.83	0.83
I-ORG	0.93	0.87	0.90
I-PER	0.98	0.99	0.98
Micro	0.94	0.91	0.93
Macro	0.94	0.91	0.92

Table 4: Intrinsic performance with BERT-NER's predictions as true labels.

	Precision	**Recall**	**F1-score**
Relation	0.66	0.61	0.63
Evidence	0.26	0.60	0.37

Table 5: Intrinsic performance with DREEAM's prediction as true labels.

5.3 Extrinsic Evaluation

While generating a large volume of new annotated synthetic texts can be accomplished with relative ease, the challenge lies in optimally utilizing this synthetic data. We conducted a series of experiments in order to address this.

DocRED In NER task, we conducted training under different scenarios. We trained the models separately on 1) the original training set $\mathcal{G}$, 2) the synthetic set $\mathcal{S}$, 3) a combination of $\mathcal{G} + \mathcal{S}$, 4) a subset of $\mathcal{G}$ by sampling documents that have $\geq$ 20% labeled tokens which left us with 1564 documents. As can be seen from Table 6, using only $\mathcal{G}$ generally yields better results. Although training solely on $\mathcal{S}$ produces acceptable results (79.14 on Weighted-F1), there is a significant performance gap between $\mathcal{G}$ and $\mathcal{S}$. Similar training strategies were applied for the RE task, except for scenario

[6] `https://github.com/princeton-nlp/SimCSE`

[7] `https://huggingface.co/dangvantuan/sentence-camembert-large`

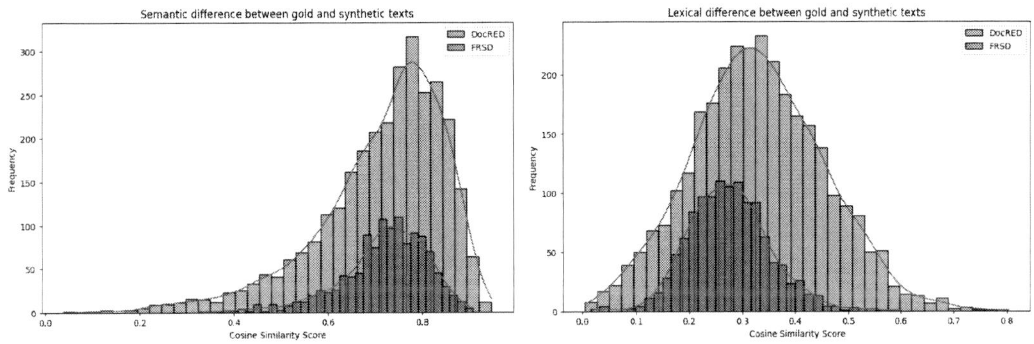

Figure 3: Distribution of the cosine similarity score between text t and t'. The left figure depicts semantic differences, while the right shows lexical differences. The text example can be found in the Appendix section A.

4, in which the model was trained using a random sample of 20% of the training set. We observed the same trend based on the scores shown in Table 7. From the evaluation results, it can be inferred that both tasks might benefit from more diverse training sets with higher semantic differences to generalize better and produce more robust performance.

FRSD For our first model BS, we randomly split $\mathcal{S}$ into three and used them as complement data to train the BS model. Results in Table 8 show the interest of using $\mathcal{S}$ as a complement training data. Notably, as shown in Tables 9 and 10, $\mathcal{S}$ enhances the performance of classes with fewer samples for Event and Attribute extraction tasks. As outlined in Section 3.4, annotations from $\mathcal{S}$ carry the risk of introducing a lot of noise due to incomplete annotation or wrongly assumed relations. Furthermore, the annotations also heavily rely on the capacity of the LLMs used. To address this issue, we tried to improve annotations by implementing a Teacher-Student learning strategy. This solution consists of training a Teacher model on $\mathcal{G}$. The Teacher model is then used to make predictions on $\mathcal{S}$. These predictions are used as annotations to pre-train a second model, the Student model. Finally, the training of the Student model is refined on the $\mathcal{G}$. For this experiment, we used only the batch of 400 texts from $\mathcal{S}$. Four training scenarios were explored: no pre-training, pre-training with $\mathcal{S}$'s annotation, pre-training on synthetic texts with annotations produced by the Teacher model, and finally, a pre-training with $\mathcal{S}$'s annotation together with those of the Teacher model. We discovered that there is an increase in the performance for classes with low samples, except for Attributes. The second observation is that using $\mathcal{S}$'s annotations alone is useful for low sample classes for Events and Entities. This significance grows when the annotations are combined with predictions from the Teacher model. The results are shown in Tables 1, 2.

	Weighted-F1	Macro-F1	Micro-F1
$\mathcal{G}$	**88.02**	**86.45**	**88.04**
$\mathcal{S}$	79.14	76.87	79.21
$\mathcal{G}+\mathcal{S}$	87.89	86.25	87.90
$\mathcal{G}_f$	**86.26**	**84.43**	**86.30**
$\mathcal{G}_f+\mathcal{S}$	85.87	84.06	85.89

Table 6: Evaluation results on DocRED's named entity recognition task.

	F1	Ign-F1	Evi-F1
$\mathcal{G}$	**61.51**±0.19	**59.7**±0.19	**52.09**±0.22
$\mathcal{S}$	44.41±0.48	43.51±0.46	31.17±0.46
$\mathcal{G}+\mathcal{S}$	60.04±0.34	58.27±0.36	50.67±0.36
$\mathcal{G}_f$	**56.12±0.28**	**55.46±0.28**	**46.99±0.28**
$\mathcal{G}_f+\mathcal{S}$	54.79±0.26	53.5±0.25	44.86±0.31

Table 7: Evaluation results on DocRED's relation extraction task. We used the same metrics that were proposed in DocRED's paper (Yao et al., 2019).

6 Conclusion

In this paper, we introduced a novel framework that leverages Knowledge Graphs and Large Language Models to generate annotated synthetic data for Information Extraction tasks. Our preliminary experiments demonstrated that while the data generated by this framework can enhance the performance of classes with limited training samples, it cannot yet serve as a substitute for the original data. Theoretically, within this framework, data anonymization and bias mitigation can be easily accomplished by modifying the input Knowledge Graphs. However,

Data	Events F1 macro	Events F1 micro	Entities F1 macro	Entities F1 micro	Attributes F1 macro	Attributes F1 micro
$\mathcal{G}$	41.83 ± 0.79	55.56 ± 0.63	65.41 ± 1.04	**81.60** ± 0.26	56.74 ± 0.86	80.02 ± 0.26
$\mathcal{G} + \mathcal{S}_{400}$	43.92 ± 1.14	55.94 ± 0.80	**65.82** ± 1.04	81.14 ± 0.14	59.17 ± 1.11	**80.86** ± 0.32
$\mathcal{G} + \mathcal{S}_{800}$	43.61 ± 0.96	56.00 ± 0.47	64.33 ± 0.94	79.91 ± 0.34	59.96 ± 1.82	80.61 ± 0.69
$\mathcal{G} + \mathcal{S}_{1200}$	**44.20** ± 1.08	**56.45** ± 0.85	63.56 ± 0.82	80.06 ± 0.38	**60.67** ± 0.95	80.46 ± 0.35

Table 8: Evaluation results for Event/Entity/Attribute extraction using BS. {400, 800, 1200} are dataset's sizes.

Classes	$\mathcal{G}$ #Samples	$\mathcal{G}$ F1-score	$\mathcal{G} + \mathcal{S}_{1200}$ #Samples	$\mathcal{G} + \mathcal{S}_{1200}$ F1-score
CIVIL_WAR_OUTBREAK	19	**57.45**	440	54.83
COUP_D_ETAT	24	44.23	198	**45.22**
DEMONSTRATION	38	4.11	1215	**12.44**
DRUG_OPERATION	13	18.48	242	**41.30**
ELECTION	27	65.73	197	**82.45**
ILLEGAL_CIVIL_DEMO.	29	**27.31**	30	20.48
NATURAL_CAUSES_DEATH	9	40.25	15	**43.02**
POLITICAL_VIOLENCE	29	**10.72**	137	3.51
POLLUTION	31	60.11	141	**68.01**
SUICIDE	22	39.27	22	**41.92**
TRAFFICKING	38	31.85	381	**45.27**

Table 9: Evaluation results on some of the Event classes with the lowest data samples based on BS.

Classes	$\mathcal{G}$ #Samples	$\mathcal{G}$ F1-score	$\mathcal{G} + \mathcal{S}_{1200}$ #Samples	$\mathcal{G} + \mathcal{S}_{1200}$ F1-score
HEIGHT	4	26.81	14	**45.56**
LATITUDE	3	41.83	4	**53.66**
LENGTH	4	23.11	13	**47.79**
LONGITUDE	5	41.83	5	**42.15**
MATERIAL_REFERENCE	14	47.36	31	**54.94**
QUANTITY_MIN	20	**46.72**	76	42.77
TIME_MAX	11	**42.81**	12	41.46
TIME_MIN	28	25.43	33	**30.20**
WEIGHT	15	74.42	24	**84.96**
WIDTH	4	4.66	11	**11.39**

Table 10: Evaluation results on some of the Attribute classes with the lowest data samples based on BS.

further research and experimentation are required to fully realize and validate these possibilities.

7 Limitation

One of the limitations of this study is that we only generated new data based on the original data's Knowledge Graphs, which led to low diversity in the dataset. Future work could involve experimenting with modified Knowledge Graphs to enhance diversity. We acknowledge that the annotations produced by our framework are far from perfect and require further enhancements. One potential improvement could be the use of a dependency tree to identify co-references and annotate them. It could also be used to extract relations between entities. Another path for improvement could be the use of attention weights from the generated texts. This could help identify the evidence of relations by pinpointing where the head and tail entities most attentively interact within the texts.

References

Piotr Bojanowski, Edouard Grave, Armand Joulin, and Tomas Mikolov. 2016. Enriching word vectors with subword information. *Transactions of the Association for Computational Linguistics*, 5:135–146.

Tom B. Brown, Benjamin Mann, Nick Ryder, Melanie Subbiah, Jared Kaplan, Prafulla Dhariwal, Arvind Neelakantan, Pranav Shyam, Girish Sastry, Amanda Askell, Sandhini Agarwal, Ariel Herbert-Voss, Gretchen Krueger, Tom Henighan, Rewon Child, Aditya Ramesh, Daniel M. Ziegler, Jeff Wu, Clemens Winter, Christopher Hesse, Mark Chen, Eric Sigler, Mateusz Litwin, Scott Gray, Benjamin Chess, Jack Clark, Christopher Berner, Sam McCandlish, Alec Radford, Ilya Sutskever, and Dario Amodei. 2020. Language models are few-shot learners. *ArXiv*, abs/2005.14165.

V. Claveau, Antoine Chaffin, and Ewa Kijak. 2021. Generating artificial texts as substitution or complement of training data. *ArXiv*, abs/2110.13016.

Claude Coulombe. 2018. Text data augmentation made simple by leveraging nlp cloud apis. *ArXiv*, abs/1812.04718.

Mathieu Dehouck and Carlos Gómez-Rodríguez. 2020. Data augmentation via subtree swapping for dependency parsing of low-resource languages. In *International Conference on Computational Linguistics*.

Xiang Deng and Huan Sun. 2019. Leveraging 2-hop distant supervision from table entity pairs for relation extraction. *ArXiv*, abs/1909.06007.

A. R. Fabbri, Simeng Han, Haoyuan Li, Haoran Li, Marjan Ghazvininejad, Shafiq R. Joty, Dragomir R. Radev, and Yashar Mehdad. 2020. Improving zero and few-shot abstractive summarization with intermediate fine-tuning and data augmentation. In *North American Chapter of the Association for Computational Linguistics*.

Albert Q. Jiang, Alexandre Sablayrolles, Arthur Mensch, Chris Bamford, Devendra Singh Chaplot, Diego de las Casas, Florian Bressand, Gianna Lengyel, Guillaume Lample, Lucile Saulnier, Lélio Renard Lavaud, Marie-Anne Lachaux, Pierre Stock, Teven Le Scao, Thibaut Lavril, Thomas Wang, Timothée Lacroix, and William El Sayed. 2023. Mistral 7b.

Sosuke Kobayashi. 2018. Contextual augmentation: Data augmentation by words with paradigmatic relations. In *Proceedings of the 2018 Conference of the North American Chapter of the Association for Computational Linguistics: Human Language Technologies, Volume 2 (Short Papers)*, pages 452–457, New Orleans, Louisiana. Association for Computational Linguistics.

Patrick Lewis, Ethan Perez, Aleksandara Piktus, Fabio Petroni, Vladimir Karpukhin, Naman Goyal, Heinrich Kuttler, Mike Lewis, Wen tau Yih, Tim Rocktäschel, Sebastian Riedel, and Douwe Kiela. 2020. Retrieval-augmented generation for knowledge-intensive nlp tasks. *ArXiv*, abs/2005.11401.

Jiachang Liu, Dinghan Shen, Yizhe Zhang, Bill Dolan, Lawrence Carin, and Weizhu Chen. 2022. What makes good in-context examples for GPT-3? In *Proceedings of Deep Learning Inside Out (DeeLIO 2022): The 3rd Workshop on Knowledge Extraction and Integration for Deep Learning Architectures*, pages 100–114, Dublin, Ireland and Online. Association for Computational Linguistics.

Youmi Ma, An Wang, and Naoaki Okazaki. 2023. DREEAM: Guiding attention with evidence for improving document-level relation extraction. In *Proceedings of the 17th Conference of the European Chapter of the Association for Computational Linguistics*, pages 1971–1983, Dubrovnik, Croatia. Association for Computational Linguistics.

Tomas Mikolov, Kai Chen, Gregory S. Corrado, and Jeffrey Dean. 2013. Efficient estimation of word representations in vector space. In *International Conference on Learning Representations*.

George A. Miller. 1995. Wordnet: a lexical database for english. *Commun. ACM*, 38(11):39–41.

Jeffrey Pennington, Richard Socher, and Christopher D. Manning. 2014. Glove: Global vectors for word representation. In *Conference on Empirical Methods in Natural Language Processing*.

Maxime Prieur, Cédric du Mouza, Guillaume Gadek, and Bruno Grilheres. 2024. Shadowfax: Harnessing textual knowledge base population. In *Proceedings of the 47th International ACM SIGIR Conference on Research and Development in Information Retrieval, SIGIR 2024, Wshington, USA, July 23-27, 2023*, Washington, USA. ACM.

Roland Roller, Eneko Agirre, Aitor Soroa Etxabe, and Mark Stevenson. 2015. Improving distant supervision using inference learning. *ArXiv*, abs/1509.03739.

Gilles Sérasset. 2015. Dbnary: Wiktionary as a lemon-based multilingual lexical resource in rdf. *Semantic Web*, 6:355–361.

Richard Shin, Christopher Lin, Sam Thomson, Charles Chen, Subhro Roy, Emmanouil Antonios Platanios, Adam Pauls, Dan Klein, Jason Eisner, and Benjamin Van Durme. 2021. Constrained language models yield few-shot semantic parsers. In *Proceedings of the 2021 Conference on Empirical Methods in Natural Language Processing*, pages 7699–7715, Online and Punta Cana, Dominican Republic. Association for Computational Linguistics.

Zhen Wan, Fei Cheng, Zhuoyuan Mao, Qianying Liu, Haiyue Song, Jiwei Li, and Sadao Kurohashi. 2023. Gpt-re: In-context learning for relation extraction using large language models. *ArXiv*, abs/2305.02105.

Xuezhi Wang, Jason Wei, Dale Schuurmans, Quoc Le, Ed Huai hsin Chi, and Denny Zhou. 2022. Self-consistency improves chain of thought reasoning in language models. *ArXiv*, abs/2203.11171.

Jason Wei, Xuezhi Wang, Dale Schuurmans, Maarten Bosma, Ed Huai hsin Chi, F. Xia, Quoc Le, and Denny Zhou. 2022. Chain of thought prompting elicits reasoning in large language models. *ArXiv*, abs/2201.11903.

Jason Wei and Kai Zou. 2019. EDA: Easy data augmentation techniques for boosting performance on text classification tasks. In *Proceedings of the 2019 Conference on Empirical Methods in Natural Language Processing and the 9th International Joint Conference on Natural Language Processing (EMNLP-IJCNLP)*, pages 6382–6388, Hong Kong, China. Association for Computational Linguistics.

Ziang Xie, Sida I. Wang, Jiwei Li, Daniel Lévy, Allen Nie, Dan Jurafsky, and A. Ng. 2017. Data noising as smoothing in neural network language models. *ArXiv*, abs/1703.02573.

Shunyu Yao, Dian Yu, Jeffrey Zhao, Izhak Shafran, Thomas L. Griffiths, Yuan Cao, and Karthik Narasimhan. 2023. Tree of thoughts: Deliberate problem solving with large language models. *ArXiv*, abs/2305.10601.

Yuan Yao, Deming Ye, Peng Li, Xu Han, Yankai Lin, Zhenghao Liu, Zhiyuan Liu, Lixin Huang, Jie Zhou, and Maosong Sun. 2019. DocRED: A large-scale document-level relation extraction dataset. In *Proceedings of the 57th Annual Meeting of the Association for Computational Linguistics*, pages 764–777, Florence, Italy. Association for Computational Linguistics.

Danqing Zhang, Tao Li, Haiyang Zhang, and Bing Yin. 2020. On data augmentation for extreme multi-label classification.

Zihao Zhao, Eric Wallace, Shi Feng, Dan Klein, and Sameer Singh. 2021. Calibrate before use: Improving few-shot performance of language models. In *Proceedings of the 38th International Conference on Machine Learning*, volume 139 of *Proceedings of Machine Learning Research*, pages 12697–12706. PMLR.

Enwei Zhu and Jinpeng Li. 2022. Boundary smoothing for named entity recognition. In *Proceedings of the 60th Annual Meeting of the Association for Computational Linguistics (Volume 1: Long Papers)*, pages 7096–7108, Dublin, Ireland. Association for Computational Linguistics.

A Example Appendix

Examples of text comparison between $\mathcal{G}$ and $\mathcal{S}$ are provided in Table 11 for English and Table 12 for French. Figure 4 illustrates a sample of Knowledge Graph K_t along with its corresponding gold text t and synthetic text t'. An example of an entity extraction prompt can be seen in Figure 5.

Knowledge Graph ***Kt***

("Australian Army":ORG, "conflict", "World War II":MISC)
("Australian Army":ORG, "country", "Australia":LOC)
("John Scanlan":PER, "military branch", "Australian Army":ORG)
("John Scanlan":PER, "conflict", "World War II":MISC)
("John Scanlan":PER, "country of citizenship", "Australia":LOC)
("Australia":LOC, "participant of", "World War II":MISC)
("Imperial Japanese Army":ORG, "conflict", "World War II":MISC)
("Imperial Japanese Army":ORG, "country", "Japan":LOC)
("Imperial Japanese Army":ORG, "country", "Japanese":LOC)
("Japan":LOC, "participant of", "World War II":MISC)
("Japan":LOC, "ethnic group", "Japanese":LOC)
("USS Sturgeon":MISC, "conflict", "World War II":MISC)
("MV Neptuna":MISC, "country", "Australia":LOC)
("HMAT Zealandia":MISC, "country", "Australia":LOC)
("Lark Force":ORG, "operator", "Australian Army":ORG)
("Lark Force":ORG, "inception", "March 1941":TIME)
("Lark Force":ORG, "conflict", "World War II":MISC)
("Lark Force":ORG, "country", "Australia":LOC)

Gold Text ***t***

During World War II, the Australian Army played a significant role in the global conflict. One notable figure within this branch of the military was John Scanlan, who served as a member of the Australian Army and participated in the war efforts. Born in Australia, Scanlan joined the army at an unknown date, eventually rising through the ranks to serve as a highly decorated soldier during World War II. His involvement in various conflicts and campaigns earned him numerous accolades, including honors such as the Distinguished Conduct Medal and the Military Cross. Scanlan's service took place under the umbrella of the Australian Army, which itself was an active participant in the war effort. This organization, based in Australia, saw many of its members deployed throughout the world, particularly in areas such as the Middle East and the Pacific theater of operations. As a result, the Australian Army found itself engaging with a variety of adversaries, including the Imperial Japanese Army, which itself represented a formidable opponent in the region. Among the many missions undertaken by the Australian Army during the war, one specific campaign stands out. This was the Lark Force, an army unit comprised primarily of Australian soldiers that was formed in March 1941. The mission of the Lark Force was to defend strategic locations in Malaya against potential invasion by Japanese forces. While they ultimately proved unsuccessful in this regard, their bravery and sacrifice in the face of overwhelming odds helped to delay Japanese advances and provide valuable intelligence to Allied forces. Notably, some members of the Lark Force were evacuated aboard the USS Sturgeon, while others were transported via the MV Neptuna and HMAT Zealandia, both of which were Australian vessels. These examples serve to illustrate the wide-ranging impact of the Australian Army during the course of the war, as well as the sacrifices and contributions made by individual soldiers like John Scanlan. Their stories help to shed light on the complexities and realities of war, providing valuable insights into the experiences of those who served in this pivotal moment in history.

Synthetic Text ***t'***

During World War II, the Australian Army played a significant role, with over 330,000 men serving overseas. Among them was John Scanlan, a soldier who served in various campaigns in the Pacific theater. Born in Australia, Scanlan enlisted in the army in 1940 and was assigned to the Lark Force, a specialized unit tasked with defending Singapore against Japanese invasion. In March 1941, the Lark Force was formally established, and Scanlan was among its founding members. The force, composed primarily of Australian infantry, artillery, and engineering units, operated mainly in Malaya and Singapore. Its primary mission was to provide defensive cover against any potential Japanese threat in the region. As the war intensified, the Lark Force found itself facing increasingly formidable opponents. The Imperial Japanese Army, which had already conquered much of Southeast Asia, launched a massive assault on Singapore in February 1942. The Lark Force, along with other Allied forces, put up a fierce resistance, but ultimately they were overwhelmed. Thousands of soldiers, including Scanlan, were captured and sent to prisoner-of-war camps in Japan. Many never returned home.

Figure 4: Sample of a knowledge graph K_t with its t and t'.

Prompt Template | **Entity Extraction**

You are a text annotator. Your objectives are to: 1/ Analyze the given text in detail, 2/ Annotate possible entities based on these entity types: person(PER), location(LOC), organization(ORG), time(TIME), numbers(NUM), and miscellaneous entity names(MISC). Response with the annotation in this format: "Possible Entities: e_1,e_2,...., e_n", where e_1 to e_n are the extracted entities

===

Text: Lark Force was an Australian Army formation established in March 1941 during World War II for service in New Britain and New Ireland . Under the command of Lieutenant Colonel John Scanlan, it was raised in Australia and deployed to Rabaul and Kavieng, aboard SS Katoomba, MV Neptuna and HMAT Zealandia, to defend their strategically important harbours and airfields . The objective of the force, was to maintain a forward air observation line as long as possible and to make the enemy fight for this line rather than abandon it at the first threat as the force was considered too small to withstand any invasion . Most of Lark Force was captured by the Imperial Japanese Army after Rabaul and Kavieng were captured in January 1942 . The officers of Lark Force were transported to Japan, however the NCOs and men were unfortunately torpedoed by the USS Sturgeon while being transported aboard the Montevideo Maru . Only a handful of the Japanese crew were rescued, with none of the between 1,050 and 1,053 prisoners aboard surviving as they were still locked below deck.

Possible Entities: (Kavieng | LOC), (SS Katoomba | MISC), (NCOs | MISC), (HMAT Zealandia | MISC), (Montevideo Maru | MISC), (1,050 | NUM), (1,053 | NUM), (March 1941 | TIME), (USS Sturgeon | MISC), (Rabaul | LOC), (Australia | LOC), (Lark Force | ORG), (Imperial Japanese Army | ORG), (Australian Army | ORG), (New Ireland | LOC), (MV Neptuna | MISC), (World War II | MISC), (Japanese | LOC), (Japan | LOC), (January 1942 | TIME), (John Scanlan | PER), (New Britain | LOC)

===

===

Text: During World War II, the Australian Army played a significant role, with over 330,000 men serving overseas. Among them was John Scanlan, a soldier who served in various campaigns in the Pacific theater. Born in Australia, Scanlan enlisted in the army in 1940 and was assigned to the Lark Force, a specialized unit tasked with defending Singapore against Japanese invasion. In March 1941, the Lark Force was formally established, and Scanlan was among its founding members. The force, composed primarily of Australian infantry, artillery, and engineering units, operated mainly in Malaya and Singapore. Its primary mission was to provide defensive cover against any potential Japanese threat in the region. As the war intensified, the Lark Force found itself facing increasingly formidable opponents. The Imperial Japanese Army, which had already conquered much of Southeast Asia, launched a massive assault on Singapore in February 1942. The Lark Force, along with other Allied forces, put up a fierce resistance, but ultimately they were overwhelmed. Thousands of soldiers, including Scanlan, were captured and sent to prisoner-of-war camps in Japan. Many never returned home.

Figure 5: Example of prompt used for entity extraction.

Texts from $\mathcal{G}$	Texts from $\mathcal{S}$
Pacific Fair is a major shopping centre in Broadbeach Waters on the Gold Coast, Queensland, Australia. It was Queensland's largest regional shopping centre until 2006. Pacific Fair was developed by Hooker Retail Developments and opened in 1977 on what was swampland with 96 specialty stores and two anchor tenants. Since then, Pacific Fair has undergone numerous expansions and has grown to have more than 300 specialty stores and four anchor tenants. In January 2014, work began on a major redevelopment project to meet the predicted regional growth on the Gold Coast. Prior to the redevelopment, the shopping centre had four main major stores including a four-level Myer, Kmart, Target, Coles and Toys 'R' Us. Daimaru operated in the centre before its Australian withdrawal, albeit briefly. It also had a 12-screen Birch Carroll and Coyle Cinema (re-opened as Event Cinemas in late 2015). Pacific Fair is a major public transport interchange on the Gold Coast, serviced by Surfside Buslines, and the Broadbeach South station located not far from the shopping centre. Nearby is The Star Gold Coast and Gold Coast Convention & Exhibition Centre. Pacific Fair fronts Little Tallebudgera Creek and is the southern end of the Surfers Riverwalk. This shopping centre was featured on the third season of The Mole.	Located in the state of Queensland, Australia, Surfers Riverwalk is a scenic walkway along the banks of the Nerang River in the city of Gold Coast. This administrative territorial entity falls under the larger jurisdiction of Queensland. The Gold Coast, also situated in Queensland, is a popular tourist destination and is known for its stunning beaches, theme parks, and shopping complexes like Pacific Fair, which was established in 1977. Some well-known retail chains operating in the area include Toys 'R' Us, Myer, Kmart, Coles, and Daimaru. Transportation options include Surfside Buslines and the Broadbeach South train station. Nearby attractions include Little Tallebudgera Creek and the Gold Coast Convention & Exhibition Centre. Surfers Riverwalk offers views of both the river and the beachfront, making it a popular spot for locals and tourists alike. Event Cinemas, another prominent establishment in the area, provides entertainment options for moviegoers. Overall, the Gold Coast boasts a diverse range of businesses and amenities catering to the needs of its residents and visitors.
Lark Force was an Australian Army formation established in March 1941 during World War II for service in New Britain and New Ireland. Under the command of Lieutenant Colonel John Scanlan, it was raised in Australia and deployed to Rabaul and Kavieng, aboard SS Katoomba, MV Neptuna and HMAT Zealandia, to defend their strategically important harbours and airfields . The objective of the force, was to maintain a forward air observation line as long as possible and to make the enemy fight for this line rather than abandon it at the first threat as the force was considered too small to withstand any invasion. Most of Lark Force was captured by the Imperial Japanese Army after Rabaul and Kavieng were captured in January 1942. The officers of Lark Force were transported to Japan, however the NCOs and men were unfortunately torpedoed by the USS Sturgeon while being transported aboard the Montevideo Maru. Only a handful of the Japanese crew were rescued, with none of the between 1,050 and 1,053 prisoners aboard surviving as they were still locked below deck.	During World War II, the Australian Army played a significant role, with over 330,000 men serving overseas. Among them was John Scanlan, a soldier who served in various campaigns in the Pacific theater. Born in Australia, Scanlan enlisted in the army in 1940 and was assigned to the Lark Force, a specialized unit tasked with defending Singapore against Japanese invasion. In March 1941, the Lark Force was formally established, and Scanlan was among its founding members. The force, composed primarily of Australian infantry, artillery, and engineering units, operated mainly in Malaya and Singapore. Its primary mission was to provide defensive cover against any potential Japanese threat in the region. As the war intensified, the Lark Force found itself facing increasingly formidable opponents. The Imperial Japanese Army, which had already conquered much of Southeast Asia, launched a massive assault on Singapore in February 1942. The Lark Force, along with other Allied forces, put up a fierce resistance, but ultimately they were overwhelmed. Thousands of soldiers, including Scanlan, were captured and sent to prisoner-of-war camps in Japan. Many never returned home.

Table 11: Samples of English Gold and Synthetic texts. Highlighted words are the entities and words in Red are the entities that did not appear in the original text t.

Texts from $\mathcal{G}$	Texts from $\mathcal{S}$
Le 19 septembre 2020, un mouvement de grève a perturbé les cours au sein de l'Université du Michigan. En effet, les enseignants de l'université ont décidé de fermer les portes de toutes les salles d'étude. Les enseignants reprochent au gouvernement d'avoir ignoré leurs relances concernant le non-respect des termes du contrat signé entre les deux parties. Après avoir été annoncée sur les réseaux sociaux, la grève a entraîné une confrontation entre les enseignants et les forces de l'ordre. Monsieur Mehmet-akhif Hassan est mort après avoir été brutalement frappé sur la tête avec une matraque durant la confrontation. Il a été évacué en urgence dans une ambulance pour être conduit à l'hôpital, mais les secouristes ont déclaré son décès en route.	Le 19 septembre 2020, une grève des enseignants au Michigan a provoqué une confrontation entre ces derniers et les forces de l'ordre, entraînant également une crise dans le gouvernement. La confrontation a débouché sur un accident de la route, où Mehmet-akhif Hassan, un citoyen présent à l'endroit des événements, a été grièvement blessé. L'accident a également causé divers dégâts matériels, notamment la perte d'un ambulance. Les secouristes ont rapidement pris en charge Mehmet-akhif Hassan et l'ont emmené à l'hôpital. Les enseignants, qui avaient par ailleurs bloqué les portes de l'université, ont également protesté devant cet incident, affirmant qu'il était lié à leur conflit avec la police et le gouvernement. Ces incidents ont également affecté les relations entre les différents groupes impliqués, en particulier celles entre les enseignants et les forces de l'ordre, ainsi que celles entre les enseignants et le gouvernement.
Naomi Zhang, la multimilliardaire et fondatrice de l'entreprise "BOMO", était à la tête de l'entreprise numéro 1 dans la distribution d'alcool en Argentine. Un de ses employés, Monsieur Thibault Alekseï, d'origine serbe, était le chef d'un gang de vente d'armes à feu. Il utilisait sa voiture de fonction pour livrer de la drogue et de la cocaïne à plusieurs entreprises. Il avait livré des dizaines déntreprises, dont "POLIS". Lorsque la nouvelle avait été annoncée dans la presse, l'entreprise de Naomi Zhang avait été au cœur dún scandale médiatique et avait vu son nombre de commandes diminuer.	Naomi Zhang est une femme d'affaires influente basée en Argentine. Elle est fondatrice de BOMO, une organisation non gouvernementale qui travaille activement pour améliorer la situation de nombreuses personnes au sein du pays. Thibault Alekseï, quant à lui, est un criminel serbe vivant également en Argentine. Il est impliqué dans la distribution illégale de drogues et fait partie d'une bande organisée appelée gang. Naomi Zhang et Thibault Alekseï sont tous deux présents en Argentine, où ils exercent leur influence respective sur divers secteurs de la vie quotidienne.

Table 12: Samples of French Gold and Synthetic texts. Highlighted words are the entities and words in Red are the entities that did not appear in the original text t. Certain entities may not have been included in K_t because they have no relationship to any other entity, which would explain why they were present in t but absent from t'.

HRGraph: Leveraging LLMs for HR Data Knowledge Graphs with Information Propagation-based Job Recommendation

Azmine Toushik Wasi
Shahjalal University of Science and Technology, Bangladesh
azmine32@student.sust.edu

Abstract

Knowledge Graphs (KGs) serving as semantic networks, prove highly effective in managing complex interconnected data in different domains, by offering a unified, contextualized, and structured representation with flexibility that allows for easy adaptation to evolving knowledge. Processing complex Human Resources (HR) data, KGs can help in different HR functions like recruitment, job matching, identifying learning gaps, and enhancing employee retention. Despite their potential, limited efforts have been made to implement practical HR knowledge graphs. This study addresses this gap by presenting a framework for effectively developing HR knowledge graphs from documents using Large Language Models. The resulting KG can be used for a variety of downstream tasks, including job matching, identifying employee skill gaps, and many more. In this work, we showcase instances where HR KGs prove instrumental in precise job matching, yielding advantages for both employers and employees. Empirical evidence from experiments with information propagation in KGs and Graph Neural Nets, along with case studies underscores the effectiveness of KGs in tasks such as job and employee recommendations and job area classification. Code and data are available at : https://github.com/azminewasi/HRGraph

1 Introduction

Knowledge Graph (KG) is a semantic network that stores real-world entities and their relationships. It uses nodes representing objects, places, or persons, connected by edges defining relationships. It can integrate diverse data, contextualize information through linking and semantic metadata, and remain flexible, accommodating dynamic knowledge changes seamlessly (Hogan et al., 2021; Wasi et al., 2024; Yang et al., 2024; Khorashadizadeh et al., 2023).

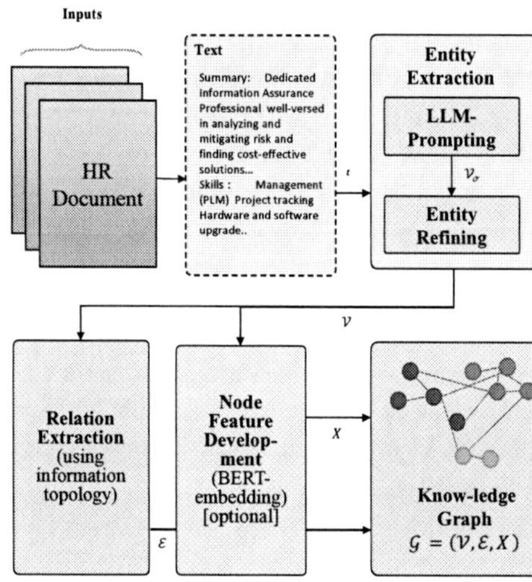

Figure 1: The overall framework of our **HRGraph**. It involves passing text data extracted from HR documents through a LLM to obtain entities and entity types, which are used to build a base knowledge graph with optional node features as BERT embeddings.

Knowledge Graphs can be highly effective for managing HR data, integrating diverse sources into a unified, structured representation (Zhang et al., 2021; Wasi et al., 2024). This is crucial for applications like recruitment and career path planning. By linking data with semantic metadata, KGs prevent misinterpretation, particularly in employee skill mapping and development. Their flexibility allows easy adaptation to new data and requirements across various HR functions. KGs enhance recruitment precision, skill and career mapping, optimize recruitment processes, identify learning gaps, improve retention strategies, and facilitate organizational knowledge sharing. For employees, KGs offer better job searches and recommendations, providing strong support from their perspective (Bourmpoulias et al., 2023; Bao et al., 2021).

In this study, we introduce a framework named **HRGraph**, aimed at constructing HR knowledge

Proceedings of the 1st Workshop on Knowledge Graphs and Large Language Models (KaLLM 2024), pages 56–62
August 15, 2024 ©2024 Association for Computational Linguistics

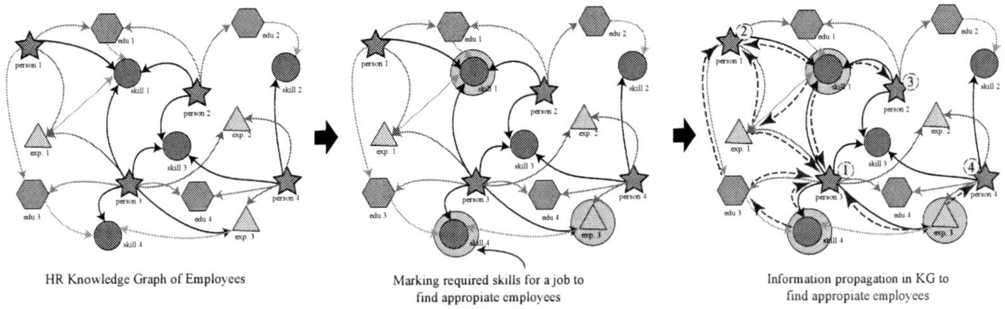

Figure 2: An overview of Job Matching and Recommendation framework using HR KGs of job applicants or employees. Using the intuition that company JDs and employee CVs or profiles should share matching entities like skills, experience, and education, we can match, find, and recommend employees from a knowledge graph. On the other hand, using a KG of many different job descriptions, we can use job-seeker skills, education, and other factors to find an appropriate employment to recommend.

graphs from various HR documents, such as Job Descriptions (JDs) and Curriculum Vitae (CVs). We illustrate the framework's utility through two practical examples as downstream tasks: employee and job recommendation using the HR knowledge graph. Our approach employs Large Language Models (LLMs) to identify and extract diverse entities, then extracts node features using pre-trained BERT, forming the knowledge graph with some post-processing. The resulting knowledge graph can be utilized for different downstream tasks. In this work, we use it for effective job matching and classification, catering to both employer and employee needs. The underlying idea is that company JDs and employee CVs or profiles should share matching entities like skills, experience, and education (an illustration of the proposal is presented in Figure 2), facilitating a comprehensive and accurate job match in both job-seeking and employee-search scenarios.

2 Related Works

2.1 Applications of Knowledge Graphs

KGs showcase versatility, excelling in applications such as semantic search, question answering, and recommendation systems (Wang et al., 2023b; Gao et al., 2020; Wasi et al., 2024). Their structured representation enhances search engine results and tailors suggestions. KGs, pivotal in Natural Language Processing (NLP), elevate information extraction and contribute to superior machine learning predictions. From enterprise knowledge management to biomedical research (Wu et al., 2023), KGs exhibit adaptability. Their integration of diverse data, contextualization, and inherent flexibility underpin effectiveness in managing and extracting insights across varied domains, including Medical AI (Wu et al., 2023), Wireless Communication Networks (He et al., 2022), Search Engines (Heist et al., 2020), and Big Data Decision Analysis (Janev et al., 2020). KGs emerge as indispensable tools, navigating dynamic information landscapes seamlessly (Hogan et al., 2021). Our work is inspired by these different uses of knowledge graphs.

2.2 HR Data and Knowledge Graphs

Though human resource knowledge graphs have good potential, limited efforts have been made in this domain. Zhang et al. (2021) adopted a top-down approach to create the ontology model of a human resource knowledge graph. The paper describes the significance of initially establishing ontology and defines entities and relationships for HR KGs. Cui (2022) presented a hypothesis to build a job description KG using NLP-based semantic entity extraction, but no detailed methodologies or experiments were presented. Wang et al. (2022) presented a job recommendation algorithm based on KGs, using word similarity to find recommendations. Upadhyay et al. (2021) uses a NER-based approach to build knowledge graphs to aid in job recommendation. However, no practical efforts have been made to implement a tangible HR knowledge graph in real-world scenarios based on LLMs and utilize one graph for multiple downstream tasks.

3 Methodology

The recent developments in LLMs, Knowledge Graph-based systems, and GNNs served as inspiration for the proposed methodology. Inspired by Wasi et al. (2024), HR knowledge graph uses Large Language Models (LLMs) for entity extraction and pre-trained NLP moels for node features enables a sophisticated representation of HR data by leveraging advanced language understanding capabilities. Existing literature presents alternative approaches, such as word similarity-based job recommendation (Wang et al., 2022) and NERs to build KGs (Upadhyay et al., 2021). Our proposed method stands out by leveraging LLMs for entity extraction and using BERT for features (length 256), offering a flexible and comprehensive approach that addresses practical challenges and enables multiple downstream tasks.

Entity Extraction and Refining. We begin by processing a job description (JD) or curriculum vitae (CV) as HR document text t, using a Large Language Model Gemini (Team, 2023). Prompts are available in Section B. This step results in the extraction of various entities ($\mathbb{V}^o$) from the text, capturing both entities and relationships. Subsequently, we perform post-processing on the entity set ($\mathbb{V}^o$) to filter out potential noises (such as KG nodes having more than 3 words or having no named entity or verbs), resulting in a refined set of entities $\mathbb{V}$.

Relation Extraction. To establish the initial connections between these entities, we leverage information topology and types, creating the initial connections set $\mathcal{E}$.

Node Feature Extraction. Employing a pre-trained BERT model, we generate feature vectors for each entity, constructing an initial feature matrix X. Thus, $\mathcal{V}$ represents the ensemble of nodes (entities) $\{v_1, v_2, v_3, \cdots v_N\}$, and $\mathcal{E}$ encompasses the collection of edges (relationships) $\{e_1, e_2, e_3, \cdots e_M\}$, where N and M signify the number of nodes and edges, respectively.

Knowledge Graph Construction. Combining $\mathcal{V}$, $\mathcal{E}$, and X forms our Knowledge Graph (KG), denoted as $\mathcal{G}^o = (\mathcal{V}, \mathcal{E}, X)$. The corresponding adjacency matrix, $\mathcal{A}$, has an element $\mathcal{A}_{ij} = 1$ if an edge connects v_i and v_j.

Each node $v \in \mathcal{V}$ and each edge $e \in \mathcal{E}$ have associated mapping functions, denoted as $\phi(v) : \mathcal{V} \rightarrow \mathcal{A}$ and $\varphi(e) : \mathcal{E} \rightarrow \mathcal{R}$. Here, $\mathcal{R}$ represents the edge type set, and $\mathcal{A}$ is the node type set, where $|\mathcal{A}| + |\mathcal{R}| > 2$. If we choose to use Knowledge Graph Embedding (KGE) (Cao et al., 2023), feature vector X can be excluded, and node embeddings can be obtained using different KGE models containing topological and structural knowledge.

4 Experiments with Knowledge Graphs

We collect 200 CVs and 200 job descriptions from online job portals, ensuring the CVs had minimal personal information and underwent manual review for privacy protection. Company details, openly available in job descriptions, were retained. The data was then manually labeled with the help of job portal filters for subsequent experiments. Any type of personally identifiable information (PII) such as names, detailed locations, email addresses, mobile numbers, etc., is thoroughly checked and removed.

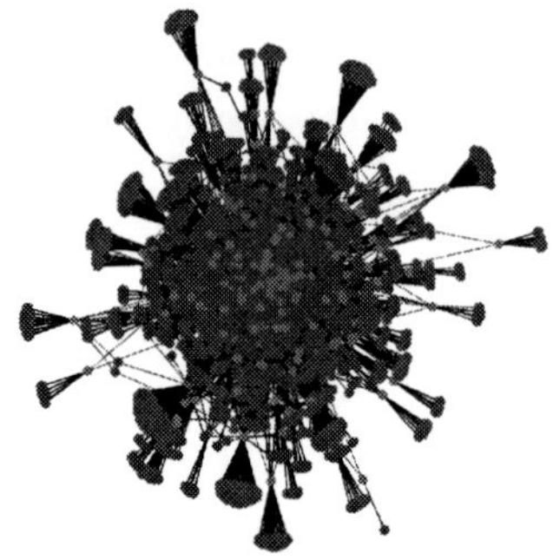

Figure 3: Our CV Knowledge Graph. Green dots are persons (CV), blue dots are skills, education and other entities

This dataset includes 20 categories of jobs and CVs targeting these jobs. The categories are: *Information Technology, Business Development, Finance, Advocate, Accountant, Engineering, Chef, Aviation, Fitness, Sales, Banking, Healthcare, Consultant, Construction, Public Relations, Human Resources, Designer, Arts, Teacher, Apparel.* In CVs, there are 10 for each category, but in job descriptions, there are more jobs in IT and engineering.

Prompts are provided in Section B. While the core design remains the same, the prompts are slightly different for Curriculum Vitae and Job Description, each tuned to its specific modality. The full inference code with examples is available in the GitHub repository.

4.1 Visualizing Knowledge Graphs

Utilizing the *Gemini* tool, we systematically gathered data and constructed two knowledge graphs for CVs and job descriptions (JDs) as HR knowledge bases, adhering to the defined methodology. To ensure relevance, entities exceeding a length of 4 were excluded. These knowledge graphs (presented in Figures 3 and 4) show that there is a huge connection between different jobs and the skills, education, and experience required. By utilizing these relationships, many downstream tasks can be done.

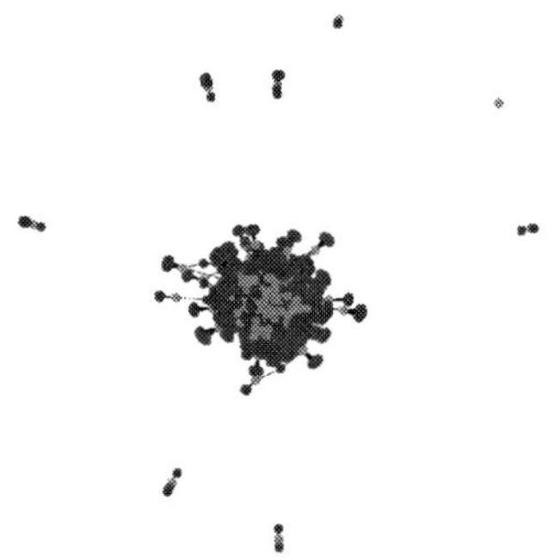

Figure 4: Our Job Description Knowledge Graph. Red dots are Jobs, blue dots are skills, education and other entities

5 Downstream Tasks

5.1 Information Propagation on HRGraph

Figure 2 provides an overview of our Job Matching and Recommendation Framework utilizing HR Knowledge Graphs for job applicants or employees. Leveraging the job description graph, we identify matching skill, education, and experience nodes, forming a targeted sub-graph with 3-hop neighbouring nodes. Node centrality within this sub-graph allows us to efficiently find and rank all relevant job nodes.

5.2 Task 01: Recommendation

The information propagation framework predicts the top N ranked jobs for each individual, enabling us to assess prediction accuracy and precision, thereby optimizing job recommendations. Similarly, in the task described above, we extend the methodology from Job Recommendation, utilizing the CV Knowledge Graph to identify employees based on matching skill, education, and experience. R denotes random recommendations, D denotes job recommendation using LLM entities directly for the top 5 recommendations. Table 1 shows that knowledge graph information propagation and ranking can provide very strong recommendations with good accuracy. Case studies are provided in Appendix A.

5.3 Task 02: Job Area Classification

In this task, we use KG-based job area classification on the CVs using two basic popular GNNs: GCN (Kipf and Welling, 2017) and GAT (Veličković et al., 2018). We compared the results with traditional and normally used deep learning models. Table 2 shows that Knowledge Graph-based GNN models are equally effective and slightly better than other models. More details are provided in Appendix A.

Table 1: Recommendation Results (↑)

N	Task	Avg. Acc.	Avg. Prec.
2	Job Rec.	0.668	0.675
2	Employee Rec.	0.684	0.685
5	Job Rec.	0.748	0.764
5	Employee Rec.	0.784	0.792
10	Job Rec.	0.702	0.700
10	Employee Rec.	0.715	0.708
D	Job Rec.	0.670	0.655
D	Employee Rec.	0.620	0.665
R	Job Rec.	0.323	0.312
R	Employee Rec.	0.373	0.361

Table 2: Job Area Classification Results (↑)

Model	Accuracy	Precision	Recall
Tfidf+LogR.	0.745	0.770	0.740
Tfidf+DecT.	0.655	0.670	0.655
Tfidf+RF	0.680	0.675	0.680
Tfidf+GBC	0.775	0.805	0.775
Tfidf+MLP	0.655	0.670	0.655
Transformer	0.660	0.645	0.675
GCN	0.785	0.800	0.795
GAT	0.775	0.835	0.775

6 Discussion

We believe that transforming HR data into a knowledge graph holds a great promise in shaping the future of human resources data collection, management, and utilization. By envisioning HR data in this interconnected graph, organizations can unlock unprecedented insights, streamline recruitment processes, identify talent gaps, and foster employee growth. This approach not only enhances decision-making but also paves the way for a dynamic and adaptive HR ecosystem that propels organizational success in an ever-evolving landscape.

7 Conclusion

This study introduces a framework leveraging LLMs and GNNs to construct HR knowledge graphs from documents, working as a HR knowledge base for different HR tasks. The resulting KGs enhance various HR functions, including job matching, job area classification, and many more, demonstrating their efficacy through empirical evidence, benefiting both employers and employees.

Limitations

The framework's primary limitation lies in its dependence on LLMs, which, although powerful, can be unreliable and prone to hallucinations (Wang et al., 2023a). Given our model's exclusive reliance on LLMs for entity extraction, we observed instances where they deviated from the provided instructions. Also, a more sophisticated job-matching algorithm can be designed. Further research can be conducted on this to examine it in the future.

Ethical Considerations

In conducting this research, strict ethical guidelines were followed to ensure the privacy and confidentiality of the individuals whose data was used. The primary focus was on handling personally identifiable information (PII) with the utmost care to protect the identity and privacy of all individuals.

Data Anonymization. To safeguard privacy, all PII such as names, detailed locations, email addresses, and mobile numbers were meticulously identified and removed from the dataset. This process involved thorough checks to ensure no traceable information was left that could potentially identify any individual.

Consent and Permissions. The original dataset was accessed with proper permissions and in compliance with the relevant data use agreements. By adhering to these agreements, we ensured that the data was used within the scope of its intended purpose, respecting the conditions under which the data was collected.

Privacy Protection. In this research, the dataset utilized was curated from an existing collection of CVs, ensuring that all personally identifiable information (PII) was meticulously removed to maintain privacy and adhere to ethical guidelines. The original data sources were accessed with proper permissions, and stringent anonymization techniques were applied to eliminate any traces of identity.

Secure Data Handling. Throughout the data curation and analysis process, secure data handling practices were implemented. This included using encrypted storage solutions and restricting access to the data to only those team members who required it for their specific research tasks. These measures were crucial in preventing unauthorized access and potential data breaches.

Ethical Use of Data. The research team was committed to using the data ethically, ensuring that the analysis and interpretations were fair and unbiased. The data was used solely for the purposes of this research and not for any commercial or exploitative activities. Additionally, findings were reported in a way that protected the anonymity of the individuals in the dataset.

Transparency and Accountability Transparency in our methods and accountability in our processes were maintained throughout the research. Detailed documentation of our data handling and anonymization procedures was kept, ensuring that the steps taken to protect privacy could be reviewed and verified by external parties if necessary.

Acknowledgements

We would like to express my sincere gratitude to Nikita Bhutani for her immense support of my ideas and her extraordinary efforts as an advisor in finding valuable resources for the study. We also extend my thanks to Estevam Hruschka for his insightful reviews and feedback. Additionally, I am particularly grateful to the NLP4HR Workshop (Hruschka et al., 2024) at EACL 2024 for providing me with the opportunities to be mentored and to develop my work.

References

Xiaona Bao, Chuan Xu, and Xiaona Bao. 2021. Analysis of knowledge graph on the subject of domestic human resource management practice. *E3S Web of Conferences*, 251:03098.

Stylianos Bourmpoulias, Dimitris Zeginis, and Konstantinos Tarabanis. 2023. An entity event knowledge graph for human resources management in public administration: the case of education personnel. In *2023 IEEE 25th Conference on Business Informatics (CBI)*, pages 1–8.

Jiahang Cao, Jinyuan Fang, Zaiqiao Meng, and Shangsong Liang. 2023. Knowledge graph embedding: A survey from the perspective of representation spaces.

Xin Cui. 2022. Knowledge graph with job recommendation.

Yang Gao, Yi-Fan Li, Yu Lin, Hang Gao, and Latifur Khan. 2020. Deep learning on knowledge graph for recommender system: A survey.

Shiwen He, Yeyu Ou, Liangpeng Wang, Hang Zhan, Peng Ren, and Yongming Huang. 2022. Representation learning of knowledge graph for wireless communication networks.

Nicolas Heist, Sven Hertling, Daniel Ringler, and Heiko Paulheim. 2020. Knowledge graphs on the web – an overview.

Aidan Hogan, Eva Blomqvist, Michael Cochez, Claudia D'amato, Gerard De Melo, Claudio Gutierrez, Sabrina Kirrane, José Emilio Labra Gayo, Roberto Navigli, Sebastian Neumaier, Axel-Cyrille Ngonga Ngomo, Axel Polleres, Sabbir M. Rashid, Anisa Rula, Lukas Schmelzeisen, Juan Sequeda, Steffen Staab, and Antoine Zimmermann. 2021. Knowledge graphs. *ACM Computing Surveys*, 54(4):1–37.

Estevam Hruschka, Thom Lake, Naoki Otani, and Tom Mitchell, editors. 2024. *Proceedings of the First Workshop on Natural Language Processing for Human Resources (NLP4HR 2024)*. Association for Computational Linguistics, St. Julian's, Malta.

Valentina Janev, Damien Graux, Hajira Jabeen, and Emanuel Sallinger, editors. 2020. *Knowledge Graphs and Big Data Processing*. Lecture Notes in Computer Science. Springer International Publishing.

Hanieh Khorashadizadeh, Nandana Mihindukulasooriya, Sanju Tiwari, Jinghua Groppe, and Sven Groppe. 2023. Exploring in-context learning capabilities of foundation models for generating knowledge graphs from text. In *TEXT2KG/BiKE@ESWC*.

Thomas N. Kipf and Max Welling. 2017. Semi-supervised classification with graph convolutional networks.

Gemini Team. 2023. Gemini: A family of highly capable multimodal models.

Chirayu Upadhyay, Hasan Abu-Rasheed, Christian Weber, and Madjid Fathi. 2021. Explainable job-posting recommendations using knowledge graphs and named entity recognition. In *2021 IEEE International Conference on Systems, Man, and Cybernetics (SMC)*, pages 3291–3296.

Petar Veličković, Guillem Cucurull, Arantxa Casanova, Adriana Romero, Pietro Liò, and Yoshua Bengio. 2018. Graph attention networks.

Hongxing Wang, Zhenhao Gu, and Mengyu Gu. 2022. Job recommendation algorithm based on knowledge graph. In *2022 IEEE 8th International Conference on Computer and Communications (ICCC)*, pages 2023–2027.

Weixuan Wang, Barry Haddow, Alexandra Birch, and Wei Peng. 2023a. Assessing the reliability of large language model knowledge.

Yu Wang, Nedim Lipka, Ryan A. Rossi, Alexa Siu, Ruiyi Zhang, and Tyler Derr. 2023b. Knowledge graph prompting for multi-document question answering.

Azmine Toushik Wasi, Taki Hasan Rafi, Raima Islam, and Dong-Kyu Chae. 2024. BanglaAutoKG: Automatic Bangla knowledge graph construction with semantic neural graph filtering. In *Proceedings of the 2024 Joint International Conference on Computational Linguistics, Language Resources and Evaluation (LREC-COLING 2024)*, pages 2100–2106, Torino, Italia. ELRA and ICCL.

Xuehong Wu, Junwen Duan, Yi Pan, and Min Li. 2023. Medical knowledge graph: Data sources, construction, reasoning, and applications. *Big Data Mining and Analytics*, 6(2):201–217.

Shenghao Yang, Weizhi Ma, Peijie Sun, Min Zhang, Qingyao Ai, Yiqun Liu, and Mingchen Cai. 2024. Common sense enhanced knowledge-based recommendation with large language model. In *Proceedings of the 29th International Conference on Database Systems for Advanced Applications (DASFAA)*.

Su Zhang, Xuefeng Wang, Wenxin Lu, Yiwei Lu, and Bangpeng Deng. 2021. Construction of human resource ontology model for knowledge graph. In *2021 IEEE 4th International Conference on Big Data and Artificial Intelligence (BDAI)*, pages 150–153.

A Experimental Details

A.1 Implementation Details

TF-IDF Vectorizer: The model employs a TF-IDF Vectorizer with an n-gram range of 1 to 5, capturing diverse word combinations, and a maximum feature limit set to a calculated vocabulary size. The vocabulary size, determined as the mean plus three times the standard deviation of the data, ensures a comprehensive representation of relevant terms. Additionally, English stopwords are excluded to focus on meaningful content during the vectorization process.

Traditional Models: After getting vectors from TF-IDF Vectorizers, we use different methods to classify. *LogR.* means *Logistic Regression*, *DecT.* means *Decision Tree*, *RF* means *Random Forest* and *GBC* denotes *Gradient Boosting Classifier*. Logistic Regression employs L1 regularization with the 'liblinear' solver. The Decision Tree Classifier has a maximum depth limited to 5. The RandomForest Classifier consists of 50 decision trees and uses a fixed random state for reproducibility. The Gradient Boosting Classifier incorporates an ensemble of 50 weak learners.

MLP: The MLP model is a simple feedforward neural network with multiple hidden layers, including dropout regularization for each layer. It consists of fully connected layers with decreasing dimensions from 2048 to 64 (halved in each layer), all utilizing the ReLU activation function. The output layer employs the softmax activation function for multi-class classification.

Transformer : The transformer model, integrated with AutoML and the Hugging Face Transformers library, utilizes the AutoTokenizer to preprocess text data. The *AutoModelForSequence-*

Classification class is employed with the *distilbert-base-uncased* model, configured to handle sequence classification tasks with a number of unique labels corresponding to the classes in the training data.

Graph Neural Network-Based Models: Both GCN (Kipf and Welling, 2017) and GAT (Veličković et al., 2018) model used are the default models from Pytorch Geometric library, with 64 hidden channels and 4 layers. Fine-tuning GNNs will improve the results.

A.2 Case Study

In CV No. 92, it is a salesperson's CV. It has these matching entities with the job description graph: *'accounting', 'managerial', 'excel', 'office', 'outlook', 'microsoft word', 'policies', 'sales', 'sap', 'time management'*. The top 5 matches job descriptions were: 150, 84, 103, 123, 163. The labels on them are ACCOUNTANT, SALES, SALES, FINANCE, Sales respectively. While the individual's primary expertise lies in sales, the inclusion of the 'accounting' skill prompted a recommendation for an accountant role. Additional skills such as 'managerial,' 'excel,' and 'policies' contributed to suggestions within the finance industry. This exemplifies the Knowledge Graph's ability to provide nuanced explanations for recommendations, offering insights into the diverse factors influencing job suggestions. It can be very effective to make career-switch moves for job-seekers.

B Prompts

If the information is a CV, use the following prompt:

> You are an entity extraction expert, you can identify and extract different types of entities from a text. Here is some information from a CV. Your task is to find and enlist all the information entities like education (degree, grade, school name), skills (which skills the person has), qualifications (skills), experience (action verb and nouns), and any other helpful token that is important for a job, and share them in a list where entities are separated by commas. Do not write anything else. Just the small entities separated by commas in a dictionary (JSON). Each entity can have only 1-2 words.
>
> `<Insert CV text here>`

If the information is a job description, use the following prompt:

> You are an entity extraction expert, you can identify and extract different types of entities from a text. Here is some information from a job description. Your task is to find and enlist all the information entities like education (degree requirement), skills (which skills the job needs), qualifications (skills), experience (action verb and nouns), and any other helpful token that is important for a job, and share them in a list where entities are separated by commas. Do not write anything else. Just the small entities separated by commas in a dictionary (JSON). Each entity can have only 1-2 words.
>
> `<Insert job description text here>`

Here is an example of the expected output:

> "Education": ["ABC University", "CGPA 3.00", "Computer Science and Engineering", "BSc"], "Skills": ["C", "Python", "R", "Machine Learning", "Communication", "Team Work"], "Experience": "ABX InfoTech": ["Team Management", "Assistant Manager"], "STech": ["Manager", "Senior Engineer", "AWS"]

Adapting Multilingual LLMs to Low-Resource Languages with Knowledge Graphs via Adapters

Daniil Gurgurov[1,2] **Mareike Hartmann**[2] **Simon Ostermann**[1]
[1]German Research Center for Artificial Intelligence (DFKI)
[2]Department of Language Science and Technology, Saarland University
daniil.gurgurov@dfki.de, mareikeh@coli.uni-saarland.de, simon.ostermann@dfki.de

Abstract

This paper explores the integration of graph knowledge from linguistic ontologies into multilingual Large Language Models (LLMs) using adapters to improve performance for low-resource languages (LRLs) in sentiment analysis (SA) and named entity recognition (NER). Building upon successful parameter-efficient fine-tuning techniques, such as K-ADAPTER (Wang et al., 2021) and MAD-X (Pfeiffer et al., 2020), we propose a similar approach for incorporating knowledge from multilingual graphs, connecting concepts in various languages with each other through linguistic relationships, into multilingual LLMs for LRLs. Specifically, we focus on eight LRLs —Maltese, Bulgarian, Indonesian, Nepali, Javanese, Uyghur, Tibetan, and Sinhala — and employ language-specific adapters fine-tuned on data extracted from the language-specific section of ConceptNet, aiming to enable knowledge transfer across the languages covered by the knowledge graph. We compare various fine-tuning objectives, including standard Masked Language Modeling (MLM), MLM with full-word masking, and MLM with targeted masking, to analyze their effectiveness in learning and integrating the extracted graph data. Through empirical evaluation on language-specific tasks, we assess how structured graph knowledge affects the performance of multilingual LLMs for LRLs in SA and NER, providing insights into the potential benefits of adapting language models for low-resource scenarios.

1 Introduction

In recent years, the advancement of multilingual Large Language Models (LLMs) (Devlin et al., 2019; Conneau et al., 2020; Xue et al., 2021) has revolutionized the field of natural language processing (NLP), enabling impressive performance across various languages. However, these models often struggle with low-resource languages (LRLs), where limited data availability affects their effectiveness (Wu and Dredze, 2020). To address this limitation, researchers have explored integrating external knowledge sources into multilingual LLMs to enhance their performance in both high-resource and low-resource contexts (Wang et al., 2021; Lauscher et al., 2020; Pfeiffer et al., 2020) via adapters (Houlsby et al., 2019) and full fine-tuning.

Adapters, introduced by Houlsby et al. (2019), are small modules inserted between the layers of a model and trained while the model is kept frozen. Previous work has used such Adapters to integrate external knowledge into LLMs. For instance, Wang et al. (2021) demonstrated improvements in relation classification, entity typing, and question answering tasks by integrating graph knowledge from Wikidata (Vrandečić and Krötzsch, 2014) into RoBERTa (Liu et al., 2019) using adapters. Similarly, Lauscher et al. (2020) enhanced BERT (Devlin et al., 2019) with graph knowledge from ConceptNet (Speer et al., 2017), achieving significant performance gains on tasks requiring common-sense knowledge. However, these efforts primarily focused on the English language. In contrast, Pfeiffer et al. (2020) addressed low-resource languages by integrating textual knowledge from Wikipedia into XLM-R (Conneau et al., 2020) via language adapters. Their approach demonstrated improvements over the baseline model for named entity recognition (NER) task.

Motivated by recent advancements in the integration of graph knowledge into language models, particularly for English, this paper investigates the incorporation of graph knowledge from linguistic ontologies, specifically ConceptNet, into multilingual LLMs particularly for LRLs. Injecting such data might be beneficial due to the scarcity of training data for these languages and the additional semantic and multilingual information provided by knowledge graphs (Miller, 1995; Speer

Proceedings of the 1st Workshop on Knowledge Graphs and Large Language Models (KaLLM 2024), pages 63–74
August 15, 2024

et al., 2017). Our focus is on a subset of LRLs, aiming to extend the success observed in graph knowledge integration to linguistically diverse and resource-scarce contexts. We work with Maltese, Bulgarian, Indonesian, Nepali, Javanese, Uyghur, Tibetan, and Sinhala, identified as low-resource according to Joshi et al. (2020). Our primary objective is to evaluate whether injecting multilingual graph knowledge, connecting various languages through linguistic relationships, into pre-trained multilingual LLMs through adapters improves performance for LRLs. We train language-specific adapters on ConceptNet data using different objective functions, including standard Masked Language Modeling (MLM) (Devlin et al., 2019), MLM with full-word masking (Cui et al., 2021), and MLM with targeted masking, and evaluate the downstream performance of the adapted model on sentiment analysis (SA) and NER tasks.

Our work extends existing advancements by proposing an approach that utilizes adapters to integrate graph knowledge specifically for LRLs, following a modular design similar to the one introduced by Pfeiffer et al. (2020). Our contributions include:

- **Low-Resource Languages Focus:** Unlike prior works on graph knowledge integration (Lauscher et al., 2020; Wang et al., 2021), our research concentrates explicitly on improving multilingual LLMs through the external graph knowledge injection for low-resource scenarios.

- **Exploiting Various Knowledge Sources and Types:** We investigate the integration of language adapters based on Wikipedia and ConceptNet, both individually and in combination. This expands the approach of Pfeiffer et al. (2020), which solely utilized Wikipedia data, enabling a comprehensive assessment of different knowledge sources' impact on model performance. We assume that language models can benefit from the multilingual connections in ConceptNet.

- **Single-Language Training Approach:** In contrast to the multilingual transfer learning approach used by Pfeiffer et al. (2020), which primarily focuses on cross-lingual adaptation, our methodology involves training language and task adapters using data in the same LRL. This training strategy aims to maximize model performance and adaptability to the specific linguistic characteristics of each target language.

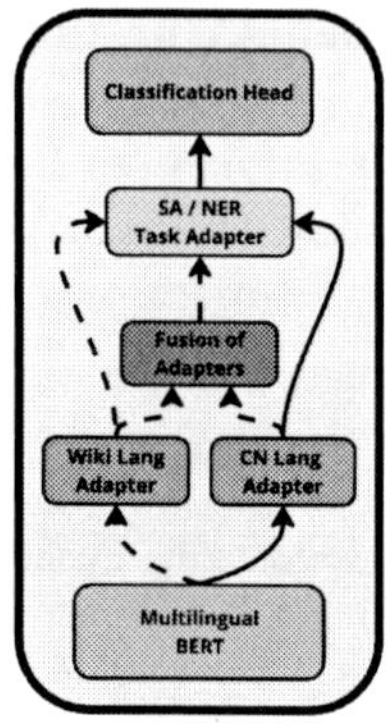

Figure 1: Proposed method. One of the Wiki or ConceptNet language adapters is used during inference. The outputs then go to a task adapter, which is followed by a classification head. If fusion is specified, the fusion mechanism is activated.

Our study provides insights into the potential benefits of adapting multilingual LLMs for low resource scenarios, contributing to the ongoing exploration of multilingual language model adaptation and graph knowledge integration.

The complete code for our experiments is publicly available on GitHub[1].

2 Related Work

Our work extends recent advancements in integrating external graph knowledge into pre-trained LLMs (Lauscher et al., 2020; Wang et al., 2021) and adapting pre-trained multilingual LLMs to specific languages (Pfeiffer et al., 2020). We use the methodologies proposed in these studies as a foundation for enhancing the performance of multilingual LLMs on downstream tasks, particularly for LRLs. To this end, we provide the overview of these methods as well as other strategies of adapting multilingual LLMs to LRLs (Artetxe et al., 2020; Muller et al., 2021; Vernikos and Popescu-Belis, 2021; Pfeiffer et al., 2022).

2.1 Adapter-based Knowledge Integration

In our approach, we draw inspiration from recently proposed adapter-based knowledge integration techniques, particularly the concept of K-Adapters (Wang et al., 2021) and the work by

[1]https://github.com/d-gurgurov/Injecting-Commonsense-Knowledge-into-LLMs

Lauscher et al. (2020). K-Adapters introduced a novel approach for injecting knowledge into pre-trained models like RoBERTa (Liu et al., 2019) without modifying their original parameters. This method utilizes two types of adapters dedicated to factual and linguistic knowledge, demonstrating improvements in tasks such as entity typing and question answering. Factual adapters are trained with a relation classification objective using data aligned from Wikipedia text to Wikidata triplets (Vrandečić and Krötzsch, 2014), while linguistic adapters are trained with a dependency relation prediction objective using linguistic information obtained from available dependency parsers.

Similarly, Lauscher et al. (2020) explored injecting external knowledge, specifically from ConceptNet (Speer et al., 2017) and the Open Mind Common Sense (OMCS) corpus (Singh et al., 2002), into language models. They introduced two boosted models: CN-ADAPT and OM-ADAPT. CN-ADAPT involves creating a synthetic corpus through random traversal of the ConceptNet graph, with adapter parameters learned through Masked Language Modeling (MLM) training on this synthetic corpus. In OM-ADAPT, adapter parameters are learned directly through MLM training on the OMCS corpus. Both models employ a parameter-efficient adapter-based architecture (Houlsby et al., 2019), injecting bottleneck adapters into BERT's (Devlin et al., 2019) transformer layers.

An approach similar to ours is presented in Hou et al. (2022), who however make stronger assumptions on the training data (such as the alignment of entities in the data with a knowledge graph) and rather train models to represent entities explicitly.

2.2 Language Adapters

In our exploration of injecting graph knowledge for LRL scenarios, we follow the MAD-X architecture presented by Pfeiffer et al. (2020). MAD-X offers an efficient approach to adapt pre-trained language models to LRLs by utilizing a modular structure consisting of language adapters, task-specific adapters, and invertible adapters.

The MAD-X framework utilizes language adapters as a fundamental component to adapt the model to specific languages. These adapters are trained on language-specific Wikipedia data and stacked onto the pre-trained model, allowing the model to capture language-specific nuances and patterns effectively. Following the enhanced bottleneck architecture (Pfeiffer et al., 2021), the language adapter involves down- and up-projections with ReLU activation and is trained via MLM on unlabeled data.

During downstream task training, such as named entity recognition (NER), the fixed language adapter corresponding to the source language is used, ensuring adaptability to different languages without changing the underlying multilingual model. The embeddings are passed through the fixed language adapter before entering the task adapter, facilitating efficient adaptation to diverse linguistic contexts and specific task requirements.

Additionally, MAD-X introduces invertible adapters to mitigate the mismatch between multilingual and target language vocabulary. These invertible adapters are stacked on top of the embedding layer, with their respective inverses preceding the output embedding layer.

Task-specific adapters are then stacked on top of the language and invertible adapters to capture task-specific knowledge and specialize a language model in a certain task.

These insights from the MAD-X framework serve as a valuable reference for our research on injecting structured graph knowledge into multilingual LLMs for low-resource cases.

2.3 Adapting LLMs to Low-Resource Languages

Various other strategies have been proposed to address the challenges of adapting multilingual LLMs to LRLs, particularly for languages with limited pre-training data. Pfeiffer et al. (2022) propose X-MOD, a modular multilingual architecture that integrates shared and language-specific parameters to overcome the curse of multilinguality (Conneau et al., 2020), allowing efficient handling of linguistic diversity and supporting the extension to new languages with minimal performance impact on pre-trained languages. Additionally, Artetxe et al. (2020) train a new embedding layer with a corresponding target-language tokenizer to extend monolingual models to new languages, aiding language extension while maintaining model stability. Moreover, approaches based on transliteration and subword mappings have been proposed to incorporate additional languages into multilingual models, contributing to the expansion of multilingual capabilities of LLMs (Muller et al., 2021; Vernikos and Popescu-Belis, 2021). Hangya et al. (2022) present a bootstrapping-based approach for

ConceptNet Relationship	Natural Language Predicate
Antonym	is the opposite of
DerivedFrom	is derived from
EtymologicallyDerivedFrom	is etymologically derived from
EtymologicallyRelatedTo	is etymologically related to
FormOf	is a form of
HasContext	has context of
IsA	is a type of
RelatedTo	is related to
SimilarTo	is similar to
Synonym	is a synonym of
SymbolOf	is a symbol of
DistinctFrom	is distinct from

Table 1: Predefined mapping from ConceptNet relations to natural language predicates used for training ConceptNet-based Language Adapters.

enhancing low-resource languages in multilingual LLMs, which relies on unsupervised word translation pairs from monolingual corpora.

3 Injecting External Knowledge into LLMs for LRLs

This section describes our approach for enhancing multilingual LLMs for LRLs by injecting external knowledge. We discuss the use of language adapters trained on ConceptNet and Wikipedia data, explore Adapter Fusion (Pfeiffer et al., 2021) for combining knowledge sources, and describe task adapters for fine-tuning multilingual LLMs for specific tasks. Our proposed method is illustrated in Figure 1.

3.1 Language Adapters

We use language adapters for integrating external knowledge into multilingual LLMs and adapting these models to a specific language. In our study, two types of language adapters are employed: those trained on ConceptNet data and those trained on Wikipedia.

3.1.1 ConceptNet Data Preparation

ConceptNet-based language adapters are trained on knowledge extracted from ConceptNet, providing a rich source of linguistic relationships and semantic information across various languages. Data preparation involves retrieving and formatting data from ConceptNet and converting it into natural text[2]. The number of triples extracted for the chosen languages are given in Table 2. These triples were converted into natural language using a predefined mapping from ConceptNet relationships to natural language predicates. This mapping allows for a straightforward method for injecting the graph knowledge through MLM-like objectives. The relationship mapping includes all possible connections from the ontology for the selected languages and is as specified in Table 1. An example of constructing a natural language sentence from an extracted triple is as follows: the triple *(kiel, RelatedTo, eat)* is converted into the sentence *"kiel is related to eat"*. In this context, "kiel" is the Maltese word for "eat." The natural language predicates are always kept in English, resulting in the generated text for a triple being multilingual.

3.1.2 ConceptNet-based Language Adapters

The ConceptNet language adapters are sequential bottleneck adapters (Pfeiffer et al., 2021), similar to the ones used in MAD-X, with modifications to exclude invertible adapter layers for simplicity. Further, different objective functions were used for various downstream tasks at hand. For Sentiment Analysis (SA), we used the standard MLM objective, whereas for Named Entity Recognition (NER) another self-designed objective function, targeted Masked Language Modeling (TLM), was used for training the language adapters on the graph knowledge. The latter objective implies predicting the masked tokens not included in a natural language predicates specified in Table 1. Following the earlier provided example with the sentence *"kiel is related to eat"*, only either the word *"kiel"* or *"eat"* would be masked.

[2]For the extraction process, we utilized a dedicated self-built module for fetching data from CN, built on top of the CN API (`https://github.com/commonsense/conceptnet5/wiki/API`) for an easier extraction of per-language data. Code available on `https://github.com/d-gurgurov/Conceptnet-Embeddings`

3.1.3 Wikipedia-based Language Adapters

In contrast, the language adapters trained on Wikipedia data utilize the Wikimedia dataset[3] for selected LRLs. This dataset provides a diverse and extensive collection of textual information scraped from Wikipedia for each language of interest. The number of articles available for each language is as in Table 2. The adapter architecture for Wikipedia language adapters is the same as the ConceptNet language adapters and uses the standard MLM objective function[4].

3.2 Fusion of Language Adapters

In our search of enhancing multilingual LLMs for LRLs, we extend our investigation to the fusion of knowledge sources through Adapter Fusion (Pfeiffer et al., 2021). The Adapter Fusion mechanism facilitates the integration of knowledge extracted from ConceptNet and Wikipedia-based language adapters, providing a non-destructive method to combine multiple pre-trained adapters for new downstream tasks.

An adapter fusion block introduces a set of parameters that dynamically combines adapters and the shared pre-trained model at each layer of the transformer. The fusion layer incorporates Key, Value, and Query matrices at each layer to learn contextual activation of each adapter. This dynamic combination is achieved through a contextual activation mechanism similar to attention mechanisms (Vaswani et al., 2017).

We activate the fusion layer with two language adapters for each language - the Wikipedia adapter and the ConceptNet adapter. This fusion layer is introduced to allow the model to learn the optimal way to dynamically compose the knowledge from different sources. The learnable weights (Query, Key, and Value) within adapter fusion should enable the model to identify and activate the most relevant information from each adapter based on the context of the task.

3.3 Task Adapters

To fine-tune multilingual LLMs for specific downstream tasks such as sentiment analysis (SA) and named entity recognition (NER), we employ task adapters stacked on top of language adapters.

Language	ISO	CN	Wiki	mBERT?
Bulgarian	bg	58060	297516	✓
Indonesian	ms	44190	689034	✓
Nepali	ne	7497	33040	✓
Javanese	jv	5082	73311	✓
Maltese	mt	8578	6310	
Uyghur	ug	3225	5979	
Tibetan	bo	9532	7090	
Sinhala	si	3350	20454	

Table 2: Number of ConceptNet triples and Wikipedia articles per language. The last column indicates if the respective language was included in the mBERT pretraining data.

The architecture of the task adapters follows the established design, featuring a stack of task-specific adapters on the top layers of a multilingual LLM and language adapter. For our study, we specifically focus on SA and NER, aiming to evaluate the impact of external knowledge injection on sentiment classification and entity recognition in LRLs, as these tasks are the most accessible in terms of labeled data availability for the selected languages.

To maintain the knowledge of the pre-trained model and language adapters during task adaptation, we adopt a weight freezing strategy, as in MAD-X. This involves preventing further fine-tuning of the weights in the pre-trained model and language adapters when training the task adapters. By doing so, we ensure that the foundational knowledge captured by the language adapters, whether sourced from Wikipedia, ConceptNet, or their fusion, remains unchanged.

The task adapters are stacked on top of the language adapters, like in the original MAD-X architecture. This stacking configuration facilitates the flow of information from the base model and the external knowledge sources through the language adapters to the task-specific adapters.

4 Experiments

In this section, we detail the experiments and data used for conducting the study.

4.1 Languages

The focus languages, classified as low-resource according to Joshi et al. (2020), are Maltese, Bulgarian, Indonesian, Nepali, Javanese, Uyghur, Tibetan, and Sinhala, as presented in Table 2. These languages serve as a subset of underrepresented languages for injecting external knowl-

[3]https://huggingface.co/datasets/wikimedia/wikipedia

[4]All extracted ConceptNet data used for the language adapters, along with the language adapters themselves, can be found on HuggingFace (https://huggingface.co/DGurgurov).

Model/Language	bg	ms	ne	jv	mt	ug	bo	si
				Sentiment Analysis (SA)				
mBERT	0.860	0.888	0.565	0.728	0.557	0.696	0.687	0.646
mBERT+TA	0.885	0.917	0.565	**0.761**	0.598	0.734	0.801	0.661
mBERT+Wiki+TA	**0.893**	**0.919**	**0.584**	0.746	**0.702**	0.706	**0.816**	**0.663**
mBERT+CN+TA	**0.893**	0.915	**0.636**	0.751	**0.658**	0.699	**0.803**	0.653
mBERT+F(CN&Wiki)+TA	0.882	0.906	**0.627**	0.750	**0.662**	**0.784**	**0.804**	**0.689**
				Named Entity Recognition (NER)				
mBERT	**0.919**	**0.934**	0.694	**0.575**	0.595	0.402	0.520	0.197
mBERT+TA	0.917	**0.934**	0.644	0.564	0.601	0.383	0.575	0.172
mBERT+Wiki+TA	0.915	0.932	0.610	0.543	**0.603**	**0.411**	**0.576**	0.172
mBERT+CN+TA	0.915	0.928	0.649	0.571	0.576	**0.403**	0.544	**0.244**
mBERT+F(CN&Wiki)+TA	0.888	0.889	**0.713**	0.503	0.563	0.401	0.540	0.165

Table 3: Experimental Results. All numbers are averaged over 3 independent runs. The scores in **bold** are the ones that outperform both baseline models.

edge through ConceptNet and Wikipedia-based language adapters. The choice is bounded to the ConceptNet and downstream tasks data available for the languages. While Bulgarian, Indonesian, Nepali and Javanese data were used for pre-training mBERT (Devlin et al., 2019), which is the multilingual LLM we will use for our experiments, Maltese, Tibetan, Uyghur and Sinhala were not included in the pre-training dataset.

4.2 Tasks

Two tasks considered for empirical evaluation are Sentiment Analysis (SA) and Named Entity Recognition (NER). Datasets for SA for all the languages are acquired from different sources (Martínez-García et al., 2021; Purwarianti and Crisdayanti, 2019; Cortis and Davis, 2019; Dingli and Sant, 2016; Singh et al., 2020; Wongso et al., 2021; Li et al., 2022; Zhu et al., 2023; Ranathunga and Liyanage, 2021) and available in our HuggingFace repositories[5]. For NER, the datasets are obtained from the WikiANN project (Pan et al., 2017). All datasets for both SA and NER contain various amounts of data, depending on language and task, and described in more detail in Appendix A. We use the vanilla F1 score (Sokolova et al., 2006) for SA performance monitoring and the "seqeval" F1 score (Nakayama, 2018) for NER.

While these datasets do not allow for a full assessment of the impact of injected graph knowledge on LRLs due to a lack of labeled data for other tasks, they serve as a good starting point for measuring the effects of multilingual graph knowledge integration on LRLs.

4.3 Baselines

In establishing baseline models for our study, we fine-tune the widely used mBERT (bert-base-multilingual-cased) (Devlin et al., 2019) from the transformer library (Wolf et al., 2020). The focus is on two baseline scenarios for each task—SA and NER.

The first baseline involves fine-tuning mBERT directly on the respective datasets for SA and NER. We employ common hyperparameters for training, including a learning rate of $\{1e-4, 2e-4\}$, a batch size of 64, $\{50, 100\}$ epochs with best-model-saving, and a dropout rate of $\{0.5, 0.2\}$, respectively for each task. The choice of hyperparameters is aligned with standard practices in transformer-based model training and our own experiments on the given datasets.

For the second baseline (mBERT+TA), we introduce a single task adapter on top of mBERT and fine-tune it on the SA and NER datasets, while keeping the parameters of mBERT frozen, using the same hyperparameters as used for the first baseline configuration. This single adapter architecture allows us to explore the effectiveness of a more compact adaptation strategy compared to the traditional fine-tuning approach.

For all models, the best checkpoint for evaluation is selected based on validation loss performance.

[5] https://huggingface.co/DGurgurov

4.4 Language Adapter Training

In this section, we provide technical details of the training process for language adapters, focusing on both ConceptNet (*CN*) and Wikipedia (*Wiki*) variants. We use sequential bottleneck architecture without invertible layers for training language adapters.

We maintain identical hyperparameters during the training of both Wikipedia and ConceptNet language adapters: reduction factor 16, learning rate $5e-05$, train and eval batch size 16,training steps 50,000 for CN and 100,000 for Wiki. These hyperparameters ensure a stable and uniform training environment for both variants. The training process is monitored through loss and accuracy metrics on the validation sets.

4.5 Task Adapters Training

In this setting, we stack task-specific adapters on top of language adapters and train the task adapters while keeping the language adapters frozen. After empirical investigations, we employ similar hyperparameters to those used for training the baselines: a learning rate of $\{1e-5, 1e-4\}$, a batch size of 64, $\{50, 100\}$ epochs with best-model saving, and a dropout of $\{0.5, 0.2\}$ for SA and NER, respectively. The experiment involves stacking the task adapters on top of either Wikipedia-based (*Wiki+TA*) or ConceptNet-based (*CN+TA*) language adapters, as well as on top of the fusion of both (*F(CN&Wiki)+TA*) (Pfeiffer et al., 2021).

4.6 Objective Functions

In this section, we compare different objective functions used for training language adapters on graph knowledge and examine their influence on the performance on the downstream tasks at hand. We experiment with three objectives for language modeling - standard token Masked Language Modeling (MLM) (Devlin et al., 2019), full-word Masked Language Modeling (FLM) (Cui et al., 2021), and targeted Masked Language Modeling (TLM). MLM and FLM were implemented as provided by the Transformers library, and TLM was self-designed. MLM masks individual tokens with a 15% probability, FLM performs the same but masks full words, and TLM masks targeted words which are not part of the natural language predicates list extracted from ConceptNet with a 50% probability. The implied goal of TLM is to create the connections between the words of a LRL to the words of other languages, which might come in bigger quantities, within the parameters of a model. The downstream results for all the objectives are as in Table 4. Upon the inspection of the results, different objective functions were chosen for SA and NER, according to the outcomes of the experiments. MLM was utilized as an objective for the language adapters used for SA, and TLM was chosen as an objective for the language adapters used for NER.

5 Results and Discussion

The experimental results, summarized in Table 3, demonstrate the results of different model configurations in improving SA and NER tasks across LRLs. This section discusses the performance of each model configuration and provide insights into the impact of external knowledge through language and task adapters on enhancing multilingual LLMs for LRLs. All scores are an average over three independent runs.

5.1 Sentiment Analysis

In SA, the performance of various model configurations on different languages reveals interesting insights. First, considering the baseline performance of fully fine-tuned mBERT across all languages, we observe moderate to high F1-scores. However, when single task-specific adapters are added to mBERT, we notice consistent improvements across all languages, indicating the effectiveness of using parameter-efficient fine-tuning techniques for adapting the model for specific languages, especially in low-resource scenarios. This confirms the findings by Li and Liang (2021), He et al. (2021), and Jukić and Snajder (2023).

When incorporating language adapters trained on CN and Wiki, relatively good results are observed. For nearly all languages, using language adapters trained on CN and Wiki leads to performance gains compared to the baselines-mBERT and mBERT with a single task adapter. The CN language adapter boosts the performance for Bulgarian, Nepalese, Maltese, and Tibetan over both baselines. As for the Wiki language adapters, they improve the scores for Bulgarian, Indonesian, Nepalese, Maltese, Tibetan, and Sinhala when compared to both mBERT and mBERT with a single adapter. The fusion of language adapters yields improvements over the baselines for Nepalese, Maltese, Uyghur, Tibetan, and Sinhala.

Sentiment Analysis (SA)									
Configuration	Objective	bg	ms	ne	jv	mt	ug	bo	si
	MLM	0.893	0.915	**0.636**	0.751	0.658	**0.699**	0.803	**0.653**
CN+TA	FLM	**0.898**	0.916	0.575	**0.756**	0.639	0.685	**0.811**	0.650
	TLM	0.893	**0.918**	0.625	0.749	**0.661**	0.638	0.797	**0.653**
	MLM	0.882	0.906	0.627	**0.750**	0.662	**0.784**	0.804	**0.689**
F(CN&Wiki)+TA	FLM	0.877	0.906	**0.669**	0.745	0.640	0.677	0.806	0.661
	TLM	**0.884**	**0.912**	0.598	0.742	**0.667**	0.712	**0.816**	0.659

Named Entity Recognition (NER)									
Configuration	Objective	bg	ms	ne	jv	mt	ug	bo	si
	MLM	0.915	**0.932**	**0.657**	**0.603**	0.471	0.341	0.559	0.196
CN+TA	FLM	**0.918**	0.930	0.626	0.578	0.476	0.398	**0.572**	0.242
	TLM	0.915	0.928	0.649	0.571	**0.576**	**0.403**	0.544	**0.244**
	MLM	**0.889**	**0.901**	0.670	**0.504**	0.540	0.373	0.514	**0.261**
F(CN&Wiki)+TA	FLM	0.887	0.900	0.688	0.496	**0.580**	0.387	0.509	0.250
	TLM	0.888	0.889	**0.713**	0.503	0.563	**0.401**	**0.540**	0.165

Table 4: Comparison of various objective functions used for training ConceptNet based Language Adapters-Token Masked Language Modeling (**MLM**), Full-Word Masked Language Modeling (**FLM**), and Targeted Masked Language Modeling (**TLM**). Maximum score per configuration in **bold**. SA results are based on MLM, and NER results are based on TLM.

5.2 Named Entity Recognition

In NER, the performance trends across different model configurations and languages exhibit similar patterns to SA but with some notable differences. mBERT demonstrates moderate to high F-1 scores across languages, indicating its ability to recognize named entities to some extent. However, the addition of single task-specific adapters leads to marginal improvements in only some cases, suggesting that named entity recognition might not benefit significantly from single task-specific adapter fine-tuning compared to SA. The improvements are only observed for Maltese and Tibetan.

When incorporating language adapters, particularly those trained on CN and Wiki, we observe mixed results. Utilizing CN language adapters leads to slight improvements over the baselines only in the case of Uyghur and Sinhala. Wiki language adapters, on the other hand, give improvements over both baseline models only for Maltese, Uyghur, and Tibetan. The combination of CN and Wiki adapters shows positive impact only on Nepalese.

5.3 Effects of Data Quantity and Language Presence in LLM pre-training Data

The data quantity of external data sources might play a crucial role in the performance of language adapters and their impact on downstream tasks. Looking at the data quantities provided in Table 2, languages like Maltese, Nepali, Uyghur, Tibetan, and Sinhala have notably fewer CN and Wiki resources compared to languages like Bulgarian and Indonesian. Despite this, language adapters trained on these limited resources still contribute to performance enhancements in SA and NER tasks for these languages compared to the baseline models. This indicates the effectiveness of leveraging even small amounts of external knowledge for adapting LLMs to low-resource languages.

Another interesting observation is the performance improvement in languages like Maltese, Uyghur, Tibetan, and Sinhala, which are not included in the mBERT pre-training data. This emphasizes that the method might be more useful for languages absent in the pre-training corpus as mBERT benefits from this adaptation using task-specific and language adapters, allowing them to effectively learn from external knowledge sources and adapt to new languages.

5.4 Take-aways

The experimental results shed light on the effectiveness of integrating graph knowledge from linguistic ontologies into multilingual LLMs via adapters for LRLs. Across both SA and NER tasks, we observe that single task-specific adapters generally lead to performance improvements, emphasizing the benefits of parameter-efficient fine-tuning for specific tasks (Li and Liang, 2021; He et al., 2021; Jukić and Snajder, 2023).

In turn, the impact of language adapters trained on external knowledge sources such as CN and Wiki varies across languages and tasks. CN-based adapters generally show promise in enhancing SA but not NER. Wiki language adapters are also more beneficial for SA than NER.

The combination of both ConceptNet and Wikipedia adapters through the Adapter Fusion demonstrates competitive performance, in some cases outperforming individual adapters alone, suggesting that leveraging diverse knowledge sources can effectively enhance the capabilities of multilingual LLMs for low resource scenarios.

Our findings underscore the partial effectiveness of our method in leveraging external graph knowledge to enhance SA and NER tasks for individual LRLs. This highlights the need for further research to develop more effective strategies for adapting multilingual LLMs to low-resource contexts using various types of knowledge. Further, the results emphasize that each LRL needs an individual approach when building the dedicated NLP tools, where some languages might benefit from a certain method and the others might not need it.

6 Conclusion

In this study, we investigated the integration of structured graph knowledge into multilingual LLMs for LRLs using language adapters and task-specific adapters. We explored the use of ConceptNet and Wikipedia data for training language adapters, and we examined Adapter Fusion as a method to combine knowledge sources. Additionally, we implemented task adapters for fine-tuning LLMs for specific downstream tasks such as Sentiment Analysis (SA) and Named Entity Recognition (NER).

Our experiments revealed insights into the effectiveness of different model configurations in improving SA and NER tasks performance across LRLs. We observed a positive effect of incorporating external graph and textual knowledge through language adapters for a number of languages, including Bulgarian, Indonesian, Maltese, Nepali, Uyghur, Tibetan, and Sinhala, some of which did not possess extensive data for training both language adapters and task adapters. Fusion of knowledge sources yielded improvements in less cases, suggesting the need for further refinement in this area.

Overall, our findings underscore the importance of parameter-efficient fine-tuning methods and the potential benefits of leveraging external knowledge for enhancing multilingual LLMs in low resource contexts. However, there are limitations to our approach, including the choice of objective functions and the need for tasks better suited to leverage external knowledge.

Limitations and Future Work

Our approach shows several limitations that should be taken into consideration in future investigations aiming to integrate graph knowledge into multilingual LLMs for enhancing LRL performance. Firstly, the choice of objective function employed for learning graph knowledge plays a critical role in effectively acquiring underlying knowledge. The objectives we explored may not be optimally suited for this purpose, highlighting the need for more tailored approaches to graph knowledge acquisition. Secondly, the tasks we selected for evaluating the effectiveness of knowledge injection may not inherently require the type of knowledge provided by graph sources. Future work should explore tasks that better leverage the acquired knowledge. Thirdly, our study was limited to a subset of LRLs, and expanding the scope to include a broader range of languages would provide a more comprehensive assessment of our approach's effectiveness. Lastly, larger models should be explored as backbones to build upon.

Acknowledgments

We are thankful to the anonymous reviewers for their insightful comments and suggestions. This research was supported by the EU-funded LT-Bridge project, GA No. 952194; and the EU-funded project DisAI - Improving scientific excellence and creativity in combating disinformation with artificial intelligence and language technologies, GA No. 101079164.

References

Mikel Artetxe, Sebastian Ruder, and Dani Yogatama. 2020. On the cross-lingual transferability of monolingual representations. In *Proceedings of the 58th Annual Meeting of the Association for Computational Linguistics*, pages 4623–4637, Online. Association for Computational Linguistics.

Alexis Conneau, Kartikay Khandelwal, Naman Goyal, Vishrav Chaudhary, Guillaume Wenzek, Francisco Guzmán, Edouard Grave, Myle Ott, Luke Zettlemoyer, and Veselin Stoyanov. 2020. Unsupervised cross-lingual representation learning at scale. In *Proceedings of the 58th Annual Meeting of the Association for Computational Linguistics*, pages 8440–8451, Online. Association for Computational Linguistics.

Keith Cortis and Brian Davis. 2019. A social opinion gold standard for the Malta government budget 2018. In *Proceedings of the 5th Workshop on Noisy User-generated Text (W-NUT 2019)*, pages 364–369, Hong Kong, China. Association for Computational Linguistics.

Yiming Cui, Wanxiang Che, Ting Liu, Bing Qin, and Ziqing Yang. 2021. Pre-training with whole word masking for chinese bert. *IEEE/ACM Transactions on Audio, Speech, and Language Processing*, 29:3504–3514.

Jacob Devlin, Ming-Wei Chang, Kenton Lee, and Kristina Toutanova. 2019. BERT: Pre-training of deep bidirectional transformers for language understanding. In *Proceedings of the 2019 Conference of the North American Chapter of the Association for Computational Linguistics: Human Language Technologies, Volume 1 (Long and Short Papers)*, pages 4171–4186, Minneapolis, Minnesota. Association for Computational Linguistics.

Alexiei Dingli and Nicole Sant. 2016. Sentiment analysis on maltese using machine learning. In *Proceedings of The Tenth International Conference on Advances in Semantic Processing (SEMAPRO 2016)*, pages 21–25.

Viktor Hangya, Hossain Shaikh Saadi, and Alexander Fraser. 2022. Improving low-resource languages in pre-trained multilingual language models. In *Proceedings of the 2022 Conference on Empirical Methods in Natural Language Processing*, pages 11993–12006, Abu Dhabi, United Arab Emirates. Association for Computational Linguistics.

Ruidan He, Linlin Liu, Hai Ye, Qingyu Tan, Bosheng Ding, Liying Cheng, Jiawei Low, Lidong Bing, and Luo Si. 2021. On the effectiveness of adapter-based tuning for pretrained language model adaptation. In *Proceedings of the 59th Annual Meeting of the Association for Computational Linguistics and the 11th International Joint Conference on Natural Language Processing (Volume 1: Long Papers)*, pages 2208–2222, Online. Association for Computational Linguistics.

Yifan Hou, Wenxiang Jiao, Meizhen Liu, Carl Allen, Zhaopeng Tu, and Mrinmaya Sachan. 2022. Adapters for enhanced modeling of multilingual knowledge and text. In *Findings of the Association for Computational Linguistics: EMNLP 2022*, pages 3902–3917.

Neil Houlsby, Andrei Giurgiu, Stanislaw Jastrzebski, Bruna Morrone, Quentin De Laroussilhe, Andrea Gesmundo, Mona Attariyan, and Sylvain Gelly. 2019. Parameter-efficient transfer learning for nlp. In *International Conference on Machine Learning*, pages 2790–2799. PMLR.

Pratik Joshi, Sebastin Santy, Amar Budhiraja, Kalika Bali, and Monojit Choudhury. 2020. The state and fate of linguistic diversity and inclusion in the NLP world. In *Proceedings of the 58th Annual Meeting of the Association for Computational Linguistics*, pages 6282–6293, Online. Association for Computational Linguistics.

Josip Jukić and Jan Snajder. 2023. Parameter-efficient language model tuning with active learning in low-resource settings. In *Proceedings of the 2023 Conference on Empirical Methods in Natural Language Processing*, pages 5061–5074, Singapore. Association for Computational Linguistics.

Anne Lauscher, Olga Majewska, Leonardo F. R. Ribeiro, Iryna Gurevych, Nikolai Rozanov, and Goran Glavaš. 2020. Common sense or world knowledge? investigating adapter-based knowledge injection into pretrained transformers. In *Proceedings of Deep Learning Inside Out (DeeLIO): The First Workshop on Knowledge Extraction and Integration for Deep Learning Architectures*, pages 43–49, Online. Association for Computational Linguistics.

Siyu Li, Kui Zhao, Jin Yang, Xinyun Jiang, Zhengji Li, and Zicheng Ma. 2022. Senti-exlm: Uyghur enhanced sentiment analysis model based on xlm. *Electronics Letters*, 58(13):517–519.

Xiang Lisa Li and Percy Liang. 2021. Prefix-tuning: Optimizing continuous prompts for generation. In *Proceedings of the 59th Annual Meeting of the Association for Computational Linguistics and the 11th International Joint Conference on Natural Language Processing (Volume 1: Long Papers)*, pages 4582–4597, Online. Association for Computational Linguistics.

Yinhan Liu, Myle Ott, Naman Goyal, Jingfei Du, Mandar Joshi, Danqi Chen, Omer Levy, Mike Lewis, Luke Zettlemoyer, and Veselin Stoyanov. 2019. Roberta: A robustly optimized BERT pretraining approach. *CoRR*, abs/1907.11692.

Antonio Martínez-García, Toni Badia, and Jeremy Barnes. 2021. Evaluating morphological typology in zero-shot cross-lingual transfer. In *Proceedings of the 59th Annual Meeting of the Association for Computational Linguistics and the 11th International Joint Conference on Natural Language Processing (Volume 1: Long Papers)*, pages 3136–3153.

George A Miller. 1995. Wordnet: a lexical database for english. *Communications of the ACM*, 38(11):39–41.

Benjamin Muller, Antonios Anastasopoulos, Benoît Sagot, and Djamé Seddah. 2021. When being unseen from mBERT is just the beginning: Handling new languages with multilingual language models. In *Proceedings of the 2021 Conference of the North American Chapter of the Association for Computational Linguistics: Human Language Technologies*, pages 448–462, Online. Association for Computational Linguistics.

Hiroki Nakayama. 2018. seqeval: A python framework for sequence labeling evaluation. Software available from https://github.com/chakki-works/seqeval.

Xiaoman Pan, Boliang Zhang, Jonathan May, Joel Nothman, Kevin Knight, and Heng Ji. 2017. Cross-lingual name tagging and linking for 282 languages. In *Proceedings of the 55th Annual Meeting of the Association for Computational Linguistics (Volume 1: Long Papers)*, pages 1946–1958, Vancouver, Canada. Association for Computational Linguistics.

Jonas Pfeiffer, Naman Goyal, Xi Lin, Xian Li, James Cross, Sebastian Riedel, and Mikel Artetxe. 2022. Lifting the curse of multilinguality by pre-training modular transformers. In *Proceedings of the 2022 Conference of the North American Chapter of the Association for Computational Linguistics: Human Language Technologies*, pages 3479–3495, Seattle, United States. Association for Computational Linguistics.

Jonas Pfeiffer, Aishwarya Kamath, Andreas Rücklé, Kyunghyun Cho, and Iryna Gurevych. 2021. AdapterFusion: Non-destructive task composition for transfer learning. In *Proceedings of the 16th Conference of the European Chapter of the Association for Computational Linguistics: Main Volume*, pages 487–503, Online. Association for Computational Linguistics.

Jonas Pfeiffer, Ivan Vulić, Iryna Gurevych, and Sebastian Ruder. 2020. MAD-X: An Adapter-Based Framework for Multi-Task Cross-Lingual Transfer. In *Proceedings of the 2020 Conference on Empirical Methods in Natural Language Processing (EMNLP)*, pages 7654–7673, Online. Association for Computational Linguistics.

Ayu Purwarianti and Ida Ayu Putu Ari Crisdayanti. 2019. Improving bi-lstm performance for indonesian sentiment analysis using paragraph vector. In *2019 International Conference of Advanced Informatics: Concepts, Theory and Applications (ICAICTA)*, pages 1–5. IEEE.

Surangika Ranathunga and Isuru Udara Liyanage. 2021. Sentiment analysis of sinhala news comments. *Transactions on Asian and Low-Resource Language Information Processing*, 20(4):1–23.

Oyesh Mann Singh, Sandesh Timilsina, Bal Krishna Bal, and Anupam Joshi. 2020. Aspect based abusive sentiment detection in nepali social media texts. In *2020 IEEE/ACM International Conference on Advances in Social Networks Analysis and Mining (ASONAM)*, pages 301–308.

Push Singh, Thomas Lin, Erik T Mueller, Grace Lim, Travell Perkins, and Wan Li Zhu. 2002. Open mind common sense: Knowledge acquisition from the general public. In *On the Move to Meaningful Internet Systems 2002: CoopIS, DOA, and ODBASE: Confederated International Conferences CoopIS, DOA, and ODBASE 2002 Proceedings*, pages 1223–1237. Springer.

Marina Sokolova, Nathalie Japkowicz, and Stan Szpakowicz. 2006. Beyond accuracy, f-score and roc: a family of discriminant measures for performance evaluation. In *Australasian joint conference on artificial intelligence*, pages 1015–1021. Springer.

Robyn Speer, Joshua Chin, and Catherine Havasi. 2017. Conceptnet 5.5: An open multilingual graph of general knowledge. In *Proceedings of the AAAI conference on artificial intelligence*, volume 31.

Ashish Vaswani, Noam Shazeer, Niki Parmar, Jakob Uszkoreit, Llion Jones, Aidan N. Gomez, Lukasz Kaiser, and Illia Polosukhin. 2017. Attention is all you need. *CoRR*, abs/1706.03762.

Giorgos Vernikos and Andrei Popescu-Belis. 2021. Subword mapping and anchoring across languages. In *Findings of the Association for Computational Linguistics: EMNLP 2021*, pages 2633–2647, Punta Cana, Dominican Republic. Association for Computational Linguistics.

Denny Vrandečić and Markus Krötzsch. 2014. Wikidata: a free collaborative knowledgebase. *Communications of the ACM*, 57(10):78–85.

Ruize Wang, Duyu Tang, Nan Duan, Zhongyu Wei, Xuanjing Huang, Jianshu Ji, Guihong Cao, Daxin Jiang, and Ming Zhou. 2021. K-Adapter: Infusing Knowledge into Pre-Trained Models with Adapters. In *Findings of the Association for Computational Linguistics: ACL-IJCNLP 2021*, pages 1405–1418, Online. Association for Computational Linguistics.

Thomas Wolf, Lysandre Debut, Victor Sanh, Julien Chaumond, Clement Delangue, Anthony Moi, Pierric Cistac, Tim Rault, Remi Louf, Morgan Funtowicz, Joe Davison, Sam Shleifer, Patrick von Platen, Clara Ma, Yacine Jernite, Julien Plu, Canwen Xu, Teven Le Scao, Sylvain Gugger, Mariama Drame, Quentin Lhoest, and Alexander Rush. 2020. Transformers: State-of-the-art natural language processing. In *Proceedings of the 2020 Conference on Empirical Methods in Natural Language Processing: System Demonstrations*, pages 38–45, Online. Association for Computational Linguistics.

Wilson Wongso, David Samuel Setiawan, and Derwin Suhartono. 2021. Causal and masked language modeling of javanese language using transformer-based architectures. In *2021 International Conference on Advanced Computer Science and Information Systems (ICACSIS)*, pages 1–7. IEEE.

Shijie Wu and Mark Dredze. 2020. Are all languages created equal in multilingual BERT? In *Proceedings of the 5th Workshop on Representation Learning for NLP*, pages 120–130, Online. Association for Computational Linguistics.

Linting Xue, Noah Constant, Adam Roberts, Mihir Kale, Rami Al-Rfou, Aditya Siddhant, Aditya Barua, and Colin Raffel. 2021. mT5: A massively multilingual pre-trained text-to-text transformer. In *Proceedings of the 2021 Conference of the North American Chapter of the Association for Computational Linguistics: Human Language Technologies*, pages 483–498, Online. Association for Computational Linguistics.

Yulei Zhu, Baima Luosai, Liyuan Zhou, Nuo Qun, and Tashi Nyima. 2023. Research on sentiment analysis of tibetan short text based on dual-channel hybrid neural network. In *2023 IEEE 4th International Conference on Pattern Recognition and Machine Learning (PRML)*, pages 377–384.

Appendix

A SA and NER Data Details

Table 5 and 6 provide a more detailed description of the datasets used for training task adapters.

Language	ISO code	#train	#val	#test
Bulgarian	bg	20000	10000	10000
Indonesian	ms	20000	1000	1000
Maltese	mt	100	100	100
Nepali	ne	100	100	100
Javanese	jv	100	100	100
Uyghur	ug	100	100	100
Tibetan	bo	100	100	100
Sinhala	si	100	100	100

Table 6: Named Entity Recognition Data Details

Language	ISO code	Source	#pos	#neg	#train	#val	#test
Bulgarian	bg	Martínez-García et al., 2021	6652	1271	5412	838	1673
Indonesian	ms	Purwarianti and Crisdayanti, 2019	7319	4005	7926	1132	2266
Maltese	mt	Cortis and Davis, 2019; Dingli and Sant, 2016	271	580	595	85	171
Nepali	ne	Singh et al., 2020	680	1019	1189	255	255
Javanese	jv	Wongso et al., 2021	12500	12500	17500	5025	2475
Uyghur	ug	Li et al., 2022	2450	353	1962	311	530
Tibetan	bo	Zhu et al., 2023	5006	5000	7004	1501	1501
Sinhala	si	Ranathunga and Liyanage, 2021	2487	2516	3502	750	751

Table 5: Sentiment Analysis Data Details

Ontology-guided Knowledge Graph Construction from Maintenance Short Texts

Zeno van Cauter
Technische Universiteit Eindhoven
z.m.v.cauter@tue.nl

Nikolay Yakovets
Technische Universiteit Eindhoven
n.yakovets@tue.nl

Abstract

Large-scale knowledge graph construction remains infeasible since it requires significant human-expert involvement. Further complications arise when building graphs from domain-specific data due to their unique vocabularies and associated contexts. In this work, we demonstrate the ability of open-source large language models (LLMs), such as Llama-2 and Llama-3, to extract facts from domain-specific Maintenance Short Texts (MSTs). We employ an approach which combines ontology-guided triplet extraction and in-context learning. By using only 20 semantically similar examples with the Llama-3-70B-Instruct model, we achieve performance comparable to previous methods that relied on fine-tuning techniques like SpERT and REBEL. This indicates that domain-specific fact extraction can be accomplished through inference alone, requiring minimal labeled data. This opens up possibilities for effective and efficient semi-automated knowledge graph construction for domain-specific data.

1 Introduction

Knowledge Graphs (KGs) have emerged as a powerful tool for representing complex relationships between entities across various domains and in aiding in various tasks (e.g., in search, recommendation systems, and others) (Hogan et al., 2021).

Constructing a KG presents several challenges. The process requires extracting structured information from unstructured data, such as text, using Information Extraction (IE) techniques. Much research has focused on large, publicly available general-purpose KGs like DBPedia, YAGO, or Wikidata, as well as on domain-specific KGs in areas like medicine (Li et al., 2020) or railway safety (Liu et al., 2021). More recent studies have explored the use of KGs to support industrial maintenance activities (Hossayni et al., 2020; Stewart et al., 2022). However, building a maintenance KG involves overcoming several additional obstacles: off-the-shelf Natural Language Processing solutions often fail to handle domain-specific data adequately, existing benchmarks do not align with industrial realities, the costs of annotating domain-specific data can be prohibitive, and the typically low volume of domain-specific data makes it challenging to train robust models that generalize well to new instances (Brundage et al., 2021; Dima et al., 2021). Additional difficulties arise when data evolves (e.g., triggering changes in the label space) necessitating computationally-expensive retraining or fine-tuning of models in traditional approaches.

In-context-learning (Dong et al., 2022) and ontology-guided KG construction from Text2KGBench (Mihindukulasooriya et al., 2023) offer the ability to overcome some of these challenges. Both these methods are dynamic and adaptable to changes in the ontology or label space without the need for re-training. In-context learning does not require large collection of annotated labeled data upfront but only at time of inference. Ontology-guided KG construction allows for seamless changes to the ontology if desired. This makes these methods particularly useful in domains where ontologies evolve over time.

Recently, Large Language Models (LLMs) have demonstrated remarkable capabilities in the ability to perform information extraction (Xu et al., 2023). However, most of this work focuses on general domain datasets, e.g. ACE datasets [1,2], CoNLL2003 (Tjong Kim Sang and De Meulder, 2003) or TacRED (Zhang et al., 2017) and little work exists on specialized domain-specific datasets. An annotated dataset of fine-grained schema and corpora for information extraction of Maintenance Short Texts (MST) recently became publicly available:

[1] https://catalog.ldc.upenn.edu/LDC2005T09
[2] https://catalog.ldc.upenn.edu/LDC2006T06

Proceedings of the 1st Workshop on Knowledge Graphs and Large Language Models (KaLLM 2024), pages 75–84
August 15, 2024

MaintIE (Bikaun et al., 2024a).

In this work, we show how LLMs can assist with the knowledge graph construction on domain-specific texts. Our contributions are as follows:

1. We evaluate the LLama-2 (Touvron et al., 2023a) and LLama-3[3] family models on ontology-guided KG construction using in-context-learning on a dataset of Maintenance Short Texts (Bikaun et al., 2024a).
2. We show that, using only a few in-context examples, Llama-3-70B-Instruct can extract fact extracts comparable to previous state-of-the-art with a near-zero hallucination rate. We find that for other models of the Llama-family, hallucinations come into play where generated triples contain objects/subjects from (mostly) in-context examples.
3. We study the effects of choosing certain token prediction penalties and the effects on hallucinations. We show that by carefully selecting these parameters can minimize the number of hallucinations, but that the wrong settings can stimulate this behaviour.
4. Finally, we show that the pruning of such hallucinations is relatively easy and increases performance (in both precision and F1) by a large margin. Performing this pruning makes smaller models such as Llama-3-8B a suitable alternative.

Our work implies that LLMs are well-suited for building domain-specific knowledge graphs, even with limited supervised data. In addition, if large-scale data annotation is required, LLMs can be combined with a human-in-the-loop process that pre-annotates data at an incremental rate. Our code, prompts and data are publicly available[4].

2 Task description

In this work, we consider the task of LLM-assisted KG construction as automatically extracting graph structured information (subject, object and (directional) relation) from unstructured text data. In line with Text2KGBench, we also regard this task as "Given an ontology and text corpora, the goal is to construct prompts to instruct the model to extract facts relevant to the ontology". An example of how this is setup in the prompt is given in Figure 1.

[3]https://ai.meta.com/blog/meta-llama-3/

[4]https://github.com/zeno17/MaintIE2KGBench

3 Methodology

3.1 Data

MaintIE (Bikaun et al., 2024a) provides a collection of Maintenance Short Texts (MST's) which encapsulates information from Maintenance Work Orders (MWOs) in a lexically-normalised concise format (Bikaun et al., 2024b). It comes in 2 annotation versions: 1) Fine-grained, spanning 224 entity classes or 2) Course-grained, spanning 6 entity classes. The fine-grained version is the result of pure intensive expert annotation, and the course-grained version was created by performing pre-annotation using fine-tuned SpERT (Eberts and Ulges, 2019) which was followed by expert correction. An example text with corresponding triplets is provided below.

```
Text:
cabin lights require replacing
Ground truth triples:
hasPart(cabin,lights)
hasAgent(require,lights)
hasPatient(require,replacing)
```

As both versions come with the same 6 relation types, we opt for the course-grained data as it is more numerous (7.000 compared to 1.067). From this, we filter out MST's that don't have actual triples annotated to them. This follows Text2KGBench which 1) also only uses triple-containing texts and 2) whose evaluation framework is not equipped to measure performance over non-triple containing texts. This only filters out 272 examples or 3.9% of the data.

From the remaining 6.728 examples, we create a 75/25 train-test split (or 5.046/1.682 examples respectively). During the experiments, the examples given to the model in the context are drawn from the train split, and performance is measured over the held-out test-split. More on this is covered in Subsection 3.5.

3.2 Prompt

For the prompting, we include a basic instruction, an ontology, k examples and the test sentence. The prompt template is provided in Figure 1. This differs from Text2KGBench as follows: 1) we feed multiple examples to model, and 2) we do not provide relation constraints to the model (which entities can have which relations). We do not provide the relation constraints as this takes a considerable amount of space in the context-window of the LLM.

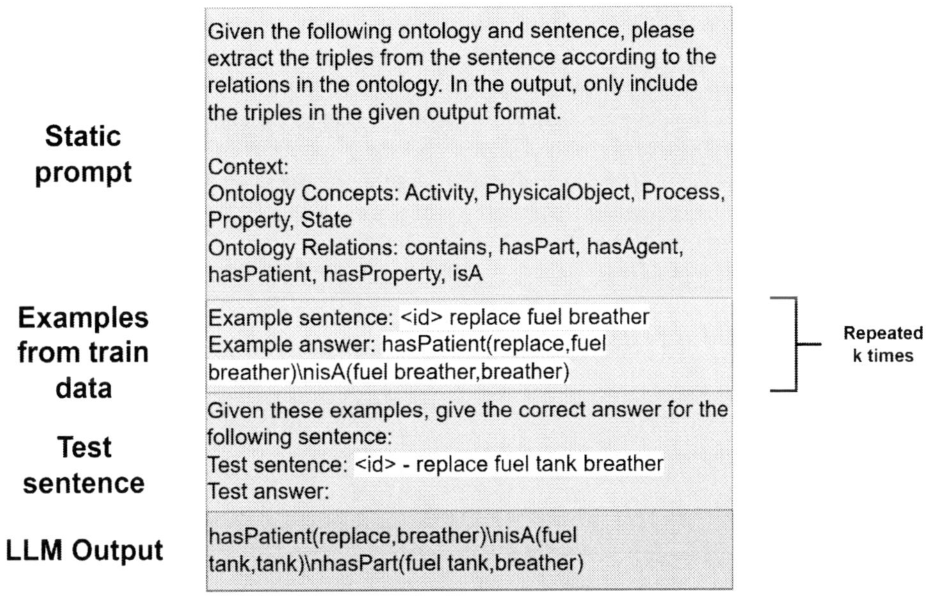

Figure 1: Used prompt template

While this space is limited for the course-grained data (5 entity types, 6 relations), the amount of space required can grow intractably for larger ontologies (e.g. the fine-grained dataset has 224 entity types and 6 relations). We consider this an avenue for future work.

3.3 Metrics

For evaluation Text2KGBench focuses on three dimensions: 1) fact extraction performance 2) ontology conformance, and 3) hallucination rate. Below, we provide brief explanations of the evaluation metrics, where we deviate from them and why.

1. **Fact Extraction**: From the generated text, triplets of the form "relation(subject, object)" are extracted using regular expressions. The extracted triples are then compared to the set of ground truth triples, and performance is measured using Precision, Recall and F1-score. Any triple that is not an exact match for relation type, object or subject is considered incorrect.

2. **Ontology Conformance**: Is the predicted relation in the provided ontology (provided in Figure 1). In this work, we limit ourselves to the relations: ['contains', 'hasPart', 'hasAgent', 'hasPatient', 'hasProperty', 'isA'].

3. **Hallucination rate**: Whether the LLM predicts relations that are not in the ontology, or objects/subjects that are not in the provided text. As Text2KGBench introduces two benchmark datasets based on Wikidata and DBpedia. This data carries more linguistically variation for the entities, and therefore they use a loose regime where objects/subjects are matched through stemmed words (using the Porter stemming algorithm (Van Rijsbergen et al., 1980)). In our work, we only count exact matches as correct because the MaintIE data is of limited vocabulary variation. We only consider exact matches and anything outside of that we consider a hallucination. For example, if the word "filter" is in the target sentence, a triple containing "filters" as an object/subject is considered a hallucination. This is important in a maintenance setting as, for example, having a singular or multiple component carries different semantics or may not even possible (e.g. if a machine only has the component once).

3.4 Models

LLMs are neural-inspired models that are trained on immense amounts of data. While initially designed for machine translation (Vaswani et al., 2017), adaptations such as encoder-only BERT (Devlin et al., 2018) or decoder-only GPT (Radford and Narasimhan, 2018) found use for a plethora of tasks. Recently, GPT-based models have been found to be the most versatile and flexible through its generative nature, including for generative information extraction (Xu et al., 2023).

LLaMa (Touvron et al., 2023a,b)[5], is an open-source LLM, and comes in different sizes and both only pre-trained and instruction-tuned versions.

In this work, we will assess several releases of the Llama family and assess their capabilities of performing fact extraction in the maintenance domain. We consider the following versions:

1. Llama-2-7B[6]
2. Llama-2-70B[7]
3. Llama-3-8B[8]
4. Llama-3-8B-Instruct[9]
5. Llama-3-70B[10]
6. Llama-3-70B-Instruct[11]

3.5 In-Context Learning

In-context-learning (ICL) is a technique of providing an LLM with a few examples to create a demonstration context. It then combines a query question with this context to form a prompt, which is fed into a language model for prediction. The model is expected to discern the pattern in the demonstration and make the appropriate prediction (Dong et al., 2022).

The model's context length is a hard limit on how many examples can be used, and the number of examples that necessary or effective can differ per model. In the context of maintenance data, availability is an important bottleneck as human annotated data is time-consuming and expensive. For this reason, we will experiment how many examples the model needs to be provided with in the context to do an effective fact extraction. For every example in the test set, semantically similar examples are retrieved using *sentence-transformers*[12] (Reimers and Gurevych, 2019) and the all-mpnet-base-v2 model[13]. In Text2KGBench, the models are only provided a single example (k=1). In our case, we will experiment with k $\in \{1, 2, 3, 5, 10, 20, 50, 100, 150\}$ except for Llama-2 where 100 and 150 examples are not possible due to hitting the context length limit. Still, this is a high number of examples which is possible largely because the maintenance short text data is of limited length.

3.6 Token prediction penalties

Text2KGBench demonstrated that ontology-guided information extraction suffers from hallucinations. This means triples are generated where the relation does not conform to the ontology or where subjects and objects that were not in the test sentence in the first place. During early experimentation, we found that the used LLM's tend to do (among others) the following: 1) repeat the same tokens until maximum sequence length was reached, and 2) provide lengthy explanations despite only asking for triples, including the generation of code.

For our LLM implementation, the parameters "frequency penalty" and "presence penalty" can be used. These change the logits if the LLM uses same tokens repeatedly or encourages it to use different tokens than already seen. Using Llama-3-8B (for computational reasons) we experiment with different settings in the full available range ([-2, 2]) to see how restricting the output logits affects the LLMs performance. As ontology conformance is generally high (and thus relation hallucination rate low), we look at the averaged hallucination rate of the object and subject. From our preliminary findings, we decided to run all other experiments with a frequency penalty of 0 and a presence penalty of -1.

3.7 Hallucination types

Next, we inspect some intricacies of the hallucinations that we found. We select the predictions from Llama-3-8B on 10 examples with frequency penalty 0, and presence penalty 2, which has the highest combined subject-object hallucination rate in our work (0.22 and 0.21 respectively). However, a solid inspection framework grows fast in complexity considering hallucination intricacies, let alone proving direct causality. We scope our approach in order to provide some quantitative inspection, and leave a hallucination inspection framework for future work. In the end, we limit ourselves to the following:

1. We only expand upon subject/object halluci-

[5]https://ai.meta.com/blog/meta-llama-3/

[6]https://huggingface.co/meta-llama/Llama-2-7b

[7]https://huggingface.co/meta-llama/Llama-2-70b

[8]https://huggingface.co/meta-llama/Meta-Llama-3-8B

[9]https://huggingface.co/meta-llama/Meta-Llama-3-8B-Instruct

[10]https://huggingface.co/meta-llama/Meta-Llama-3-70B

[11]https://huggingface.co/meta-llama/Meta-Llama-3-70B-Instruct

[12]https://github.com/UKPLab/sentence-transformers

[13]https://huggingface.co/sentence-transformers/all-mpnet-base-v2

nations for simplicity.

2. We only consider subjects consisting of 1 word (e.g. "replace" but not "change out" or "chain hoist) due to difficulties with proper stemming.

3. We adopt an assumed hierarchy of errors of most probable cause of the hallucination, which is as follows (in order):
   (a) The stemmed subject/object is in a stemmed sentence (this matches e.g. replace and replacing).
   (b) The subject/object is in one of the examples provided to the LLM.
   (c) The stemmed subject/object is in one of the stemmed examples.

3.8 Hallucination-filtered performance

Lastly, we look at what the fact extraction performance can be without hallucinations. If a triple contains a relation not in the provided ontology, or a subject/object which is not in the original input string, then it simply cannot be a factual triple. These conditions can be verified automatically and triples that violate them filtered from the fact extraction process. This leads to less produced triples, but the remaining extracted triples should match better with the ground truth and thus increase precision.

4 Results

4.1 Fact Extraction

Figure 2 shows how effective each LLM is at obtaining correct facts and hallucination rate versus the number of examples. It can be seen that there are stark differences between model performance with both highest and lowest performance coming from the instruction-tuned and untuned Llama-3-70B respectively. Conversely, for Llama-3-8B instruction-tuning seems to decrease performance across the board. In addition, Llama-3-8B-Instruct has a visibly lower ontology conformance compared to the other models which all adhere to the provided ontology systematically. Eventually, Llama-3-70B-Instruct obtains 0.77 F1-score when given 150 examples. For both versions of Llama-3-8B, further increasing the number of examples to a 150 hurts performance compared to fewer examples. The scores of k=20 (which we consider a low amount) are also displayed in Table 1.

4.2 Token prediction penalties

Figure 3 shows how Llama-3-8B's performance varies when tuning different parameters as described in Subsection 3.6. It can be seen that shifting frequency penalty and token penalty leads to an optimal fact extraction performance on an off-diagonal line. In addition, the lower right triangle is the generally lower performing side in terms of fact extraction. Conversely, this lower performance is combined with an increasing hallucination rate.

4.3 Ontology conformance & Hallucination rate

Text2KGBench reports that ontology conformance is consistently high across a variety of ontologies, which resonates with our results. In Figure 2 the ontology conformance is near 1 for all models, with the exception to this are Llama-2-7b and Llama-3-8B-Instruct where we see a decline throughout the number of examples. This means that the LLM's generally adhere to the provided Ontology, at a much higher rate found for the Text2KGBench benchmark.

Next, we look at how performance and hallucination progresses as the number of in-context examples increases in Figure 4. For Llama-3-8B-Instruct, the hallucination rate first increases follow by stabilization. Both Llama-3-8B and Llama-3-8B-Instruct suffer from a the hallucination rate and this is relatively stable as the number of examples increases. On the contrary, Llama-3-70B-Instruct does not suffer from this problem and sees a steady performance increase while the hallucination rate actually goes down. Thus, this seems to be a model-dependent issue.

4.4 Hallucination types

From inspection, we found that most subject/object hallucinations conform to the following scenarios: 1) objects/subjects contain tokens from the examples provided in the context, 2) objects/subjects being changed from plural to singular or vice versa, 3) object/subject verbs having active instead or passive form or vice versa. In some cases, these observations are not mutually exclusive for a single sentence. For example: if a test sentence contains "replaced", an extracted triple has a subject 'replace', and the word "replace" occurs in an example, then both 1) and 3) are true simultaneously. For relation hallucinations, the LLM sometimes used the provided ontology concepts as a relation (e.g. Phys-

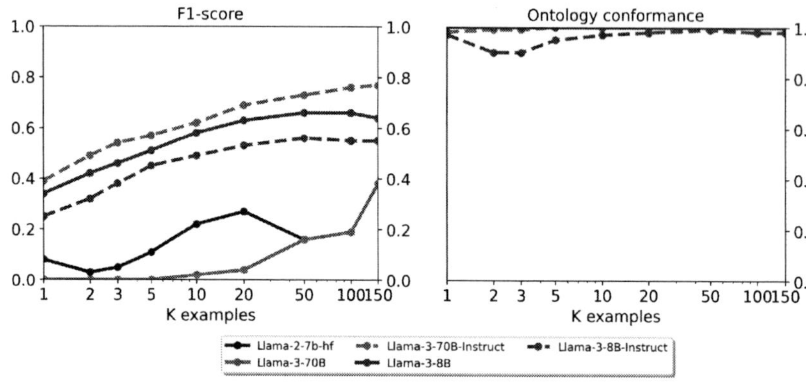

Figure 2: Left: Per-model performance on fact extraction. Right: Ontology conformance. Higher is better. Scale is logarithmic

Model	P (↑)	R (↑)	F1 (↑)	OC (↑)	SH (↓)	RH (↓)	OH (↓)
REBEL (MaintIE)	-	-	0.77	-	-	-	-
Llama-2-7b-hf	0.31	0.26	0.27	1.00	0.03	0.00	0.01
Llama-3-8B	0.62	0.70	0.63	1.00	0.03	0.00	0.03
Llama-3-8B-Instruct	0.48	0.70	0.53	0.98	0.08	0.02	0.09
Llama-3-70B	0.04	0.04	0.04	1.00	0.00	0.00	0.00
Llama-3-70B-Instruct	0.67	0.74	0.69	1.00	0.00	0.00	0.01

Table 1: Per-Model Fact Extraction Performance, Ontology Conformance and Hallucination rate. Scores reported are Precision, Recall, F1-score, Ontology Conformance, Subject Hallucination, Relation Hallucination and Objection Hallucination. Number of examples (k) is 20. For P, R, F1 and OC higher is better (↑). For SH, RH and OH lower is better (↓).

icalObject, Process, etc.), or it combined them into new relations (e.g. the relation hasProcess from the concept Process, hasState from State, etc.). It also occured the generated answer contained Python code (despite being asked not to) where certain lines contained substrings matching a "r(a,b)" form which were extracted unintentionally.

Figure 5 partially quantifies some of these aspects and it can be seen that for both subject and both, a large part of hallucinations overlap with being present in the context examples.

4.4.1 Hallucination-filtered performance

If triples that contain a hallucinated relation, object or subject are pruned, we obtain the performance as reported in Table 2. We observe that by applying a simple filter for triples of which we know they are non-factual, all models gain a significant amount of performance. The exception being Llama-3-70B-Instruct as it already obtained high performance with near-zero hallucination rate. We observe that for all models, the precision improves (as expected) compared to the results in Table 1. This heuristic pruning of extracted triples can thus be a useful way of increasing fact extraction performance, specifically smaller models which require less compute power.

5 Discussion

Firstly, we will draw a comparison to the results of MaintIE (Bikaun et al., 2024a). Since we only focus on triplet extraction without entity recognition, a comparison must be done between our work and MaintIE's evaluation of REBEL on loose relation extraction (as it only requires agreement on the relation type and entity spans) (Bikaun et al., 2024a). In a supervised fine-tuning setting called curriculum learning, MaintIE (Bikaun et al., 2024a) obtained an F1-score of 0.77. For comparison, Llama-3-70B-Instruct matches this score by using 150 examples and obtains 0.69 F1-score using only 20 semantically similar in-context examples, making the performance remarkably close. The effectiveness of using only a few semantically similar examples can significantly improve the model's

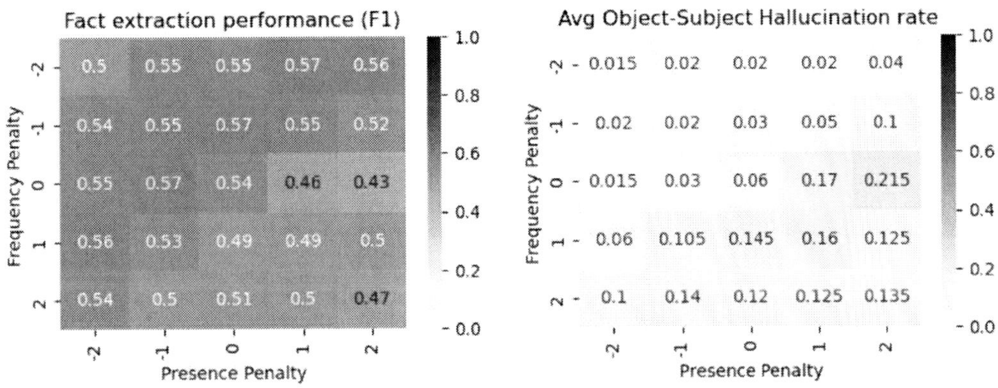

Figure 3: Fact extraction performance and hallucination rate for different settings of frequency and presence penalties. Selected model was Llama-3-8B. Number of in-context examples was set to 10. Left: higher is better. Right: lower is better.

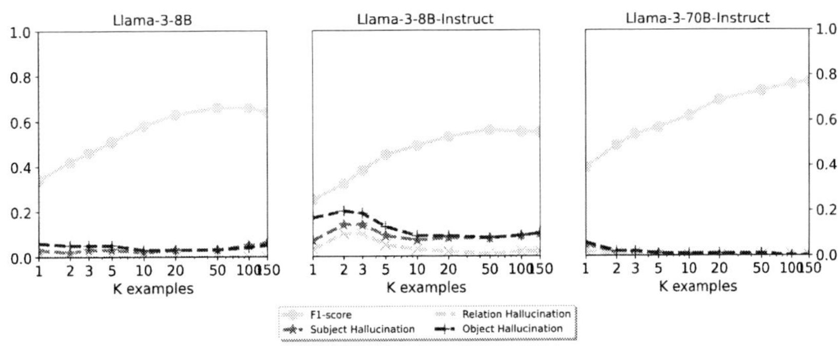

Figure 4: Number of in-context examples versus hallucination rate. Llama-3-8B, Llama-3-8B-Instruct and Llama-3-70B-Instruct selected for their overall performance.

ability to recognize patterns in the data.

However, this performance is only close when comparing it to the largest state-of-the-art open and instruction-tuned models. For Llama-3-70B, its low performance is explained that a significant portion of its "generations" are empty, which means its low performance is caused by the model's failure to even generate a sequence with triples at all. The associated performance in terms of hallucination is therefore void, given that empty generations by default don't contain tokens that fall outside the given sentence of the ontology. Llama-3-70B without instruction-tuning is thus incapable of performing fact extraction, while instruction-tuning Llama-3-8B slightly decreases performance rather than improve it.

Second, we would like to draw a comparison methodologically between REBEL, SpERT and LLMs and review differences and corresponding consequences. Both REBEL and SpERT use a fine-tuning approach that requires the labelled data to be available upfront. For SpERT, a relation classifier is used and as it constrains its output to a label space, it doesn't suffer from hallucinations. LLMs do not require this labelled data for fine-tuning, and, in this work, we have shown that even with few examples they can already be effective. However, this at-inference requirement of LLM comes with the drawback of hallucinations and is a subject of research (McKenna et al., 2023; Agrawal et al., 2023).

Thirdly, we will discuss how these hallucinations can be dealt with. We find that changing token penalties can simultaneously maximize fact extraction performance and minimize hallucination rate. By stimulating the model to diversify through presence penalty, the generated hallucinated triples will contain objects/subjects that are outside of the target sentence, likely sourced by in-context-examples. The exact reason for why

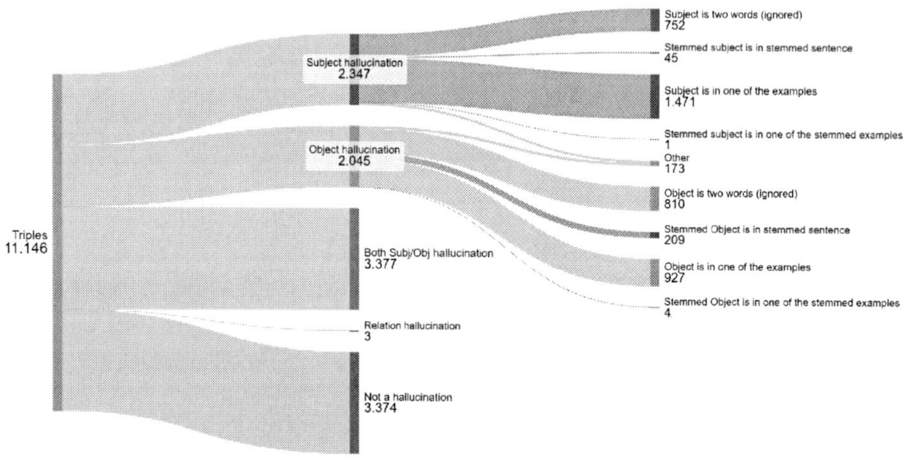

Figure 5: Types of hallucinations and subject sub-classifications. Based on predictions from Llama-3-8B with frequency penalty 0 and presence penalty 2. These parameter values induce a relatively high number of hallucinations.

	Before pruning			After pruning		
Model	P	R	F1	P	R	F1
REBEL (MaintIE)	-	-	0.77	-	-	-
Llama-2-7b-hf	0.31	0.26	0.27	0.32	0.26	0.28
Llama-3-8B	0.62	0.70	0.63	0.64	0.70	0.65
Llama-3-8B-Instruct	0.48	0.70	0.53	0.58	0.69	0.61
Llama-3-70B	0.04	0.04	0.04	0.04	0.04	0.04
Llama-3-70B-Instruct	0.67	0.74	0.69	0.68	0.74	0.69

Table 2: Fact extraction performance where hallucinations are pruned. Scores reported are Precision, Recall, F1-score where higher is better. Number of examples (k) is 20.

this occurs is unclear, and we consider an extended evaluation framework an interesting area for further research. Despite these hallucinations occurring, it is relatively straight-forward to prune them. Hallucinations are fairly easy to detect in this setting, as the relation must conform to the provided ontology and the subject/object must occur in the target text. The filtering of these verifiable hallucinations generally leads to a higher precision and thus higher F1-score, while ensuring ontology conformity in a domain-specific setting.

Lastly, we would like to discuss the implications of our findings. Building domain-specific Knowledge Graphs is a time-consuming effort, and building NLP-pipelines to do this often requires considerable resources. Our work implies that an incremental human-in-the-loop process could significantly assist with fact extraction. In (Bikaun et al., 2024a), pre-annotation was done by fully fine-tuning SpERT on an already annotated corpus and annotating a second corpus. Our work implies that by using LLMs and in-context learning, pre-annotation could start both earlier (using few examples) and continuously (building the number of examples as you go) using inference-only. This could considerably reduce workload for domain experts that need to be involved.

6 Conclusion

This study explores the use of Large Language Models for constructing knowledge graphs from Maintenance Short Texts. We assess models from the Llama family, focusing on fact extraction through two main methods: 1) ontology-guided triplet extraction and 2) in-context learning. Utilizing these techniques with the Llama-3-70B-Instruct model, we achieve fact extraction performance comparable to the current state-of-the-art methods that require fine-tuning. During this process, the issue of hallucinations (incorrect or fabricated information) can arise, often exacerbated by suboptimal settings for token prediction penalties. However, for the Llama-3-70B-Instruct model, hallucinations are almost non-existent. For other models, it's feasible to prune hallucinated triples from the output. This capability extends even to smaller models like Llama-3-8B, making them viable alternatives. This approach facilitates human-in-the-loop pre-annotation for domain-specific datasets, potentially reducing the time investment required from domain experts. Our work shows that Large Language Models are a fitting solution for Knowledge Graph construction, specifically where labelled data is scarce or the ontology dynamic.

Acknowledgments

This work was made possible by the TKI MATTER grant. We also would like to thank Mykola Pechenizkiy, Tyler Bikaun and Simon Koop for their comments.

References

Garima Agrawal, Tharindu Kumarage, Zeyad Alghami, and Huan Liu. 2023. Can knowledge graphs reduce hallucinations in llms?: A survey. *arXiv preprint arXiv:2311.07914*.

Tyler Bikaun, Tim French, Michael Stewart, Wei Liu, and Melinda Hodkiewicz. 2024a. Maintie: A fine-grained annotation schema and benchmark for information extraction from maintenance short texts.

Tyler Bikaun, Melinda Hodkiewicz, and Wei Liu. 2024b. MaintNorm: A corpus and benchmark model for lexical normalisation and masking of industrial maintenance short text. In *Proceedings of the Ninth Workshop on Noisy and User-generated Text (W-NUT 2024)*, pages 68–78, San Ġiljan, Malta. Association for Computational Linguistics.

Michael P. Brundage, Thurston Sexton, Melinda Hodkiewicz, Alden Dima, and Sarah Lukens. 2021. Technical language processing: Unlocking maintenance knowledge. *Manufacturing Letters*, 27:42–46.

Jacob Devlin, Ming-Wei Chang, Kenton Lee, and Kristina Toutanova. 2018. Bert: Pre-training of deep bidirectional transformers for language understanding. *arXiv preprint arXiv:1810.04805*.

Alden Dima, Sarah Lukens, Melinda Hodkiewicz, Thurston Sexton, and Michael P. Brundage. 2021. Adapting natural language processing for technical text. *Applied AI Letters*, 2(3):e33.

Qingxiu Dong, Lei Li, Damai Dai, Ce Zheng, Zhiyong Wu, Baobao Chang, Xu Sun, Jingjing Xu, and Zhifang Sui. 2022. A survey on in-context learning. *arXiv preprint arXiv:2301.00234*.

Markus Eberts and Adrian Ulges. 2019. Span-based joint entity and relation extraction with transformer pre-training. In *European Conference on Artificial Intelligence*.

Aidan Hogan, Eva Blomqvist, Michael Cochez, Claudia d'Amato, Gerard De Melo, Claudio Gutierrez, Sabrina Kirrane, José Emilio Labra Gayo, Roberto Navigli, Sebastian Neumaier, et al. 2021. Knowledge graphs. *ACM Computing Surveys (Csur)*, 54(4):1–37.

Hicham Hossayni, Imran Khan, Mohammad Aazam, Amin Taleghani-Isfahani, and Noel Crespi. 2020. Semkore: Improving machine maintenance in industrial iot with semantic knowledge graphs. *Applied Sciences*, 10(18).

Linfeng Li, Peng Wang, Jun Yan, Yao Wang, Simin Li, Jinpeng Jiang, Zhe Sun, Buzhou Tang, Tsung-Hui Chang, Shenghui Wang, and Yuting Liu. 2020. Real-world data medical knowledge graph: construction and applications. *Artificial Intelligence in Medicine*, 103:101817.

Jintao Liu, Felix Schmid, Keping Li, and Wei Zheng. 2021. A knowledge graph-based approach for exploring railway operational accidents. *Reliability Engineering & System Safety*, 207:107352.

Nick McKenna, Tianyi Li, Liang Cheng, Mohammad Hosseini, Mark Johnson, and Mark Steedman. 2023. Sources of hallucination by large language models on inference tasks. In *Findings of the Association for Computational Linguistics: EMNLP 2023*, pages 2758–2774, Singapore. Association for Computational Linguistics.

Nandana Mihindukulasooriya, Sanju Tiwari, Carlos F Enguix, and Kusum Lata. 2023. Text2kgbench: A benchmark for ontology-driven knowledge graph generation from text. In *International Semantic Web Conference*, pages 247–265. Springer.

Alec Radford and Karthik Narasimhan. 2018. Improving language understanding by generative pre-training.

Nils Reimers and Iryna Gurevych. 2019. Sentence-bert: Sentence embeddings using siamese bert-networks. In *Conference on Empirical Methods in Natural Language Processing*.

Michael Stewart, Melinda Hodkiewicz, Wei Liu, and Tim French. 2022. Mwo2kg and echidna: Constructing and exploring knowledge graphs from maintenance data. *Proceedings of the Institution of Mechanical Engineers, Part O: Journal of Risk and Reliability*, page 1748006X221131l.

Erik F. Tjong Kim Sang and Fien De Meulder. 2003. Introduction to the CoNLL-2003 shared task: Language-independent named entity recognition. In *Proceedings of the Seventh Conference on Natural Language Learning at HLT-NAACL 2003*, pages 142–147.

Hugo Touvron, Thibaut Lavril, Gautier Izacard, Xavier Martinet, Marie-Anne Lachaux, Timothée Lacroix, Baptiste Rozière, Naman Goyal, Eric Hambro, Faisal Azhar, et al. 2023a. Llama: Open and efficient foundation language models. *arXiv preprint arXiv:2302.13971*.

Hugo Touvron, Louis Martin, Kevin Stone, Peter Albert, Amjad Almahairi, Yasmine Babaei, Nikolay Bashlykov, Soumya Batra, Prajjwal Bhargava, Shruti Bhosale, et al. 2023b. Llama 2: Open foundation and fine-tuned chat models. *arXiv preprint arXiv:2307.09288*.

C.J. Van Rijsbergen, S.E. Robertson, and M.F. Porter. 1980. *New Models in Probabilistic Information Retrieval*. British Library research & development reports. Computer Laboratory, University of Cambridge.

Ashish Vaswani, Noam Shazeer, Niki Parmar, Jakob Uszkoreit, Llion Jones, Aidan N Gomez, Łukasz Kaiser, and Illia Polosukhin. 2017. Attention is all you need. *Advances in neural information processing systems*, 30.

Derong Xu, Wei Chen, Wenjun Peng, Chao Zhang, Tong Xu, Xiangyu Zhao, Xian Wu, Yefeng Zheng, and Enhong Chen. 2023. Large language models for generative information extraction: A survey. *arXiv preprint arXiv:2312.17617*.

Yuhao Zhang, Victor Zhong, Danqi Chen, Gabor Angeli, and Christopher D. Manning. 2017. Position-aware attention and supervised data improve slot filling. In *Proceedings of the 2017 Conference on Empirical Methods in Natural Language Processing (EMNLP 2017)*, pages 35–45.

Educational Material to Knowledge Graph Conversion: A Methodology to Enhance Digital Education

Miquel Canal-Esteve and Yoan Gutiérrez
Research Group of Language Processing and Information System
University of Alicante, Spain

Abstract

This article argues that digital educational content should be structured as knowledge graphs (KGs). Unlike traditional repositories such as Moodle, a KG offers a more flexible representation of the relationships between concepts, facilitating intuitive navigation and discovery of connections. In addition, it integrates effectively with Large Language Models, enhancing personalized explanations, answers, and recommendations. This article studies different proposals based on semantics and knowledge modelling to determine the most appropriate ways to strengthen intelligent educational technologies.

1 Introduction

Knowledge graphs (KGs) structure complex information into nodes and relationships, allowing an intuitive and manipulable representation of knowledge. This structure facilitates the integration of information from diverse sources, improves the ability to perform precise semantic searches, and enhances the inference of new knowledge from existing data (Kejriwal, 2022; Zhu et al., 2023). Given these capabilities, KGs have shown significant potential across various domains, including education (Ain et al., 2023).

In the educational environment, KGs can transform how educational information is organized and accessed. They integrate data from multiple sources, such as textbooks, research articles and online resources, to link key concepts, theories and relevant authors (Dang et al., 2021). In addition, integration with Large Language Models (LLMs) can enhance this approach, enabling detailed explanations and accurate answers (Zhu et al., 2023). This approach facilitates the search for specific information for students and educators and helps identify hidden relationships between different topics, promoting deeper, interdisciplinary learning (Abu-Salih and Alotaibi, 2024).

Although many KGs have been proposed in the literature, due to their complexity, they are often limited to small environments (Yuan et al., 2024). The construction of KGs has traditionally required laborious data extraction and linking processes based on natural language processing (NLP) and data mining techniques (Zhu et al., 2023). However, in recent years, LLMs have revolutionized the field of NLP, demonstrating a remarkable ability to understand and generate natural language and programming. The potential of LLMs for automatic KG generation is an emerging area of research (Pan et al., 2023; Melnyk et al., 2022).

To address the problem of converting educational materials into KGs for improved content structuring, navigation, and personalization with large language models, this paper explores several key areas:

- Identifying the advantages of using KGs in the educational environment.
- Highlighting the most relevant KGs in education and their significant contributions.
- Examining the latest models based on LLMs that facilitate the conversion from text to KG.
- Proposing an innovative approach to enhance the educational material to KG task.

2 Advantages of using knowledge graphs in the educational environment

2.1 Representation and efficient access to knowledge

As indicated in Dang et al. (2021), representation and efficient access to knowledge is fundamental in KGs applied in education. These graphs allow large amounts of information to be organized and visualized in a structured manner, facilitating understanding and retrieval of relevant data. Abu-Salih

Proceedings of the 1st Workshop on Knowledge Graphs and Large Language Models (KaLLM 2024), pages 85–91
August 15, 2024

and Alotaibi (2024) note that KGs significantly improve semantic searchability, allowing students and educators to access the specific information they need quickly.

2.2 Enhancement of learning and discovery of connections

According to Ain et al. (2023), KGs facilitate a more flexible and dynamic representation of concepts and their interrelationships, allowing students to explore and better understand how different topics are connected. This approach improves information retention and fosters deeper and more contextualized learning.

Furthermore, KGs can significantly improve the ability of educational systems to provide personalized and relevant recommendations. Chicaiza and Valdiviezo-Diaz (2021) demonstrate that systems can suggest materials integrated into the student's learning process by mapping the relationships between concepts and educational resources. This optimizes the learning process by aligning with each student's progress and specific interests and facilitates discovering new connections and areas of interest that might not be evident in a more traditional, linear learning environment.

2.3 Personalization and integration with LLMs

Research by Li et al. (2019) analyses the use of KGs in online learning platforms. The authors find that these graphs improve the organization of educational content and facilitate learning personalization. Educational systems using KGs can provide content recommendations based on each learner's progress and interests.

In addition, KGs can play a crucial role in creating intelligent tutoring systems. According to Li and Wang (2023), these graphs enable virtual tutors to provide more detailed explanations tailored to the individual needs of learners.

3 Review of knowledge graphs in education

This section discusses three recent studies that review using KGs and ontologies in education. Each study addresses different aspects and applications of these technologies, assessing their impact and challenges. The conclusions of each of these studies are then presented, providing a comprehensive view of the current and future state of KGs in education. Additionally, we add the article (Chen et al., 2018) that proposes a methodology to build KGs in the educational environment. The proposed scheme will be relevant to the proposed method in Section 5.

Abu-Salih and Alotaibi (2024) conclude that KGs are transforming education by providing personalized learning experiences and enriched data for curriculum planning. However, they face challenges such as a lack of standardized formats, limited interoperability, incomplete data, and scalability issues. Future research is suggested to address these limitations and explore integrating advanced language models and creating multidomain KGs.

Stancin et al. (2020) highlights the crucial role of ontologies in educational systems, facilitating structured knowledge representation and curriculum management. Although there is no single methodology for their construction, researchers combine several methodologies. Recent literature review shows an increase in the use of ontologies in education, highlighting their importance and future potential.

Khoiruddin et al. (2023) reviews the development of ontologies in e-learning, highlighting methodologies such as NeON and METHONTOLOGY, and the roles of domain experts, developers, and end users. It uses metrics such as Relationship Richness to assess the quality of ontologies. He concludes that a proper understanding and application of these methods and metrics can improve the efficiency and effectiveness of e-learning systems.

Finally, Chen et al. (2018) describes a system called KnowEDu developed to automatically construct KGs in education using pedagogical and learning assessment data. KnowEdu uses NLP algorithms to extract meaningful instructional concepts and educational relationships from heterogeneous data. The methods and results of this study provide a solid foundation for the practical implementation of educational KGs. However, this methodology does not allow for an automatic transition from text to KG.

4 Text-to-Knowledge graph conversion models

Many integrations exist between LLMs and KGss, but these only cover one of the text-to-knowledge graph process's tasks, as seen in the review (Pan et al., 2023). An analysis of models that perform the complete task of moving from text to KG is shown below. Several common features and differences are observed in these models. The models are commonly evaluated in Zero-Shot, One-Shot, and Few-Shot scenarios, measuring various datasets' accuracy and semantic relatedness capability. The differences lie in the base LLMs chosen, the fine-tuning techniques applied, and the specific architectures used. The results show that, although there are improvements in certain configurations, there is still ample room to optimize the accuracy and efficiency of KG generation.

For instance, in the study by Giglou et al. (2023) several models are evaluated on the text to OWL conversion task in Zero-Shot, including BERT-Large (Devlin et al., 2019), PubMed-BERT (Gu et al., 2021), BART-Large (Lewis et al., 2020), Flan-T5-Large (Chung et al., 2022), Flan-T5-XL (Chung et al., 2022), BLOOM-1b7 (Workshop et al., 2022), BLOOM-3b (Workshop et al., 2022), GPT-3 (Brown et al., 2020), GPT-3.5 (OpenAI, 2023), LLaMA (Touvron et al., 2023) and GPT-4 (OpenAI et al., 2023). These models were tested on the term typing task using different datasets: WordNet (Miller, 1995), GeoNames (Rebele et al., 2016), NCI (National Cancer Institute, National Institutes of Health, 2022), SNOMEDCT_US (SNOMED International, 2023) and MEDCIN (Medicomp Systems, 2023). The best results were 91.7 for WordNet (Miller, 1995), but significantly lower for the other datasets, with scores of 43.3, 16.1, 37.7 and 29.8, respectively, evidencing considerable room for improvement in the models' ability for this task. They were also evaluated in the entity classification task with the GeoNames (Rebele et al., 2016), UMLS (Bodenreider, 2004), and schema.org datasets, showing scores of 67.8, 78.1 and 74.4, again suggesting considerable room for improvement. Finally, in the relationship recognition task with the UMLS (Bodenreider, 2004) dataset, a result of 49.5 was obtained, reflecting once again the need for improvement.

Moreover, the same article presents two tuned models: Flan-T5-Large (Chung et al., 2022) and Flan-T5-XL (Chung et al., 2022), which show remarkable improvements in several datasets of the evaluated tasks. For example, for the datasets of the first task, the results were improved to 32.8, 43.4 and 51.8. The results improved to 79.3 and 91.7 in the entity classification task, and in the relationship recognition task, 53.1 was achieved.

Similarly, in the study by Mihindukulasooriya et al. (2023) Vicuna-13B (Chiang et al., 2023) and Alpaca-LoRA-13B (Taori et al., 2023; Hu et al., 2022) are evaluated in Zero-Shot on the Fact Extraction task using the F1 metric for different subsets of the Wikidata-TekGen (Vrandečić and Krötzsch, 2014) and DBpedia-WebNLG (Gardent et al., 2017) datasets. The best result for the Wikidata dataset (Vrandečić and Krötzsch, 2014) is 0.38 for Vicuna (Chiang et al., 2023) and 0.28 for Alpaca (Taori et al., 2023; Hu et al., 2022) and for the DBpedia dataset (Gardent et al., 2017) it is 0.3 for Vicuna (Chiang et al., 2023) and 0.25 for Alpaca (Taori et al., 2023; Hu et al., 2022). As in the previous case, it is evident that there is much room for improvement.

Furthermore, in the study by Zhu et al. (2023), a comprehensive evaluation of Extended Language Models (LLMs) such as GPT-4 (OpenAI et al., 2023) and ChatGPT(OpenAI, 2023) in KG construction and reasoning tasks is performed by experiments on eight datasets and four representative tasks: entity and relationship extraction, event extraction, link prediction, and question and answer. The results show that, although GPT-4 achieves an F1 score of 31.03 in relation extraction on DuIE2.0 (Li et al., 2019) on zero-shot and 41.91 on one-shot, as well as an F1 score of 34.2 on MAVEN (Wang et al., 2020) for event extraction on zero-shot, and a hits@1 of 32.0 on FB15K-237 (Toutanova et al., 2015) for link prediction on zero-shot, these results are improbable.

The paper by Melnyk et al. (2022) presents an innovative approach for generating KGs from text in multiple stages. This approach is divided into two main phases: first, the generation of nodes using the pre-trained language model T5-large (Chung et al., 2022) and then the construction of edges using the information from the generated nodes. This method seeks to overcome the limitations of traditional graph linearization approaches by breaking the process into manageable and separately optimizable steps. The model was evaluated on three datasets: WebNLG 2020 (Castro Ferreira et al., 2020), TEKGEN (Agarwal et al., 2021) and New York Times (Riedel et al., 2010), obtaining F1 scores of 0.722, 0.707 and 0.918 respectively, demonstrating its effectiveness. However, it highlights the need for further improvement, especially in edge generation, to optimize the system's performance in various applications.

Finally, in the study by Ain et al. (2023), embeddings-based methods, such as SIFRank (Sun et al., 2020) and SIFRankplus, which is an extension made by the authors, enhanced with SqueezeBERT (Iandola et al., 2020), achieved an F1-score of 40.38% in keyphrase extraction. In concept weighting, the SBERT-based (Reimers and Gurevych, 2019) strategy achieved an accuracy of 13.9% and an F1-score of 20.6% for the top ten ranked concepts, superior results to the benchmark models with which they were purchased. Despite these advances, the results highlight the need to improve the accuracy and performance of the techniques to ensure the effective construction of KGs.

5 Proposed methodology

This section presents an innovative methodology for automatically using an LLM to generate KGs from educational materials. Existing models like BERT-Large, GPT-4, Vicuna-13B, PubMedBERT, BART-Large, Flan-T5, BLOOM, GPT-3, GPT-3.5, LLaMA, and Alpaca-LoRA-13B have shown progress in converting text to KGs but still have significant limitations, as seen in the previous section. For example, in term typing tasks, scores were 43.3 for GeoNames, 16.1 for NCI, 37.7 for SNOMEDCT_US, and 29.8 for MEDCIN, compared to 91.7 for WordNet. In entity classification, the highest scores were 78.1 for UMLS and 74.4 for schema.org. Fact extraction tasks showed Vicuna-13B scoring 0.38 and Alpaca-LoRA-13B scoring 0.28 on Wikidata-TekGen. These results highlight the need for new strategies to improve model performance in text-to-knowledge graph conversion in general and particularly in education.

To address these limitations, we propose a methodology that involves creating an expert model in natural language and KG language. This model is subsequently refined to convert learning materials into KGs, following a learning object structure that offers a guided and comprehensive teaching experience with multimedia educational content. The methodology comprises two phases: continuous pre-training using a large dataset of KGs and specific fine-tuning with didactic materials.

During pre-training, a diverse dataset of KGs from sources like Wikidata (Vrandečić and Krötzsch, 2014), DBpedia (Lehmann et al., 2015), and YAGO (Rebele et al., 2016) will be used to train the model with masking and self-supervised learning. This will enhance the model's understanding of semantic relationships and hierarchical structures, improving its ability to generate coherent and accurate graphs.

Continual pre-training allows the model to become more expert in its domain, enhancing semantic understanding, training on structured data, flexibility, generalization, bias reduction, and leveraging existing resources (Wu et al., 2024).

In the fine-tuning phase, diverse educational materials will be gathered, and their corresponding KGs will be created manually or semi-automatically. This process will necessitate defining a KG schema or leveraging an existing one from the literature that aligns with the proposed use case. Specifically, the of the IEEE Computer Society (2020) provides a comprehensive schema and vocabulary for metadata that could be particularly useful. Alongside this standard, methodologies and schemes described in the studies by (Wölfel et al., 2024) and (Chen et al., 2018) will also be considered.

Although KGs are not used in Wölfel et al. (2024), it becomes clear that a small amount of domain-specific data, such as slides and lecture transcripts, can be extremely valuable for building knowledge-based and generative educational chatbots. Slides are enriched with semantic annotations, identifying entities such as definitions, quotes, and examples. This enables knowledge-based to provide accurate and relevant responses by mining directly from this structured data.

Chen et al. (2018) describes a system developed to build educational KGs using pedagogical and learning assessment data automatically. The methods used in this study for extracting instructional concepts and identifying meaningful educational relationships will provide a solid foundation for the proposed KG scheme. Integrating these methodologies is expected to improve the system's effectiveness in automatically generating KGs from educational materials.

6 Conclusion

In conclusion, this article argues that structuring digital educational content as KGs rather than traditional repositories provides significant advantages. KGs offer a flexible, navigable representation of concept relationships, enhancing learning personalization and integration with LLMs. A methodology to automatically generate KGs from educational texts is proposed, promising to transform access to and organization of educational information for more profound, personalized learning.

References

Bilal Abu-Salih and Salihah Alotaibi. 2024. A systematic literature review of knowledge graph construction and application in education. *Heliyon*, 10(3):e25383.

Oshin Agarwal, Heming Ge, Siamak Shakeri, and Rami Al-Rfou. 2021. Knowledge graph based synthetic corpus generation for knowledge-enhanced language model pre-training. In *Proceedings of the 2021 Conference of the North American Chapter of the Association for Computational Linguistics: Human Language Technologies*, pages 3554–3565, Online. Association for Computational Linguistics.

Qurat Ul Ain, Mohamed Amine Chatti, Komlan Gluck Charles Bakar, Shoeb Joarder, and Rawaa Alatrash. 2023. Automatic construction of educational knowledge graphs: A word embedding-based approach. *Information*, 14(10):526.

Olivier Bodenreider. 2004. The unified medical language system (umls): integrating biomedical terminology. *Nucleic acids research*, 32(Database issue), D267–D270.

Tom B. Brown, Benjamin Mann, Nick Ryder, Melanie Subbiah, Jared Kaplan, Prafulla Dhariwal, Arvind Neelakantan, Pranav Shyam, Girish Sastry, Amanda Askell, Sandhini Agarwal, Ariel Herbert-Voss, Gretchen Krueger, Tom Henighan, Rewon Child, Aditya Ramesh, Daniel M. Ziegler, Jeffrey Wu, Clemens Winter, Christopher Hesse, Mark Chen, Eric Sigler, Mateusz Litwin, Scott Gray, Benjamin Chess, Jack Clark, Christopher Berner, Sam McCandlish, Alec Radford, Ilya Sutskever, and Dario Amodei. 2020. Language Models are Few-Shot Learners. *arXiv e-prints*, arXiv:2005.14165.

Thiago Castro Ferreira, Claire Gardent, Nikolai Ilinykh, Chris van der Lee, Simon Mille, Diego Moussallem, and Anastasia Shimorina. 2020. The 2020 bilingual, bi-directional WebNLG+ shared task: Overview and evaluation results (WebNLG+ 2020). In *Proceedings of the 3rd International Workshop on Natural Language Generation from the Semantic Web (WebNLG+)*, pages 55–76, Dublin, Ireland (Virtual). Association for Computational Linguistics.

Penghe Chen, Yu Lu, Vincent W. Zheng, Xiyang Chen, and Boda Yang. 2018. Knowedu: A system to construct knowledge graph for education. *IEEE Access*, 6:31553–31563.

Wei-Lin Chiang, Zhuohan Li, Zi Lin, Ying Sheng, Zhanghao Wu, Hao Zhang, Lianmin Zheng, Siyuan Zhuang, Yonghao Zhuang, Joseph E. Gonzalez, Ion Stoica, and Eric P. Xing. 2023.

Janneth Chicaiza and Priscila Valdiviezo-Diaz. 2021. A comprehensive survey of knowledge graph-based recommender systems: Technologies, development, and contributions. *Information*, 12(6):232.

Hyung Won Chung, Le Hou, Shayne Longpre, Barret Zoph, Yi Tay, William Fedus, Yunxuan Li, Xuezhi Wang, Mostafa Dehghani, Siddhartha Brahma, Albert Webson, Shixiang Shane Gu, Zhuyun Dai, Mirac Suzgun, Xinyun Chen, Aakanksha Chowdhery, Alex Castro-Ros, Marie Pellat, Kevin Robinson, Dasha Valter, Sharan Narang, Gaurav Mishra, Adams Yu, Vincent Zhao, Yanping Huang, Andrew Dai, Hongkun Yu, Slav Petrov, Ed H. Chi, Jeff Dean, Jacob Devlin, Adam Roberts, Denny Zhou, Quoc V. Le, and Jason Wei. 2022. Scaling Instruction-Finetuned Language Models. *arXiv e-prints*, arXiv:2210.11416.

Fu-Rong Dang, Jin-Tao Tang, Kun-Yuan Pang, Ting Wang, Sha-Sha Li, and Xiao Li. 2021. Constructing an educational knowledge graph with concepts linked to wikipedia. *Journal of Computer Science and Technology*, 36:1200–1211.

Jacob Devlin, Ming-Wei Chang, Kenton Lee, and Kristina Toutanova. 2019. BERT: Pre-training of deep bidirectional transformers for language understanding. In *Proceedings of the 2019 Conference of the North American Chapter of the Association for Computational Linguistics: Human Language Technologies, Volume 1 (Long and Short Papers)*, pages 4171–4186, Minneapolis, Minnesota. Association for Computational Linguistics.

Claire Gardent, Anastasia Shimorina, Shashi Narayan, and Laura Perez-Beltrachini. 2017. Creating training corpora for NLG micro-planners. In *Proceedings of the 55th Annual Meeting of the Association for Computational Linguistics (Volume 1: Long Papers)*, pages 179–188, Vancouver, Canada. Association for Computational Linguistics.

Hamed Giglou, Jennifer D'Souza, and Sören Auer. 2023. LLMs4OL: Large Language Models for Ontology Learning. *arXiv e-prints*, arXiv:2307.16648.

Yu Gu, Robert Tinn, Hao Cheng, Michael Lucas, Naoto Usuyama, Xiaodong Liu, Tristan Naumann, Jianfeng Gao, and Hoifung Poon. 2021. Domain-specific language model pretraining for biomedical natural language processing. *ACM Trans. Comput. Healthcare*, 3(1).

Edward J. Hu, Yelong Shen, Phillip Wallis, Zeyuan Allen-Zhu, Yuanzhi Li, Shean Wang, Lu Wang, and Weizhu Chen. 2022. *LoRA: Low-rank adaptation of large language models*. Accessed: 2023-05-21.

Forrest Iandola, Albert Shaw, Ravi Krishna, and Kurt Keutzer. 2020. SqueezeBERT: What can computer vision teach NLP about efficient neural networks? In *Proceedings of SustaiNLP: Workshop on Simple and Efficient Natural Language Processing*, pages 124–135, Online. Association for Computational Linguistics.

Mayank Kejriwal. 2022. Knowledge graphs: A practical review of the research landscape. *Information*, 13(4):161.

Muhammad Khoiruddin, Sri Kusumawardani, Indriana Hidayah, and Silmi Fauziati. 2023. A review of ontology development in the e-learning domain: Methods, roles, evaluation. *2023 International Conference on Computer, Control, Informatics and its Applications (IC3INA)*.

Jens Lehmann, Robert Isele, Max Jakob, Anja Jentzsch, Dimitris Kontokostas, Pablo N Mendes, Sebastian Hellmann, Mohamed Morsey, Patrick van Kleef, Sören Auer, and Christian Bizer. 2015. Dbpedia – a large-scale, multilingual knowledge base extracted from wikipedia. *Semantic Web*, 6(2):167–195.

Mike Lewis, Yinhan Liu, Naman Goyal, Marjan Ghazvininejad, Abdelrahman Mohamed, Omer Levy, Veselin Stoyanov, and Luke Zettlemoyer. 2020. BART: Denoising sequence-to-sequence pre-training for natural language generation, translation, and comprehension. In *Proceedings of the 58th Annual Meeting of the Association for Computational Linguistics*, pages 7871–7880, Online. Association for Computational Linguistics.

Linqing Li and Zhifeng Wang. 2023. Knowledge Graph Enhanced Intelligent Tutoring System Based on Exercise Representativeness and Informativeness. *arXiv e-prints*, arXiv:2307.15076.

S. Li, J. Tang, M.Y. Kan, D. Zhao, S. Li, and H. Zan. 2019. Duie: A large-scale chinese dataset for information extraction. *Natural Language Processing and Chinese Computing*, 11839.

Medicomp Systems. 2023. MEDCIN. Accessed: 2024-05-21.

Igor Melnyk, Pierre Dognin, and Payel Das. 2022. Knowledge Graph Generation From Text. *arXiv e-prints*, arXiv:2211.10511.

Nandana Mihindukulasooriya, Sanju Tiwari, Carlos F. Enguix, and Kusum Lata. 2023. Text2KGBench: A Benchmark for Ontology-Driven Knowledge Graph Generation from Text. *arXiv e-prints*, arXiv:2308.02357.

George A. Miller. 1995. Wordnet: a lexical database for english. *Commun. ACM*, 38(11):39–41.

National Cancer Institute, National Institutes of Health. 2022. NCI Thesaurus. Accessed: 2024-05-21.

Learning Technology Standards Committee of the IEEE Computer Society. 2020. Ieee standard for learning object metadata. *IEEE Std 1484.12.1-2020*, pages 1–50.

OpenAI. 2023. ChatGPT: Language Model. Accessed: 2024-05-21.

OpenAI, Josh Achiam, Steven Adler, Sandhini Agarwal, Lama Ahmad, Ilge Akkaya, Florencia Leoni Aleman, Diogo Almeida, Janko Altenschmidt, Sam Altman, Shyamal Anadkat, Red Avila, Igor Babuschkin, Suchir Balaji, Valerie Balcom, Paul Baltescu, Haiming Bao, Mohammad Bavarian, Jeff Belgum, Irwan Bello, Berdine, and et al. 2023. GPT-4 Technical Report. *arXiv e-prints*, arXiv:2303.08774.

Shirui Pan, Linhao Luo, Yufei Wang, Chen Chen, Jiapu Wang, and Xindong Wu. 2023. Unifying Large Language Models and Knowledge Graphs: A Roadmap. *arXiv e-prints*, arXiv:2306.08302.

Thomas Rebele, Fabian Suchanek, Johannes Hoffart, Joanna Biega, Erdal Kuzey, and Gerhard Weikum. 2016. Yago: A multilingual knowledge base from wikipedia, wordnet, and geonames. *International Semantic Web Conference*, pages 177–185.

Nils Reimers and Iryna Gurevych. 2019. Sentence-BERT: Sentence embeddings using Siamese BERT-networks. In *Proceedings of the 2019 Conference on Empirical Methods in Natural Language Processing and the 9th International Joint Conference on Natural Language Processing (EMNLP-IJCNLP)*, pages 3982–3992, Hong Kong, China. Association for Computational Linguistics.

S. Riedel, L. Yao, and A. McCallum. 2010. Modeling relations and their mentions without labeled text. *Machine Learning and Knowledge Discovery in Databases. ECML PKDD 2010. Lecture Notes in Computer Science*, 6323.

SNOMED International. 2023. US Edition of SNOMED CT. Accessed: 2024-05-21.

K. Stancin, P. Poscic, and D. Jaksic. 2020. Ontologies in education – state of the art. *Education and Information Technologies*, 25:5301–5320.

Yi Sun, Hangping Qiu, Yu Zheng, Zhongwei Wang, and Chaoran Zhang. 2020. Sifrank: A new baseline for unsupervised keyphrase extraction based on pre-trained language model. *IEEE Access*, 8:10896–10906.

Rohan Taori, Ishaan Gulrajani, Tianyi Zhang, Yann Dubois, Xuechen Li, Carlos Guestrin, Percy Liang, and Tatsunori B. Hashimoto. 2023. Stanford Alpaca: An instruction-following LLaMA model. Accessed: 2023-05-21.

Kristina Toutanova, Danqi Chen, Patrick Pantel, Hoifung Poon, Pallavi Choudhury, and Michael Gamon. 2015. Representing text for joint embedding of text and knowledge bases. In *Proceedings of the 2015 Conference on Empirical Methods in Natural Language Processing*, pages 1499–1509, Lisbon, Portugal. Association for Computational Linguistics.

Hugo Touvron, Thibaut Lavril, Gautier Izacard, Xavier Martinet, Marie-Anne Lachaux, Timothée Lacroix, Baptiste Rozière, Naman Goyal, Eric Hambro, Faisal Azhar, Aurelien Rodriguez, Armand Joulin, Edouard Grave, and Guillaume Lample. 2023. LLaMA: Open and Efficient Foundation Language Models. *arXiv e-prints*, arXiv:2302.13971.

Denny Vrandečić and Markus Krötzsch. 2014. Wikidata: a free collaborative knowledgebase. *Commun. ACM*, 57(10):78–85.

Xiaozhi Wang, Ziqi Wang, Xu Han, Wangyi Jiang, Rong Han, Zhiyuan Liu, Juanzi Li, Peng Li, Yankai Lin, and Jie Zhou. 2020. MAVEN: A Massive General Domain Event Detection Dataset. In *Proceedings of the 2020 Conference on Empirical Methods in Natural Language Processing (EMNLP)*, pages 1652–1671, Online. Association for Computational Linguistics.

BigScience Workshop, Teven Le Scao, Angela Fan, Christopher Akiki, Ellie Pavlick, Suzana Ilić, Daniel Hesslow, Roman Castagné, Alexandra Sasha Luccioni, François Yvon, Matthias Gallé, Jonathan Tow, Alexander M. Rush, Stella Biderman, Albert Webson, Pawan Sasanka Ammanamanchi, Thomas Wang, Benoît Sagot, Niklas Muennighoff, Albert Villanova del Moral, and et al. 2022. BLOOM: A 176B-Parameter Open-Access Multilingual Language Model. *arXiv e-prints*, arXiv:2211.05100.

Tongtong Wu, Linhao Luo, Yuan-Fang Li, Shirui Pan, Thuy-Trang Vu, and Gholamreza Haffari. 2024. Continual Learning for Large Language Models: A Survey. *arXiv e-prints*, arXiv:2402.01364.

Matthias Wölfel, Mehrnoush Barani Shirzad, Andreas Reich, and Katharina Anderer. 2024. Knowledge-based and generative-ai-driven pedagogical conversational agents: A comparative study of grice's cooperative principles and trust. *Big Data and Cognitive Computing*, 8(1).

Xu Yuan, Jiaxi Chen, Yingbo Wang, Anni Chen, Yiou Huang, Wenhong Zhao, and Shuo Yu. 2024. Semantic-enhanced knowledge graph completion. *Mathematics*, 12(3).

Yuqi Zhu, Xiaohan Wang, Jing Chen, Shuofei Qiao, Yixin Ou, Yunzhi Yao, Shumin Deng, Huajun Chen, and Ningyu Zhang. 2023. LLMs for Knowledge Graph Construction and Reasoning: Recent Capabilities and Future Opportunities. *arXiv e-prints*, arXiv:2305.13168.

STAGE: Simplified Text-Attributed Graph Embeddings Using Pre-trained LLMs

Aaron Zolnai-Lucas[1*], Jack Boylan[1*], Chris Hokamp[1], Parsa Ghaffari[1]

[1]Quantexa,

Correspondence: {firstname}{lastname}@quantexa.com

Abstract

We present Simplified Text-Attributed Graph Embeddings (STAGE), a straightforward yet effective method for enhancing node features in Graph Neural Network (GNN) models that encode Text-Attributed Graphs (TAGs). Our approach leverages Large-Language Models (LLMs) to generate embeddings for textual attributes. STAGE achieves competitive results on various node classification benchmarks while also maintaining a simplicity in implementation relative to current state-of-the-art (SoTA) techniques. We show that utilizing pre-trained LLMs as embedding generators provides robust features for ensemble GNN training, enabling pipelines that are simpler than current SoTA approaches which require multiple expensive training and prompting stages. We also implement diffusion-pattern GNNs in an effort to make this pipeline scalable to graphs beyond academic benchmarks.

1 Introduction

A Knowledge Graph (KG) typically includes entities (represented as nodes), relationships between entities (represented as edges), and attributes of both entities and relationships (Ehrlinger and Wöß, 2016). These attributes, referred to as metadata, are often governed by a domain-specific ontology, which provides a formal framework for defining the types of entities and relationships as well as their properties. KGs can be used to represent structured information about the world in diverse settings, including medical domain models (Koné et al., 2023), words and lexical semantics (Miller, 1995), and commercial products (Chiang et al., 2019).

Text-Attributed Graphs (TAGs) can be viewed as a subset of KGs, where some node and edge metadata is represented by unstructured or semi-structured natural language text (Yang et al., 2023). Examples of unstructured data values in TAGs could include the research article text representing the nodes of a citation graph, or the content of social media posts that are the nodes of an interaction graph extracted from a social media platform. Many real-world datasets are naturally represented as TAGs, and studying how to best represent and learn using these datasets has received attention from the fields of graph learning, natural language processing (NLP), and information retrieval.

Graph Learning and LLMs With the emergence of LLMs as powerful general purpose reasoning agents, there has been increasing interest in integrating KGs with LLMs (Pan et al., 2024). Current SoTA approaches combining graph learning with (L)LMs follow either an **iterative** or a **cascading** method. *Iterative* methods involve jointly training an LM and a GNN for the given task. While this approach can produce a task-specific feature space, it may be complex and resource-intensive, particularly for large graphs. In contrast, *cascading* methods first apply an LM to extract node features which are then used by a downstream GNN model. Cascading models demonstrate excellent performance on TAG tasks (He et al., 2024; Duan et al., 2023a), although they often require multiple stages of training targeted at each pipeline component. More recent cascading techniques implement an additional step, known as text-level enhancement (Chen et al., 2024), whereby textual features are augmented using an LLM.

Simplifying Node Representation Generation To the best of our knowledge, all existing cascading approaches require multiple rounds of data generation or finetuning to achieve satisfactory results on TAG tasks (He et al., 2024; Duan et al., 2023a; Chen et al., 2024). This bottleneck increases the difficulty of applying such methods to real-world graphs. Our proposed method, STAGE, aims to simplify existing approaches by foregoing LM finetuning, and only making use of a single pre-

*Authors contributed equally.

Proceedings of the 1st Workshop on Knowledge Graphs and Large Language Models (KaLLM 2024), pages 92–104
August 15, 2024 ©2024 Association for Computational Linguistics

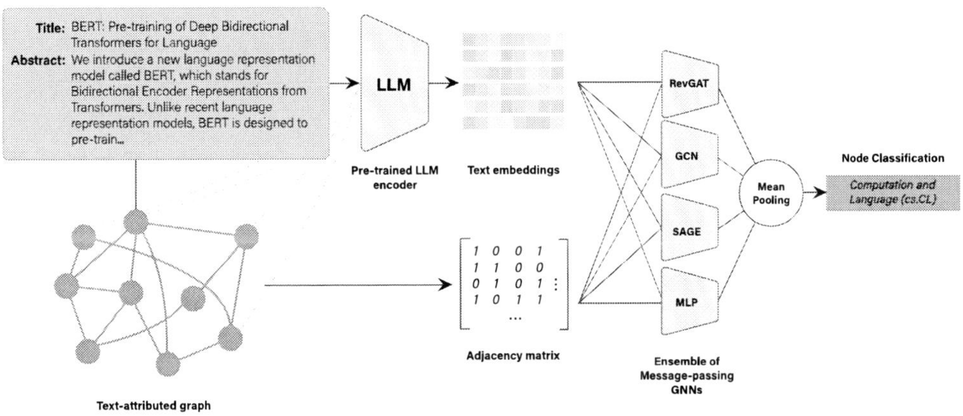

Figure 1: Our proposed approach to node classification. Firstly, the textual attributes of the input graph nodes are encoded using an off-the-shelf LLM. The text embeddings will be used alongside the graph adjacency matrix as input to train a downstream ensemble of GNNs. GNN predictions are then mean-pooled to obtain the final prediction.

trained LLM as the node embedding model, without data augmentation via prompting. We study possible configurations of this simplified pipeline and demonstrate that this method achieves competitive performance while significantly reducing the complexity of training and data preparation.

Scalable GNN Architectures The exponentially growing receptive field required during training of most message-passing GNNs is another bottleneck in both cascading and iterative approaches, becoming computationally intractable for large graphs (Duan et al., 2023b; Liu et al., 2024). Because we wish to study approaches that can be applied in real-world settings, we also explore the implementation of diffusion-pattern GNNs, such as SimpleGCN (Wu et al., 2019) and SIGN (Frasca et al., 2020), which may enable STAGE to be applied to much larger graphs beyond the relatively small academic benchmarks. Our code is available at `https://github.com/aaronzo/STAGE`.

Concretely, this work studies several ways to make learning on TAGs more efficient and scalable:

- **Single Training Stage:** We perform ensemble GNN training with a fixed LLM as the node feature generator, which significantly reduces training time by eliminating the need for multiple large model training runs.
- **No LLM Prompting:** We do not prompt an LLM for text-level augmentations such as predictions or explanations. Instead, we use only the text attributes provided in the dataset.
- **Direct Use of LLM as Text Embedding Model:** Using an off-the-shelf LLM as the embedding model makes this method adaptable to new models and datasets. We study several alternative base models for embedding generation.
- **Diffusion-pattern GNN implementation:** We contribute an investigation into diffusion-pattern GNNs which enable this method to scale to larger graphs.

The rest of the paper is organized as follows: section 2 gives an overview of related work, section 3 discusses our approach in detail, section 4 studies the performance of STAGE in various settings, and section 5 is a discussion of the experimental results.

2 Background

Text-Attributed Graphs Yan et al. (2023) suggest that integrating topological data with textual information can significantly improve the learning outcomes on various graph-related tasks. Chien et al. (2022) incorporate graph structural information into the pre-training stage of pre-trained language models (PLMs), achieving improved performance albeit with additional training overhead, while Liu et al. (2023) further adopt sentence embedding models to unify the text-attribute and

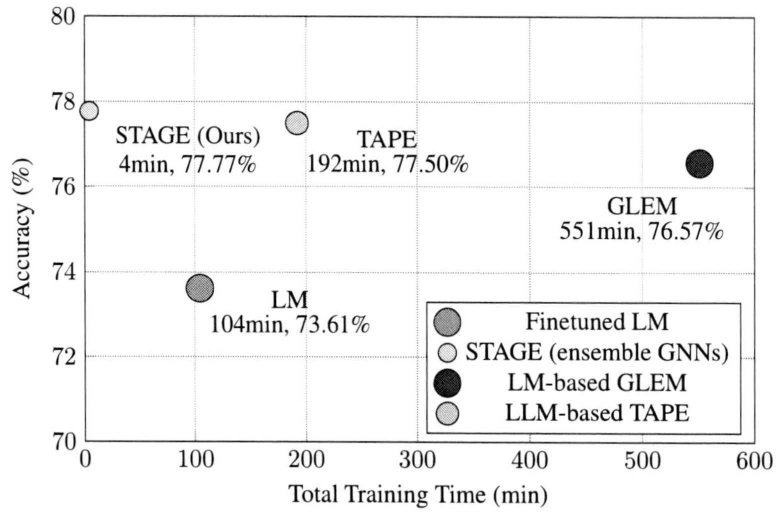

Figure 2: The performance trade-off between node classification accuracy and total training time on ogbn-arxiv for SoTA LM-GNN methods. The STAGE model uses text embeddings generated from Salesforce-Embedding-Mistral and an ensemble of GNNs (GCN, SAGE and RevGAT) and MLP. The size of each marker indicates the total number of trainable parameters. Figure adapted from (He et al., 2024).

graph structure feature space, proposing a unified model for diverse tasks across multiple datasets.

LLMs as Text Encoders General purpose text embedding models, used in both finetuned and zero-shot paradigms, are a standard component of modern NLP pipelines (Mikolov et al., 2013; Pennington et al., 2014; Reimers and Gurevych, 2019). As LLMs have emerged as powerful zero-shot agents, many studies have considered generating text embeddings as an auxiliary output (Muennighoff, 2022; Mialon et al., 2023). BehnamGhader et al. (2024) introduce LLM2Vec, an unsupervised method to convert LLMs into powerful text encoders by using bidirectional attention, masked next token prediction and contrastive learning, achieving state-of-the-art performance on various text embedding benchmarks.

Language Models and GNNs Graph Neural Networks have been successfully applied to node classification and link prediction tasks, demonstrating improved performance when combined with textual features from nodes (Kipf and Welling, 2017; Li et al., 2022b). Several studies show that finetuning pre-trained Language Models (PLMs), such as BERT (Devlin et al., 2019) and DeBERTa (He et al., 2021), enhances GNN performance by leveraging textual node features (Chen et al., 2024; Duan et al., 2023a; He et al., 2024).

Recent research has explored the integration of LLMs with GNNs, particularly for TAGs. LLMs contribute deep semantic understanding and commonsense knowledge, potentially boosting GNNs' effectiveness on downstream tasks. However, combining LLMs with GNNs poses computational challenges. Techniques like GLEM (Zhao et al., 2023) use the Expectation Maximization framework to alternate updates between LM and GNN modules.

Other approaches include the TAPE method, which uses GPT (OpenAI, 2023; OpenAI et al., 2024) models for data augmentation, enhancing GNN performance through enriched textual embeddings (He et al., 2024). SimTeG demonstrates that parameter-efficient finetuning (PEFT) PLMs can yield competitive results (Duan et al., 2023a). (Ye et al., 2024) suggest that finetuned LLMs can match or exceed state-of-the-art GNN performance on various benchmarks.

Building on these insights, the STAGE method focuses on efficient and scalable learning for TAGs by utilizing zero-shot capabilities of LLMs to generate representations without extensive task-specific tuning or auxiliary data generation.

3 Approach

Our cascading approach consists of two steps:

- A zero-shot LLM-based embedding generator is used to encode the title and abstract (or equivalent textual attribute) of each node. We denote the generated node embeddings as $\mathcal{X}$.

- An ensemble of GNN architectures are trained on $\mathcal{X}$, and their predictions are mean-pooled to obtain the final node predictions.

Ensembling the predictions from multiple GNN architectures was motivated by our observation of strong performance by different models across different datasets.

3.1 Text Embedding Retrieval

For the text embedding model, we select a general-purpose embedding LLM that ranks highly on the Massive Text Embedding Benchmark (MTEB) Leaderboard[1]. Specifically, we evaluate `gte-Qwen1.5-7B-instruct`, `LLM2Vec-Meta-Llama-3-8B-Instruct`, and `SFR-Embedding-Mistral`. MTEB ranks embedding models based on their performance across a wide variety of information retrieval, classification and clustering tasks. This model is used out-of-the-box without any finetuning. An appealing aspect of LLM-based embeddings is the possibility to add instructions alongside input text to bias the embeddings for a given task. We empirically evaluate the effect of instruction biased embeddings is in Table 2 of section 4.

Node representations $\mathcal{X}$ are generated using only the title and abstract, or equivalent textual node attributes, omitting the LLM predictions and explanations provided by (He et al., 2024). $\mathcal{X}$ will then be used as enriched node feature vectors for training a downstream GNN ensemble.

3.2 GNN Training

Using the previously generated embeddings $\mathcal{X}$ as node features, we train an ensemble of GNN models on the node classification task:

$$\text{Loss}_{\text{cls}} = \mathcal{L}_\theta\left(\phi(\text{GNN}(\mathcal{X}, \mathcal{A})), \mathbf{Y}\right), \quad (1)$$

where $\phi(\cdot)$ is the classifier, $\mathcal{A}$ is the adjacency matrix of the graph and $\mathcal{Y}$ is the label. For the GNN architectures we choose GCN (Kipf and Welling, 2017), SAGE (Hamilton et al., 2018) and RevGAT (Li et al., 2022a). We also evaluate a multi-layer perceptron (MLP) (Haykin, 1994) among our GNN models. To combine the predictions from each of the K models in the ensemble, we compute the mean prediction as follows:

$$\bar{\mathbf{p}} = \frac{1}{K}\sum_{k=1}^{K} \mathbf{p}_k, \quad (2)$$

Cross-entropy loss is used to compute the loss value.

Diffusion-based GNNs For a graph G with node features $\mathcal{X}$, a diffusion operator is a matrix A_{OP} with the same dimensions as the adjacency matrix of G. Diffused features $\mathcal{H}$ are then calculated via $\mathcal{H} = A_{\text{OP}}\mathcal{X}$.

We explored Simple-GCN (Wu et al., 2019) and SIGN (Frasca et al., 2020), both of which employ adjacency-based diffusion operators to pre-aggregate features across the graph before training. SIGN is a generalization of Simple-GCN, to extend to Personalized-PageRank (Page et al., 1998) and triangle-based operators. This allows expensive computation to be carried out by distributed computing clusters or efficient sparse graph routines such as GraphBLAS (Davis, 2019), which do not need to back-propagate through graph convolution. The prediction head can then be a shallow MLP or logistic regression. We provide implementation specifics in appendix section C to ensure repeatability.

3.3 Parameter-efficient Finetuning LLM

Motivated by the node classification performance gains seen by (Duan et al., 2023a) using PEFT, we finetune an LLM on the node classification task. Concretely, we use an LLM embedding model with a low-rank adapter (LoRA) (Hu et al., 2021a) and a densely connected classifier head. The pre-trained LLM weights remain frozen as the model trains on input text T to reduce loss according to:

$$\text{Loss}_{\text{cls}} = \mathcal{L}(\phi(\text{LLM}(T)), Y) \quad (3)$$

where $\phi(\cdot)$ is the classifier head and Y is the label. Again, we use cross-entropy loss to compute the loss value.

4 Experiments

We investigate the performance of STAGE over five TAG benchmarks: *ogbn-arxiv* (Hu et al., 2021b), a dataset of arXiv papers linked by citations; *ogbn-products* (Hu et al., 2021b), representing an Amazon product co-purchasing network; *PubMed* (Sen et al., 2008), a citation network of diabetes-related scientific publications; *Cora* (McCallum et al.,

[1]https://huggingface.co/spaces/mteb/leaderboard

Dataset	Method	h_{shallow}	h_{GIANT}	GPT3.5	LM_{finetune}	h_{TAPE}	h_{STAGE}(**OURS**)
Cora	MLP	0.6388 ± 0.0213	0.7196 ± 0.0000	0.6769	0.7606 ± 0.0378	0.8778 ± 0.0485	0.7680 ± 0.0228
	GCN	0.8911 ± 0.0015	0.8423 ± 0.0053	0.6769	0.7606 ± 0.0378	0.9119 ± 0.0158	0.8704 ± 0.0105
	SAGE	0.8824 ± 0.0009	0.8455 ± 0.0028	0.6769	0.7606 ± 0.0378	0.9290 ± 0.0307	0.8722 ± 0.0063
	RevGAT	0.8911 ± 0.0000	0.8353 ± 0.0038	0.6769	0.7606 ± 0.0378	0.9280 ± 0.0275	0.8639 ± 0.0129
	Ensemble	-	-	-	-	-	0.8824 ± 0.0155
PubMed	MLP	0.8635 ± 0.0032	0.8175 ± 0.0059	0.9342	0.9494 ± 0.0046	0.9565 ± 0.0060	0.9142 ± 0.0122
	GCN	0.8031 ± 0.0425	0.8419 ± 0.0050	0.9342	0.9494 ± 0.0046	0.9431 ± 0.0043	0.8960 ± 0.0042
	SAGE	0.8881 ± 0.0002	0.8372 ± 0.0082	0.9342	0.9494 ± 0.0046	0.9618 ± 0.0053	0.9087 ± 0.0064
	RevGAT	0.8850 ± 0.0005	0.8502 ± 0.0048	0.9342	0.9494 ± 0.0046	0.9604 ± 0.0047	0.8654 ± 0.0952
	Ensemble	-	-	-	-	-	0.9265 ± 0.0068
ogbn-arxiv	MLP	0.5336 ± 0.0038	0.7308 ± 0.0006	0.7350	0.7361 ± 0.0004	0.7587 ± 0.0015	0.7517 ± 0.0011
	GCN	0.7182 ± 0.0027	0.7329 ± 0.0010	0.7350	0.7361 ± 0.0004	0.7520 ± 0.0005	0.7377 ± 0.0010
	SAGE	0.7171 ± 0.0017	0.7435 ± 0.0014	0.7350	0.7361 ± 0.0004	0.7672 ± 0.0007	0.7596 ± 0.0040
	RevGAT	0.7083 ± 0.0017	0.7590 ± 0.0019	0.7350	0.7361 ± 0.0004	0.7750 ± 0.0012	0.7638 ± 0.0054
	Ensemble	-	-	-	-	-	0.7777 ± 0.0019
ogbn-products	MLP	0.5385 ± 0.0017	0.6125 ± 0.0078	0.7440	0.7297 ± 0.0023	0.7878 ± 0.0082	0.7277 ± 0.0054
	GCN	0.7052 ± 0.0051	0.6977 ± 0.0042	0.7440	0.7297 ± 0.0023	0.7996 ± 0.0041	0.7679 ± 0.0109
	SAGE	0.6913 ± 0.0026	0.6869 ± 0.0011	0.7440	0.7297 ± 0.0023	0.8137 ± 0.0043	0.7795 ± 0.0012
	RevGAT	0.6964 ± 0.0017	0.7189 ± 0.0030	0.7440	0.7297 ± 0.0023	0.8234 ± 0.0036	0.8083 ± 0.0051
	Ensemble	-	-	-	-	-	0.8140 ± 0.0033
tape-arxiv23	MLP	0.6202 ± 0.0064	0.5574 ± 0.0032	0.7356	0.7358 ± 0.0006	0.8385 ± 0.0246	0.7940 ± 0.0022
	GCN	0.6341 ± 0.0062	0.5672 ± 0.0061	0.7356	0.7358 ± 0.0006	0.8080 ± 0.0215	0.7678 ± 0.0024
	SAGE	0.6430 ± 0.0037	0.5665 ± 0.0032	0.7356	0.7358 ± 0.0006	0.8388 ± 0.0264	0.7894 ± 0.0024
	RevGAT	0.6563 ± 0.0062	0.5834 ± 0.0038	0.7356	0.7358 ± 0.0006	0.8423 ± 0.0256	0.7880 ± 0.0023
	Ensemble	-	-	-	-	-	0.8029 ± 0.0020

Table 1: Node classification accuracy for the Cora, PubMed, ogbn-arxiv, ogbn-products, and tape-arxiv23 datasets. The experiment is run over four seeds, with mean accuracy and standard deviation shown. The best results are coloured green (first), yellow (second), and orange (third). For h_{STAGE}, we use SFR-Embedding-Mistral as the embedding model on TA features only, and the simple task instruction to bias the embeddings. We adapt the table from (He et al., 2024) and include our results.

2000), a dataset of scientific publications categorized into one of seven classes; and *tape-arxiv23* (He et al., 2024), focusing on arXiv papers published after the 2023 knowledge cut-off for GPT3.5. We use the subset of *ogbn-products* provided by (He et al., 2024). Further details can be found in appendix Table 7.

For each experiment using Cora, PubMed or *tape-arxiv23*, 60% of the data was allocated for training, 20% for validation, and 20% for testing. For the `ogbn-arxiv` and `ogbn-products` datasets, we adopted the standard train/validation/test split provided by the Open Graph Benchmark (OGB)[2] (Hu et al., 2021b).

Our main results can be seen in Table 1. Multiple GNN models are trained using embeddings from a pre-trained LLM as node features. We ensemble the predictions across model architectures by taking the mean prediction.

Node classification accuracy is provided for various datasets, measured across multiple methods and feature types. Each column represents a specific metric or method:

- $\mathbf{h_{shallow}}$: Performance using shallow features, indicating basic attributes provided as part of each dataset
- $\mathbf{h_{GIANT}}$: Results obtained by using GIANT features as proposed by (Chien et al., 2022), designed to incorporate graph structural information into LM training
- **GPT3.5**: Accuracy when using zero-shot predictions from GPT-3.5-turbo, demonstrating the utility of state-of-the-art language models in a zero-shot setting
- $\mathbf{LM_{finetune}}$: Performance metrics reported by (He et al., 2024) after finetuning the DeBERTa (He et al., 2021) model on labeled nodes from the graph, showing the benefits of supervised finetuning
- $\mathbf{h_{TAPE}}$: Shows results for the TAPE features (He et al., 2024), which includes the original textual attributes of the node, GPT-generated predictions for each node, and GPT-generated

[2] `https://ogb.stanford.edu/`

Dataset	Method	$h_{\text{no instruction}}$	$h_{\text{task instruction}}$	$h_{\text{graph-aware-instruction}}$
Cora	MLP	0.7772 ± 0.0205	0.7680 ± 0.0228	0.7763 ± 0.0193
	GCN	0.8612 ± 0.0121	0.8704 ± 0.0105	0.8718 ± 0.0085
	SAGE	0.8833 ± 0.0125	0.8722 ± 0.0063	0.8704 ± 0.0109
	RevGAT	0.8630 ± 0.0119	0.8639 ± 0.0129	0.8676 ± 0.0125
	Ensemble	0.8930 ± 0.0086	0.8824 ± 0.0155	0.8875 ± 0.0118
PubMed	MLP	0.9305 ± 0.0052	0.9142 ± 0.0122	0.9185 ± 0.0145
	GCN	0.9021 ± 0.0034	0.8960 ± 0.0042	0.8978 ± 0.0046
	SAGE	0.9268 ± 0.0052	0.9087 ± 0.0064	0.9126 ± 0.0024
	RevGAT	0.8637 ± 0.0942	0.8654 ± 0.0952	0.9211 ± 0.0022
	Ensemble	0.9358 ± 0.0035	0.9265 ± 0.0068	0.9313 ± 0.0025
ogbn-arxiv	MLP	0.7417 ± 0.0015	0.7517 ± 0.0011	0.7519 ± 0.0028
	GCN	0.7336 ± 0.0029	0.7377 ± 0.0010	0.7367 ± 0.0045
	SAGE	0.7515 ± 0.0027	0.7596 ± 0.0040	0.7559 ± 0.0039
	RevGAT	0.7629 ± 0.0035	0.7638 ± 0.0054	0.7607 ± 0.0011
	Ensemble	0.7745 ± 0.0013	0.7777 ± 0.0019	0.7740 ± 0.0019
ogbn-products	MLP	0.6841 ± 0.0054	0.7277 ± 0.0054	0.7163 ± 0.0172
	GCN	0.7367 ± 0.0068	0.7679 ± 0.0109	0.7729 ± 0.0033
	SAGE	0.7543 ± 0.0065	0.7795 ± 0.0012	0.7811 ± 0.0049
	RevGAT	0.8016 ± 0.0078	0.8083 ± 0.0051	0.8000 ± 0.0078
	Ensemble	0.7991 ± 0.0034	0.8140 ± 0.0033	0.8090 ± 0.0037
tape-arxiv23	MLP	0.7803 ± 0.0014	0.7940 ± 0.0022	0.7948 ± 0.0025
	GCN	0.7518 ± 0.0044	0.7678 ± 0.0024	0.7703 ± 0.0025
	SAGE	0.7702 ± 0.0022	0.7894 ± 0.0024	0.7917 ± 0.0021
	RevGAT	0.7880 ± 0.0047	0.7880 ± 0.0023	0.7906 ± 0.0034
	Ensemble	0.8013 ± 0.0017	0.8029 ± 0.0020	0.8054 ± 0.0025

Table 2: Node classification accuracy for the Cora, PubMed, ogbn-arxiv, ogbn-products, and tape-arxiv23 datasets, demonstrating the effect of varying an instruction to bias the embeddings from the pre-trained LLM. The experiment is run over four seeds, with mean accuracy and standard deviation shown. The best results are coloured green (first), yellow (second), and orange (third). For all experiments, we use SFR-Embedding-Mistral as the embedding model on TA features only, and the simple task instruction to bias the embeddings.

explanations of ranked predictions to enrich node features.

- $\mathbf{h}_{\text{STAGE}}$: Reflects the model's performance training with node features generated by a pre-trained LLM.

Instruction-biased Embeddings Textual attributes for each node are passed to the embedding LLM together with a task description which remains constant for every text, prefixing each input with a task-specific system prompt. We evaluated 3 simple task descriptions:

1. A short prompt describing the classification task for the text, as used during the pre-training stage of the LLM.
2. A description of the types of relationships between texts to form a graph, along with the classification task description. Specific graph structure for each node is not included in the prompt, unlike the proposed method from (Fatemi et al., 2024).
3. No task description.

Our findings are summarized in Table 2. Further details of the instructions can be found in appendix Table 8.

Parameter-efficient Finetuning In Table 3 we investigate the effect of using parameter-efficient finetuning (PEFT) on the pre-trained LLM, as described in (Duan et al., 2023a). We also compare this against finetuning both the LLM (using PEFT) and the GNN in unison.

Embedding Model Type In Table 4, we compare the results when using different pre-trained LLMs as the text encoder.

Diffusion GNNs Included in Table 4, we study the performance of using SimpleGCN and SIGN models individually. Model selection and implementation details can be found in the appendix sections C and D.

Ablation Study To study the impact of each component in the GNN ensemble, we perform a detailed ablation study. The results can be found in 6.

Dataset	LLM + GNN Ensemble	$LLM_{finetuned}$	$LLM_{finetuned}$ + GNN Ensemble
Cora	0.8824 ± 0.0155	0.8063	**0.8856**
PubMed	0.9265 ± 0.0068	0.9513	**0.9559**
ogbn-arxiv	0.7777 ± 0.0019	0.7666	**0.7813**
ogbn-products	0.8140 ± 0.0033	0.8020	**0.8257**
tape-arxiv23	0.8029 ± 0.0020	0.8021	**0.8095**

Table 3: Effect of using parameter-efficient finetuning (PEFT) on the pre-trained LLM, as described in (Duan et al., 2023a). Comparison of GNN-only trained, LLM finetuned without GNNs, and LLM and GNN trained separately. The best results are highlighted in bold.

Dataset	Method	SFR-Embedding-Mistral	LLM2Vec	gte-Qwen1.5-7B-instruct
Cora	MLP	0.7680 ± 0.0228	0.8026 ± 0.0141	0.7389 ± 0.0136
	GCN	0.8704 ± 0.0105	0.8778 ± 0.0046	0.8621 ± 0.0105
	SAGE	0.8722 ± 0.0063	0.8773 ± 0.0062	0.8658 ± 0.0049
	RevGAT	0.8639 ± 0.0129	0.8810 ± 0.0033	0.8408 ± 0.0076
	Ensemble	0.8824 ± 0.0155	0.8898 ± 0.0066	0.8686 ± 0.0024
	Simple-GCN	0.7389 ± 0.0120	0.6983 ± 0.0120	0.7491± 0.0166
	SIGN	0.8819 ± 0.0074	0.8856 ± 0.0083	0.8575 ± 0.0157
PubMed	MLP	0.9142 ± 0.0122	0.9321 ± 0.0013	0.8808 ± 0.0107
	GCN	0.8960 ± 0.0042	0.8996 ± 0.0011	0.8591 ± 0.0041
	SAGE	0.9087 ± 0.0064	0.9231 ± 0.0056	0.8733 ± 0.0051
	RevGAT	0.8654 ± 0.0952	0.9312 ± 0.0026	0.8754 ± 0.0010
	Ensemble	0.9265 ± 0.0068	0.9357 ± 0.0031	0.8941 ± 0.0041
	Simple-GCN	0.7505 ± 0.0048	0.7400 ± 0.0037	0.7472 ± 0.0076
	SIGN	0.8868 ± 0.0062	0.9004 ± 0.0038	0.8611 ± 0.0084
ogbn-arxiv	MLP	0.7517 ± 0.0011	0.7331 ± 0.0033	0.7603 ± 0.0011
	GCN	0.7377 ± 0.0010	0.7324 ± 0.0014	0.7369 ± 0.0022
	SAGE	0.7596 ± 0.0040	0.7428 ± 0.0039	0.7664 ± 0.0029
	RevGAT	0.7638 ± 0.0054	0.7529 ± 0.0044	0.7738 ± 0.0009
	Ensemble	0.7777 ± 0.0019	0.7701 ± 0.0018	0.7817 ± 0.0011
	Simple-GCN	0.3337 ± 0.0107	0.3614 ± 0.0039	0.3463 ± 0.0181
	SIGN	0.6150 ± 0.0182	0.6035 ± 0.0084	0.6285 ± 0.0114
ogbn-products	MLP	0.7277 ± 0.0054	0.6913 ± 0.0052	0.7231 ± 0.0050
	GCN	0.7679 ± 0.0109	0.7479 ± 0.0128	0.7701 ± 0.0117
	SAGE	0.7795 ± 0.0012	0.7496 ± 0.0163	0.7921 ± 0.0069
	RevGAT	0.8083 ± 0.0051	0.7883 ± 0.0014	0.7955 ± 0.0096
	Ensemble	0.8140 ± 0.0033	0.7908 ± 0.0045	0.8104 ± 0.0041
	Simple-GCN	0.6216 ± 0.0052	0.6040 ± 0.0039	0.6219 ± 0.0039
	SIGN	0.6668 ± 0.0078	0.6621 ± 0.0009	0.6698 ± 0.0010
tape-arxiv23	MLP	0.7940 ± 0.0022	0.7772 ± 0.0033	0.8008 ± 0.0018
	GCN	0.7678 ± 0.0024	0.7541 ± 0.0042	0.7746 ± 0.0025
	SAGE	0.7894 ± 0.0024	0.7677 ± 0.0018	0.7975 ± 0.0016
	RevGAT	0.7880 ± 0.0023	0.7840 ± 0.0058	0.7954 ± 0.0028
	Ensemble	0.8029 ± 0.0020	0.7967 ± 0.0037	0.8065 ± 0.0022
	Simple-GCN	0.2516 ± 0.0027	0.2451 ± 0.0004	0.258 ± 0.0011
	SIGN	0.7186 ± 0.0041	0.6804 ± 0.0041	0.733 ± 0.0009

Table 4: Node classification accuracy for the Cora, PubMed, ogbn-arxiv, ogbn-products, and tape-arxiv23 datasets, demonstrating the effect of changing the pre-trained LLM text encoder. The experiment is run over four seeds, with mean accuracy and standard deviation shown. The best results are coloured green (first), yellow (second), and orange (third). For all experiments, we use TA features only, and the simple task instruction to bias the embeddings.

5 Analysis

Main Results (Table 1) We find that ensembling GNNs always leads to superior performance across datasets when taking the STAGE approach.

Despite the reduced computational resources and training data requirements, the STAGE method remains highly competitive across all benchmarks. The ensemble STAGE approach lags behind the TAPE pipeline by roughly 5% on Cora, 3.5% on Pubmed, 0.8% on ogbn-products, and 4% on tape-arxiv23. This is a strong result when we consider that STAGE involves training only the GNN ensemble, whereas TAPE also requires two finetuned LMs to generate node features. We see marginally superior results on the ogbn-arxiv dataset using the ensemble STAGE approach.

Instruction-biased Embedding Results (Table 2) From our findings we conclude that varying the instructions to bias embeddings has little effect on downstream node classification performance for the models we evaluated. We note that while the authors of all embedding models recommend providing instructions along with input text in order to avoid degrading performance, we did not measure a performance improvement in our experiments.

This experiment further supports our claim that an ensemble approach improves robustness across datasets and methods of node feature generation.

PEFT Results (Table 3) Finetuning each LLM gave marginal performance improvements across all datasets to varying degrees; we see the largest improvement on pubmed (3%). It is of note that finetuning significantly increases the number of trainable parameters (see Table 5) and total training time. Specifically, PEFT for 7B embedding models has over 20 million trainable parameters. On a single A100 GPU, training runs lasted 6 hours on `ogbn-arxiv`.

LLM Embedding Model Comparison (Table 4) All three LLM embedding models demonstrated comparable performance on the graph tasks, with each model exhibiting marginally better results on different datasets. Notably, there was no clear winner among them. The LLM2Vec model exhibited slightly weaker performance on the larger datasets (ogbn-arxiv, ogbn-products, tape arxiv23), while it was marginally stronger on the smaller datasets (Cora, PubMed).

Ensembling the GNN models consistently ranked among the top three models across all three LLM embedding models, delivering an average performance increase of 1%. Among the individual GNN architectures, RevGAT consistently demonstrated superior performance.

Diffusion-pattern GNN Results (Table 4) The diffusion-based GNNs yielded variable results across datasets. Specifically, SIGN emerged as the second-best performer on the Cora dataset. As expected, SIGN consistently outperformed SimpleGCN, given that it generalizes the latter. Due to its low training time, SIGN is a viable candidate for large datasets, although careful tuning of its hyper-parameters is recommended for optimal performance.

Ablation Study Results (Table 6) From our ablation study we observe that no individual GNN model outperforms any ensemble of models on any dataset. Additionally, we find that the full ensemble of MLP, GCN, SAGE and RevGAT achieve the highest and most stable accuracy scores across datasets.

Scalability An important advantage of STAGE is the lack of finetuning necessary to achieve strong results. This lies in contrast to approaches such as TAPE (He et al., 2024) and SimTeG (Duan et al., 2023a), both of which require finetuning at least one LM. Training an ensemble of GNNs and MLP head over the ogbn-arxiv dataset can be performed on a single consumer-grade GPU in less than 5 minutes. This is illustrated in Figure 2 where we compare the relationship between training time and accuracy for a number of SoTA node classification approaches. When using SIGN diffusion, training time was under 12 seconds for the ogbn-arxiv, but this came at a performance cost. Moreover, TAPE relies on text-level enhancement via LLM API calls, which adds a new dimension of cost and rate-limiting[3] to consider when adapting to other datasets.

6 Conclusions

This work introduces STAGE, a method to use pretrained LLMs as text encoders in TAG tasks without the need for finetuning, significantly reducing computational resources and training time. Additional gains can be achieved through parameter-efficient finetuning of the LLM. Data augmentation, which is orthogonal to our approach, could improve performance with general-purpose text embedding models. However, it likely remains intractable for many large-scale datasets due to the need to query a large model for each node.

We also demonstrate the effect of diffusion operators (Frasca et al., 2020) on node classification performance, decreasing TAG pipeline training time substantially. We aim to examine the scalability of diffusion-pattern GNNs on larger datasets in later work.

[3] `https://platform.openai.com/docs/guides/rate-limits`

Future work may aim to refine the integration of LLM encoders with GNN heads. Potential strategies include an Expectation-Maximization approach or a joint model configuration (Zhao et al., 2023). A significant challenge is the requirement for large, variable batch sizes during LLM finetuning due to current neighborhood sampling techniques, which necessitates increased computational power. We anticipate that overcoming these limitations will make future research more accessible and expedite iterations.

References

Parishad BehnamGhader, Vaibhav Adlakha, Marius Mosbach, Dzmitry Bahdanau, Nicolas Chapados, and Siva Reddy. 2024. Llm2vec: Large language models are secretly powerful text encoders. *Preprint*, arXiv:2404.05961.

Zhikai Chen, Haitao Mao, Hang Li, Wei Jin, Hongzhi Wen, Xiaochi Wei, Shuaiqiang Wang, Dawei Yin, Wenqi Fan, Hui Liu, and Jiliang Tang. 2024. Exploring the potential of large language models (llms) in learning on graphs. *Preprint*, arXiv:2307.03393.

Wei-Lin Chiang, Xuanqing Liu, Si Si, Yang Li, Samy Bengio, and Cho-Jui Hsieh. 2019. Cluster-gcn: An efficient algorithm for training deep and large graph convolutional networks. In *Proceedings of the 25th ACM SIGKDD International Conference on Knowledge Discovery and Data Mining*, KDD '19. ACM.

Eli Chien, Wei-Cheng Chang, Cho-Jui Hsieh, Hsiang-Fu Yu, Jiong Zhang, Olgica Milenkovic, and Inderjit S Dhillon. 2022. Node feature extraction by self-supervised multi-scale neighborhood prediction. *Preprint*, arXiv:2111.00064.

Timothy Davis. 2019. Algorithm 1000: Suitesparse:graphblas: Graph algorithms in the language of sparse linear algebra. *ACM Transactions on Mathematical Software*, 45:1–25.

Jacob Devlin, Ming-Wei Chang, Kenton Lee, and Kristina Toutanova. 2019. Bert: Pre-training of deep bidirectional transformers for language understanding. *Preprint*, arXiv:1810.04805.

Keyu Duan, Qian Liu, Tat-Seng Chua, Shuicheng Yan, Wei Tsang Ooi, Qizhe Xie, and Junxian He. 2023a. Simteg: A frustratingly simple approach improves textual graph learning. *Preprint*, arXiv:2308.02565.

Keyu Duan, Zirui Liu, Peihao Wang, Wenqing Zheng, Kaixiong Zhou, Tianlong Chen, Xia Hu, and Zhangyang Wang. 2023b. A comprehensive study on large-scale graph training: Benchmarking and rethinking. *Preprint*, arXiv:2210.07494.

Lisa Ehrlinger and Wolfram Wöß. 2016. Towards a definition of knowledge graphs. In *International Conference on Semantic Systems*.

Bahare Fatemi, Jonathan Halcrow, and Bryan Perozzi. 2024. Talk like a graph: Encoding graphs for large language models. In *The Twelfth International Conference on Learning Representations*.

Fabrizio Frasca, Emanuele Rossi, Davide Eynard, Ben Chamberlain, Michael Bronstein, and Federico Monti. 2020. Sign: Scalable inception graph neural networks. *arXiv preprint arXiv:2004.11198*.

Johannes Gasteiger, Aleksandar Bojchevski, and Stephan Günnemann. 2022. Predict then propagate: Graph neural networks meet personalized pagerank. *Preprint*, arXiv:1810.05997.

William L. Hamilton, Rex Ying, and Jure Leskovec. 2018. Inductive representation learning on large graphs. *Preprint*, arXiv:1706.02216.

Taher H. Haveliwala. 2002. Topic-sensitive pagerank. In *Proceedings of the 11th International Conference on World Wide Web*, WWW '02, page 517–526, New York, NY, USA. Association for Computing Machinery.

Simon Haykin. 1994. *Neural networks: a comprehensive foundation*. Prentice Hall PTR.

Pengcheng He, Xiaodong Liu, Jianfeng Gao, and Weizhu Chen. 2021. Deberta: Decoding-enhanced bert with disentangled attention. *Preprint*, arXiv:2006.03654.

Xiaoxin He, Xavier Bresson, Thomas Laurent, Adam Perold, Yann LeCun, and Bryan Hooi. 2024. Harnessing explanations: Llm-to-lm interpreter for enhanced text-attributed graph representation learning. *Preprint*, arXiv:2305.19523.

Edward J. Hu, Yelong Shen, Phillip Wallis, Zeyuan Allen-Zhu, Yuanzhi Li, Shean Wang, Lu Wang, and Weizhu Chen. 2021a. Lora: Low-rank adaptation of large language models. *Preprint*, arXiv:2106.09685.

Weihua Hu, Matthias Fey, Marinka Zitnik, Yuxiao Dong, Hongyu Ren, Bowen Liu, Michele Catasta, and Jure Leskovec. 2021b. Open graph benchmark: Datasets for machine learning on graphs. *Preprint*, arXiv:2005.00687.

Thomas N. Kipf and Max Welling. 2017. Semi-supervised classification with graph convolutional networks. *Preprint*, arXiv:1609.02907.

Constant Joseph Koné, Michel Babri, and Jean Marie Rodrigues. 2023. Snomed ct: A clinical terminology but also a formal ontology. *Journal of Biosciences and Medicines*.

Guohao Li, Matthias Müller, Bernard Ghanem, and Vladlen Koltun. 2022a. Training graph neural networks with 1000 layers. *Preprint*, arXiv:2106.07476.

Rui Li, Jianan Zhao, Chaozhuo Li, Di He, Yiqi Wang, Yuming Liu, Hao Sun, Senzhang Wang, Weiwei Deng, Yanming Shen, Xing Xie, and

Qi Zhang. 2022b. House: Knowledge graph embedding with householder parameterization. *Preprint*, arXiv:2202.07919.

Hao Liu, Jiarui Feng, Lecheng Kong, Ningyue Liang, Dacheng Tao, Yixin Chen, and Muhan Zhang. 2023. One for all: Towards training one graph model for all classification tasks. *Preprint*, arXiv:2310.00149.

Juncheng Liu, Bryan Hooi, Kenji Kawaguchi, Yiwei Wang, Chaosheng Dong, and Xiaokui Xiao. 2024. Scalable and effective implicit graph neural networks on large graphs. In *The Twelfth International Conference on Learning Representations*.

Andrew McCallum, Kamal Nigam, Jason D. M. Rennie, and Kristie Seymore. 2000. Automating the construction of internet portals with machine learning. *Information Retrieval*, 3:127–163.

Grégoire Mialon, Roberto Dessì, Maria Lomeli, Christoforos Nalmpantis, Ram Pasunuru, Roberta Raileanu, Baptiste Rozière, Timo Schick, Jane Dwivedi-Yu, Asli Celikyilmaz, Edouard Grave, Yann LeCun, and Thomas Scialom. 2023. Augmented language models: a survey. *Preprint*, arXiv:2302.07842.

Tomas Mikolov, Ilya Sutskever, Kai Chen, Greg Corrado, and Jeffrey Dean. 2013. Distributed representations of words and phrases and their compositionality. *Preprint*, arXiv:1310.4546.

George A. Miller. 1995. Wordnet: a lexical database for english. *Commun. ACM*, 38(11):39–41.

Niklas Muennighoff. 2022. Sgpt: Gpt sentence embeddings for semantic search. *Preprint*, arXiv:2202.08904.

OpenAI. 2023. Introducing chatgpt. Accessed: 2023-05-20.

OpenAI, Josh Achiam, Steven Adler, Sandhini Agarwal, Lama Ahmad, Ilge Akkaya, Florencia Leoni Aleman, Diogo Almeida, and Janko Altenschmidt. 2024. Gpt-4 technical report. *Preprint*, arXiv:2303.08774.

Lawrence Page, Sergey Brin, Rajeev Motwani, and Terry Winograd. 1998. The PageRank Citation Ranking: Bringing Order to the Web. Technical report, Stanford Digital Library Technologies Project.

Shirui Pan, Linhao Luo, Yufei Wang, Chen Chen, Jiapu Wang, and Xindong Wu. 2024. Unifying large language models and knowledge graphs: A roadmap. *IEEE Transactions on Knowledge and Data Engineering*, page 1–20.

Jeffrey Pennington, Richard Socher, and Christopher Manning. 2014. GloVe: Global vectors for word representation. In *Proceedings of the 2014 Conference on Empirical Methods in Natural Language Processing (EMNLP)*, pages 1532–1543, Doha, Qatar. Association for Computational Linguistics.

Nils Reimers and Iryna Gurevych. 2019. Sentence-bert: Sentence embeddings using siamese bert-networks. In *Proceedings of the 2019 Conference on Empirical Methods in Natural Language Processing*. Association for Computational Linguistics.

Prithviraj Sen, Galileo Namata, Mustafa Bilgic, Lise Getoor, Brian Galligher, and Tina Eliassi-Rad. 2008. Collective classification in network data. *AI Magazine*, 29(3):93.

Felix Wu, Amauri Souza, Tianyi Zhang, Christopher Fifty, Tao Yu, and Kilian Weinberger. 2019. Simplifying graph convolutional networks. In *Proceedings of the 36th International Conference on Machine Learning*, volume 97 of *Proceedings of Machine Learning Research*, pages 6861–6871. PMLR.

Hao Yan, Chaozhuo Li, Ruosong Long, Chao Yan, Jianan Zhao, Wenwen Zhuang, Jun Yin, Peiyan Zhang, Weihao Han, Hao Sun, et al. 2023. A comprehensive study on text-attributed graphs: Benchmarking and rethinking. *Advances in Neural Information Processing Systems*, 36:17238–17264.

Junhan Yang, Zheng Liu, Shitao Xiao, Chaozhuo Li, Defu Lian, Sanjay Agrawal, Amit Singh, Guangzhong Sun, and Xing Xie. 2023. Graphformers: Gnn-nested transformers for representation learning on textual graph. *Preprint*, arXiv:2105.02605.

Ruosong Ye, Caiqi Zhang, Runhui Wang, Shuyuan Xu, and Yongfeng Zhang. 2024. Language is all a graph needs. In *Findings of the Association for Computational Linguistics: EACL 2024*, pages 1955–1973, St. Julian's, Malta. Association for Computational Linguistics.

Jianan Zhao, Meng Qu, Chaozhuo Li, Hao Yan, Qian Liu, Rui Li, Xing Xie, and Jian Tang. 2023. Learning on large-scale text-attributed graphs via variational inference. *Preprint*, arXiv:2210.14709.

A Appendix

B Negative Results

Co-training LLM and GNN: In a similar approach to iterative methods, we investigated co-training the LLM and GNN on the `ogbn-arxiv` node classification task to facilitate a shared representation space. This proved unfeasible due to the memory requirements exceeding the capacity of one A100 GPU.

C Implementation of Diffusion Operators

We implement diffusion operators from two methods, Simple-GCN (Wu et al., 2019) and SIGN (Frasca et al., 2020). In the case of SIGN, the authors omit implementation details of the operators, so we include them here.

Let A denote the adjacency matrix of a possibly directed graph G, X its node features, and D the diagonal degree matrix of G.

We denote the *random-walk normalized* adjacency $A_{\text{RW}}\& := AD^{-1}$ and the *GCN-normalized* adjacency (Kipf and Welling, 2017)

$$A_{\text{GCN}} := (D+I)^{-1/2}(A+I)(D+I)^{-1/2} \quad (4)$$

The *Personalized PageRank* matrix is then given by (Gasteiger et al., 2022):

$$A_{\text{PPR}} := \alpha\left(I_n - (1-\alpha)A_{\text{RW}}\right)^{-1} \quad (5)$$

And we denote the *triangle-based* adjacency matrix by $\mathbf{A}_\Delta$, where $(A_\Delta)_{ij}$ counts the number of directed triangles in G that contain the edge (i, j)

Diffusion is applied to node features X by matrix multiplication. Simple-GCN takes a power k of A_{GCN} as its diffusion operator, whilst SIGN diffusion generalizes this to concatenate powers of A_{GCN}, A_{PPR} and A_Δ.

Diffusion can be calculated efficiently if sparse-matrix-sparse-matrix multiplication is avoided. For both SIGN and Simple-GCN, the order of operations for applying a power of an operator A_{op} should be

$$\underbrace{A_{\text{op}}(A_{\text{op}}(\ldots(A_{\text{op}}(X))\ldots)}_{k \text{ times}} \quad (6)$$

as opposed to $(A_{\text{op}}^k)X$, where the operator matrix A_{op} is feasible to calculate, since the former avoids sparse matrix multiplication. In SIGN, the recursive nature of eq.6 can be exploited to reuse results for calculating successive powers.

In the case of personalized pagerank diffusion, we first use a trick from (Gasteiger et al., 2022) to approximate the diffused features of personalized pagerank matrix $A_{\text{PPR}}X$ in linear time and avoid calculative A_{PPR} directly, by viewing eq.5 as *topic-sensitive* PageRank (Haveliwala, 2002). We use the random-walk normalized adjacency matrix.

The following power iteration approximates $A_{\text{PPR}}X$ (notation from (Gasteiger et al., 2022)):

$$Z^{(0)} := X$$
$$Z^{(k+1)} := (1-\alpha)AZ^{(k)} + \alpha X$$

To compute the nth diffused power, we repeat the process n times:

$$Z_0^{(0)} = X$$
$$Z_{n+1}^{(0)} = \lim_{k \to \inf} Z_n^{(k)}$$

Lastly, for triangle-based diffusion, we count triangles using linear algebra. For unweighted A we perform a single sparse matrix multiplication to obtain A^2, in which element (i, j) counts the directed paths in G for node i to node j. We then calculate

$$A_\Delta = A^T \odot A^2$$

where $\odot$ denotes the Hadamard product, which can be efficiently calculated for sparse matrices. We then normalize and diffuse features over powers of A_Δ in the same fashion as for A_{GCN}.

An implementation of these operators as GraphBLAS (Davis, 2019) code is published alongside this paper.

C.1 Parallelism of diffusion operators

All operations above can be be parallelized across columns of X, either keeping A in shared memory on one machine or keeping a copy on each executor in a distributed computing infrastructure like Apache Spark.

D Preprocessing & Model Selection for Diffusion Operators

For Simple-GCN (Wu et al., 2019), we set the degree k by selecting the highest validation accuracy from $k = 2, 3, 4$, of which $k = 2$ had the highest accuracy in each case. For SIGN (Frasca et al., 2020), we choose s, p, t from the highest validation accuracy amongst $(3, 0, 0)$ $(3, 0, 1)$ $(3, 3, 0)$, $(4, 2, 1)$ $(5, 3, 0)$. For **Cora** and **PubMed**, $(4, 2, 1)$ was chosen, and for **ogbn-arxiv**, **ogbn-products**, and **tape-arxiv23** $(3, 3, 0)$ was chosen. We chose the number of layers for the Inception NLP to match the number of layers in other GNNs tested, 4. We did not perform additional hyper-parameter tuning. When preprocessing the embeddings, we centered and scaled the data to unit variance for Simple-GCN and SIGN only.

E Model Trainable Parameters

Model	Trainable Parameter Count
RevGAT	3,457,678
GCN	559,111
SAGE	1,117,063
MLP	117,767
Simple-GCN	24,111
SIGN-(3,3,0)	500,271
SIGN-(4,2,1)	582,575
PEFT 7B LLM	>20M

Table 5: Trainable parameter counts for different models. 7B LLM refers to all finetuned LLM embedding models used during experiments (see Section 3.1)

F Ablation Study

To study the effect each model has on the GNN ensemble step of STAGE, we perform a detailed ablation study. The results are shown in Table 6.

G Datasets

In this section, we describe the characteristics of the node classification datasets we used during our work. The statistics are shown in Table 7.

H Instruction-biased Embeddings

In Table 8 we list the specific instructions used to investigate the effect of biasing embeddings.

Method	Cora	PubMed	ogbn-arxiv	ogbn-products	tape-arxiv23
Full Ensemble	0.8824 ± 0.0155	0.9265 ± 0.0068	0.7777 ± 0.0019	0.8140 ± 0.0033	0.8029 ± 0.0020
No MLP	0.8838 ± 0.0039	0.9239 ± 0.0036	0.7748 ± 0.0012	0.8093 ± 0.0021	0.8015 ± 0.0010
No GCN	0.8685 ± 0.0209	0.9240 ± 0.0076	0.7731 ± 0.0017	0.8100 ± 0.0038	0.8028 ± 0.0023
No SAGE	0.8759 ± 0.0207	0.9258 ± 0.0110	0.7739 ± 0.0020	0.8116 ± 0.0045	0.8021 ± 0.0035
No RevGAT	0.8764 ± 0.0180	0.9272 ± 0.0052	0.7717 ± 0.0007	0.8029 ± 0.0036	0.7985 ± 0.0018
Best Individual	0.8722 ± 0.0063	0.9142 ± 0.0122	0.7638 ± 0.0054	0.8083 ± 0.0051	0.7880 ± 0.0023
Best Individual Model	**SAGE**	**MLP**	**RevGAT**	**RevGAT**	**RevGAT**

Table 6: Ablation study results for the ensemble model on various datasets. The table shows the accuracy when each component is removed from the ensemble. The experiment is run over four seeds, with mean accuracy and standard deviation shown. The best results are coloured green (first), yellow (second), and orange (third). For all experiments, we use SFR-Embedding-Mistral as the embedding model on TA features only, and the simple task instruction to bias the embeddings.

Dataset	Node Count	Edge Count	Task	Metric
Cora (McCallum et al., 2000)	2,708	5,429	7-class classif.	Accuracy
Pubmed (Sen et al., 2008)	19,717	44,338	3-class classif.	Accuracy
ogbn-arxiv (Hu et al., 2021b)	169,343	1,166,243	40-class classif.	Accuracy
ogbn-products (Hu et al., 2021b) (subset)	54,025	74,420	47-class classif.	Accuracy
tape-arxiv23 (He et al., 2024)	46,198	78,548	40-class classif.	Accuracy

Table 7: Statistics of the TAG datasets

Dataset	Prompt Type	Prompt
ogbn-arxiv, arxiv_2023, cora, pubmed	Simple Task	Identify the main and secondary category of Arxiv papers based on the titles and abstracts.
ogbn-arxiv, arxiv_2023, cora, pubmed	Graph-Aware	Identify the main and secondary category of Arxiv papers based on the titles and abstracts. Your predictions will be used in a downstream graph-based prediction that for each paper can learn from your predictions of neighboring papers in a graph as well as the predictions for the paper in question. Papers in the graph are connected if one cites the other.
ogbn-products	Simple Task	Identify the main and secondary category of this product based on the titles and description.
ogbn-products	Graph-Aware	Identify the main and secondary category of this product based on the titles and description. Your predictions will be used in a downstream graph-based prediction that for each product can learn from your predictions of neighboring products in a graph as well as the predictions for the paper in question. Products in the graph are connected if they are purchased together.

Table 8: Task descriptions for embedding bias across various datasets.

Zero-Shot Fact-Checking with Semantic Triples and Knowledge Graphs

Zhangdie Yuan and **Andreas Vlachos**
Department of Computer Science and Technology
University of Cambridge
zy317,av308@cam.ac.uk

Abstract

Despite progress in automated fact-checking, most systems require a significant amount of labeled training data, which is expensive. In this paper, we propose a novel zero-shot method, which instead of operating directly on the claim and evidence sentences, decomposes them into semantic triples augmented using external knowledge graphs, and uses large language models trained for natural language inference. This allows it to generalize to adversarial datasets and domains that supervised models require specific training data for. Our empirical results show that our approach outperforms previous zero-shot approaches on FEVER, FEVER-Symmetric, FEVER 2.0, and Climate-FEVER, while being comparable or better than supervised models on the adversarial and the out-of-domain datasets.

1 Introduction

Fact-checking is the task of assessing the truthfulness of a claim, and is well-studied across multiple disciplines. Traditionally, journalists perform such a task manually, which is time-consuming. More recently, automated fact-checking systems have become of interest due to the explosion of (mis)information on social media (Adair et al., 2017; Hassan et al., 2017). In the NLP community, fact-checking is typically defined as a task consisting of three stages: claim detection, evidence retrieval, and claim verification (Guo et al., 2022). In particular, verdict prediction assumes the evidence is retrieved from sources such as Wikipedia or the web, and aims to predict the verdict of a claim given the retrieved evidence, often as a three-way classification task (Thorne et al., 2018a): SUPPORTS, REFUTES, and NEI (NOT ENOUGH INFO).

Recent work (DeHaven and Scott, 2023) has achieved strong results on canonical datasets like FEVER (Thorne et al., 2018a), mostly relying on supervised approaches. However, concerns have been expressed on whether these models learn language's and the task's nuances or merely leverage embedded biases and dataset idiosyncrasies. This argument (Gururangan et al., 2018; Poliak et al., 2018) gains empirical weight when such high-performing models are tested against adversarial fact-checking datasets such as FEVER-Symmetric (Schuster et al., 2019) and FEVER 2.0 (Thorne et al., 2019). Their underperformance (Thorne et al., 2018b) in these adversarial benchmarks exposes a lack of model robustness.

The narrative of this vulnerability extends to out-of-domain contexts as well. A pertinent example is the Climate-FEVER dataset—a platform for verifying real-world climate claims (Diggelmann et al., 2020). Supervised models, despite their commendable performance on the original FEVER dataset, suffer performance degradation when evaluated on Climate-FEVER. Additionally, earlier zero-shot fact-checking approaches (Pan et al., 2021; Wright et al., 2022) hinge on synthetic data creation for training purposes. While this data emanates from factual evidence, it largely adheres to the domain boundaries of the originating dataset. Such inherent domain confinement curtails the model's capacity for broader generalization.

In this work we propose a zero-shot method utilizing semantic triples and knowledge graphs in conjunction with pretrained Natural Language Inference (NLI) models, and does not require training data for parameter learning.

In particular, we propose to extract triples from the claim and the evidence texts to form knowledge graphs and fill potential gaps in the evidence using a universal schema model (Riedel et al., 2013) on Wikidata and Wikipedia. Crucially, our method refrains from utilizing any annotated or synthetic training data, sidestepping the pitfalls of biases and dataset artifacts that can inadvertently be encoded into models. Additionally, by decomposing the original claim into triples, our method can harness

Proceedings of the 1st Workshop on Knowledge Graphs and Large Language Models (KaLLM 2024), pages 105–115
August 15, 2024 ©2024 Association for Computational Linguistics

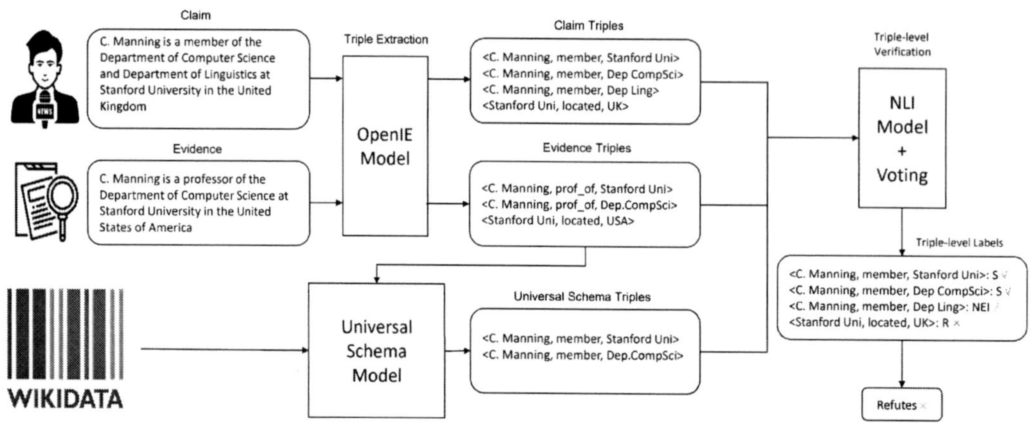

Figure 1: An overview of our zero-shot learning system. By harnessing Wikidata for training the universal schema model, incorporating on-demand training with evidence triples, and leveraging OpenIE for triple-level inference, our system achieves enhanced improvements. Label S stands for SUPPORTS and R stands for REFUTES.

the pre-trained NLI model's strengths more effectively. Both design choices position our approach to exhibit greater robustness when subjected to adversarial and out-of-domain evaluations.

As shown in Figure 1, we follow a two-stage verification process: triple-level and claim-level. For triple-level, we employ NLI models pre-trained without further fine-tuning on any fact-checking training dataset, hence a zero-shot setting. For claim-level verification, we design a simple rule-based system relying on the triple verification. In Figure 1, the process involves extracting claim and evidence sentences to generate triples. Subsequently, the universal schema is applied to obtain additional triples. The NLI model is then employed to assign triple-level labels, resulting in 2 SUPPORTS, 1 REFUTES, and 1 NEI[1]. Finally, a rule-based system is utilized to derive claim-level verification. In this example, since one claim triple is refuted, the entire claim is considered refuted. Note that we are able to use the "gap" triples filled by the universal schema model to retrieve better evidence. For example, *<Manning, member_of, Stanford>* is needed to verify the claim. However, such a triple is missing from the evidence triple extraction because the word *member* is not mentioned in the evidence. Instead, *<Manning, professor_of, Stanford>* is extracted from evidence. Therefore, with the universal schema model, *<Manning, member_of, Stanford>* will be assigned a high probability given *<Manning, prof_of, Stanford>* is observed as evidence, and the gap is filled.

[1]In the context of our study, the NLI labels have been appropriately reconfigured to align with the FEVER labels.

We evaluate our approach on the FEVER (Thorne et al., 2018a), FEVER-Symmetric (Schuster et al., 2019), FEVER 2.0 (Thorne et al., 2019), and Climate-FEVER (Diggelmann et al., 2020) datasets. Our findings show that our system consistently outperforms zero-shot NLI model baselines by a margin of approximately 2.5 percentage points and beats the previous zero-shot approach by around 3 percentage points on FEVER-Symmetric. Notably, in contrast to state-of-the-art supervised methods (DeHaven and Scott, 2023), our approach exhibits robustness on both adversarial datasets. When evaluated on the out-of-domain Climate-FEVER dataset, our method outperforms the supervised method by a margin exceeding 10 percentage points.

2 Related Work

Recent advances in natural language processing have highlighted significant challenges associated with supervised learning models. A prominent concern is the models' tendency to learn dataset-specific biases, often at the expense of genuine linguistic understanding. For instance, Schuster et al. (2019) demonstrated the effectiveness of a claim-only model that classifies each claim in isolation, without the need for associated evidence. The high performance achieved by their system over the baseline can be attributed to the idiosyncrasies inherent in the dataset's construction. Similarly, Thorne et al. (2019) highlighted the vulnerability of several FEVER systems, observing significant performance declines under adversarial conditions with simple rule-based perturbations. In other tasks such as NLI, previous works (Poliak et al., 2018; Gururangan et al., 2018) examined the susceptibility of neural models to such spurious correlations, revealing a troubling propensity for models to exploit unintended, data-specific heuristics. Taken together, these findings suggest that annotation artifacts within datasets contain discernible patterns. Such vulnerabilities underscore the necessity for more rigorous evaluation mechanisms, thus motivating the introduction of several adversarial fact-checking evaluation datasets (Guo et al., 2022).

Pan et al. (2021) presented the first work to investigate zero-shot fact verification, where they proposed a framework named Question Answering for Claim Generation (QACG). From any given evidence, QACG generates SUPPORTS, REFUTES, and NEI claims. A classifier is then trained using the generated claims instead of annotated claims, hence a zero-shot setting. To generate claims, QACG first produces QA pairs using a Question Generator fine-tuned on the processed SQuAD dataset (Zhou et al., 2018). Next, a QA-to-Claim Model is fine-tuned on the QA2D dataset (Demszky et al., 2018), which converts each QA pair into a declarative sentence. However, their experiments are limited, using only the gold evidence to evaluate various zero-shot methods, which is not practical in a real-world setting. Also, unlike their work, where training is still performed using the generated training data, our approach does not require any training for claim verification.

Knowledge graphs have long been investigated in NLP, where the first discussions of a graphical knowledge representation can date back to the 50s (Newell et al., 1959). Since then, many NLP researchers have tried to integrate knowledge graphs into various NLP tasks, notably language models with knowledge graphs (Nakashole and Mitchell, 2014; Logan IV et al., 2019; Liu et al., 2020; Wang et al., 2021a) and many downstream tasks such as question answering (Liu et al., 2020) and text classification (Hu et al., 2021). For fact-checking specifically, Ciampaglia et al. (2015) proposed to use knowledge graphs to verify simple natural language claims, considering fact-checking as a special case of link prediction. Their method uses the subject and object of the claim and then finds the shortest path between the two entities. If the claim is true, there should be such a shortest path (or an edge); otherwise, there should be no shortest path (nor edge). While the fact that a simple shortest-path computation can assess the truth of new claims is exciting, this work is limited because all the factual claims are automatically generated using triples. Therefore, it does not directly apply to recent human-generated fact-checking datasets such as FEVER, as claims in FEVER are much more complicated.

notation	description
$\mathcal{C}$	claim
$\mathcal{E}$	evidence
$\mathcal{Y}$	claim-level label of $\mathcal{C}$
$\mathbb{C}$	set of triples extracted from $\mathcal{C}$
$\mathbb{E}$	set of triples extracted from $\mathcal{E}$
c	$\mathsf{c} \in \mathbb{C}$
e	$\mathsf{e} \in \mathbb{E}$
$\mathsf{y_e}$	triple-level label of c predicted by e
y	aggregated triple-level label of c

Table 1: Notations used in our fact-checking system

3 Methodology

As introduced, the verdict prediction step of claim verification is to predict a label $\mathcal{Y} \in \{\text{SUPPORTS}, \text{REFUTES}, \text{NEI}\}$ given a claim $\mathcal{C}$ and its corresponding evidence $\mathcal{E}$, indicating if $\mathcal{C}$ is supported, refuted, or cannot be verified by $\mathcal{E}$. While we do not use any training data (manually or automatically labeled), we assume a human-annotated development set is available for fine-tuning hyperparameters of our system. In keeping with prior research, we use the same set of notations and extend it to include triples. Table 1 contains all the notations used in the methodology.

Figure 1 illustrates the structure of our system, which comprises three main steps: Triple Extraction, Triple-level Verification, and Claim-level Verification. Additionally, we have integrated an external component, the Universal Schema. This section provides comprehensive insights into each component, outlining their functionalities and operations.

3.1 Triple Extraction

A semantic triple consists of three entities: the subject, the object, and the relation between them. We denote such a triple as <*subj, rel, obj*> where all three entities are natural language words, phrases, or clauses, and no schema needs to be specified in advance. Extracting a set of triples from plain text is called open information extraction (Open IE) (Yates et al., 2007).

As illustrated in Figure 1, our system first employs an OpenIE tool to extract triples from claim $\mathcal{C}$ and evidence $\mathcal{E}$, resulting in a set $\mathbb{C}$ of claim triples and a set $\mathbb{E}$ of evidence triples. Note that this step is back-traceable. For example, for any evidence triple, we can trace back which evidence sentence it comes from and which part of that sentence forms such evidence triple.

3.2 Triple-level Verification

Given a claim triple c and a set of evidence triples $\mathbb{E}$, triple-level verification predicts a label $\mathsf{y} \in \{\text{SUPPORTS}, \text{REFUTES}, \text{NEI}\}$ for this triple. Intuitively, any evidence triple may provide signals to predicting y. Therefore, given c, for each evidence triple e in $\mathbb{E}$, we utilise an NLI model to predict a label $\mathsf{y_p}$ with a softmax score as its probability. We linearise c and e and concatenate them with a special separation token: e [SEP] c. For example, let $\mathsf{c} =$ *<Barack Obama, was born in, USA>* and $\mathsf{e} =$ *<Barack Obama, was born in, Hawaii>*, the input of the NLI model therefore is, 'Barack Obama was born in Hawaii [SEP] Barack Obama was born in USA'. Following previous work, we map NLP labels to fact-checking labels, namely ENTAILMENT to SUPPORTS, CONTRADICTION to REFUTES, and NEUTRAL to NEI.

To filter out less reliable triple-level labels $\mathsf{y_p}$, we set up two thresholds for SUPPORTS and REFUTES as hyperparameters to cut off labels with low probabilities. The remaining labels are aggregated to reach a triple-level label y for the claim triple c using one of the following voting mechanisms:

Max voting takes the label with the overall highest probability as the triple-level label.

Majority voting ensures that the label with the most supporters (i.e., most frequent appearances) is the triple-level label.

Weighted sampling samples a label according to the highest probabilities of each label.

Note that if all labels are filtered out, the triple-level label is NEI because none of the evidence triple is reliable enough for this claim triple.

3.3 Claim-level Verification

For each claim triple c in $\mathbb{C}$, a triple-level label y is predicted by the previous step. The final step is to reach a claim-level label $\mathcal{Y}$ from this set of triple-level labels using the following rule-based system also used by previous research (Stacey et al., 2022):

- If there exists a y that is REFUTES, then $\mathcal{Y}$ is REFUTES.
- If no y is REFUTES and there exists a y that is NEI, then $\mathcal{Y}$ is NEI.
- Otherwise, $\mathcal{Y}$ is SUPPORTS.

3.4 Universal Schema

The challenge of integrating a knowledge graph with our system stems from the incompatibility between a pre-determined schema and the unrestricted textual information extracted from open sources. In response, we put forward a solution that involves the implementation of the universal schema (Riedel et al., 2013), which acts as an interface between pre-defined symbolic relations such as those found in knowledge graphs, and unconstrained textual relations such as those extracted by Open IE. Universal schema can be viewed as a matrix that represents the knowledge base, comprising pairs of entities and relations.

Notably, the original knowledge graph dataset employed in previous research on Universal Schema, namely Freebase (Bollacker et al., 2008), is no longer maintained. Therefore, we undertook the task of training a novel universal schema model, utilizing a more contemporary language model architecture and incorporating data from Wikidata (Vrandečić and Krötzsch, 2014) and some corresponding texts from Wikipedia.

Task Definition. Consistent with Riedel et al. (2013), a fact, or relation instance, is denoted by the pair *rel* and *<subj, obj>*. The goal of a universal schema model is, by definition, to estimate, for a given relation *rel* and a given tuple *<subj, obj>*, the probability $p(y_{rel,<subj,obj>} = 1)$ where the random variable $y_{rel,<subj,obj>}$ represents if *<subj, obj>* is in relation *rel*. In the context of our fact-checking scenario, we leverage these *<subj, rel, obj>* triples to complete missing information.

Objective. To train our model, we adopt Bayesian Personalized Ranking (BPR) (Rendle et al., 2009). In this approach, observed true facts are assigned higher scores compared to both true and false unobserved facts. This scoring scheme serves as our optimization objective. Let σ denote the sigmoid function, θ_{f+} denote the dot product of the latent representations of a positive (θ_{f-} for negative) fact pair *rel* and *<subj, obj>*, then the objective function is $\text{Obj}_{f+,f-} = -log(\sigma(\theta_{f+} - \theta_{f-}))$.

Integration. Upon successful training of the universal schema model, it becomes feasible to predict the probability of a tuple being associated with a given relation. The integration of this component into our fact-checking system involves utilizing the universal schema model to assign scores to potential triple candidates for a given set of claim triples $\mathbb{C}$ and supporting evidence triple set $\mathbb{E}$. All possible combinations of relations in the $\mathbb{C}$ and tuples in the $\mathbb{E}$ are considered as triple candidates. The universal schema model is then used to compute the probability of each triple candidate being true. Similar to Section 3.2, a threshold is set to remove less reliable triple candidates. The triple candidates with a probability above the threshold are only utilized for triple-level verification if the available evidence triples are insufficient, i.e. when the label for the triple-level label y is NEI. In a manner akin to in-context learning, we also modify the Universal Schema model during the inference stage, upon encountering newly observed facts derived from evidence triples $\mathbb{E}$.

4 Implementation

Evidence Retrieval. To perform document level retrieval, we adopt the approach proposed by Hanselowski et al. (2018) For sentence level retrieval, we aim to demonstrate the effectiveness of our verification system without relying on any fact-checking training data. Therefore, we utilize traditional information retrieval techniques such as tf-idf weighting. In addition, we incorporate a semantic score as a weight factor, which is computed using the cosine similarity of embeddings generated by a neural model called stsb-roberta-base (Reimers and Gurevych, 2019).[2]

OpenIE Model. We utilized an AllenNLP reimplementation of a BiLSTM sequence prediction model initially proposed by Stanovsky et al. (2018) as our Open Information Extraction (OpenIE) tool. The model can recognize verbs as relations and add their corresponding subjects and objects as arguments when given a sentence as input. For instances with more than two arguments, the model produces a triple for each combination of subjects or objects. If a relation only has one argument, known as a unary relation, a placeholder is added to ensure consistency across all generated triples.

NLI Model. In our experiments, we evaluate the effectiveness of our system using both base size and large size pre-trained NLI models. The aim is to demonstrate that our system consistently outperforms the NLI baselines. In particular, we leverage the RoBERTa base and large models, which have been pretrained on the MNLI dataset. Both models follow the standard NLI format of taking a premise and a hypothesis as input in the format of "[premise] SEP [hypothesis]", where SEP denotes the special separation token. We adhere to this format throughout our experiments.

Universal Schema Model. We leverage Sentence-BERT (Reimers and Gurevych, 2019) to obtain sentence embeddings that serve as latent representations for both relations and tuples. This approach allows us to capture the semantic meaning of the sentences, which is essential for accurately representing the relations and tuples in our model. The pre-trained model "all-MiniLM-L6-v2"[3] is utilized in our study, which is based on MiniLM (Wang et al., 2020). This model has been pre-trained with a contrastive objective using diverse datasets containing sentence pairs. The cosine similarity is computed for each possible sentence pair within a batch, and cross-entropy loss is employed to compare these similarities with the true pairs.

5 Experimental Setup

Dataset. In our evaluation, we employ four benchmark datasets, FEVER, FEVER-Symmetric, FEVER 2.0, and Climate-FEVER. FEVER dataset (Thorne et al., 2018a) comprises 185,445 claims that are created by modifying sentences from Wikipedia, which are subsequently verified on Wikipedia without knowing the original sentence they were derived from. On the other hand, the FEVER-Symmetric dataset is introduced by Schuster et al. (2019) to address the biases identified in the original FEVER dataset. This dataset is constructed with a regularization procedure to downweigh the giveaway phrases that cause potential biases. Similarly, the FEVER 2.0 dataset (Thorne et al., 2019) comprises adversarial examples intentionally created by participants of the FEVER 2.0 shared task. The task required teams to generate claims specifically designed to challenge FEVER-trained models. From this dataset, we extracted all SUPPORTS and REFUTES claims, along with their corresponding gold evidence sentences, for our evaluation. The Climate-FEVER dataset (Diggelmann et al., 2020) is for

[2]https://huggingface.co/sentence-transformers/stsb-roberta-base

[3]https://huggingface.co/sentence-transformers/all-MiniLM-L6-v2

verification of real-world climate change-related claims, excluding disputed claims.

To train our universal schema model, we utilize the Wikidata5m dataset (Wang et al., 2021b), which is a knowledge graph dataset comprising one million entities. This dataset is particularly suitable for our purposes, as it includes an aligned corpus, which we leverage in conjunction with the OpenIE tool to extract open-domain triples. In our approach, all triples from the Wikidata5m dataset and the extracted triples the aligned corpus are treated as positive samples. To generate negative samples based on a given positive sample, we utilize a randomized approach where we preserve the relation and generate arbitrary tuples that exist within the dataset. This approach allows us to create negative samples that differ from the positive samples while still being relevant to the original relation.

Hyperparameters. In our experiments, claim verification does not require model-level hyperparameter tuning since no training is involved. However, as outlined before, we have a small set of three thresholds to be adjusted: a threshold for the SUPPORTS label at the triple level, a threshold for the REFUTES label at the triple level, and a threshold for filtering out Universal Schema triple candidates.[4] We adjusted their values on the FEVER dataset and did not perform any further adjustments on FEVER-Symmetric, FEVER 2.0, or Climate-FEVER. This deliberate choice was made to test the robustness of our system in handling different datasets without relying on dataset-specific optimization, an advantage of zero-shot approaches.

Figures 2 illustrates the impact of thresholds on our system, and that optimizing them is relatively straightforward as the best settings are clustered in the region. It is worth noting that the optimal threshold for REFUTES is considerably higher compared to SUPPORTS, indicating that our system is more stringent in assigning a triple-level REFUTES label than SUPPORTS. This difference is justified by the fact that, as explained in Section 3.3, a single refuted claim triple is sufficient to refute the entire claim, therefore it helps being cautious when assigning a REFUTES label to claim triples.

[4]The specifics concerning the hyperparameters of the Universal Schema model can be found in Appendix A. Note that the aforementioned thresholds were identified by conducting a search with a fixed Universal Schema model.

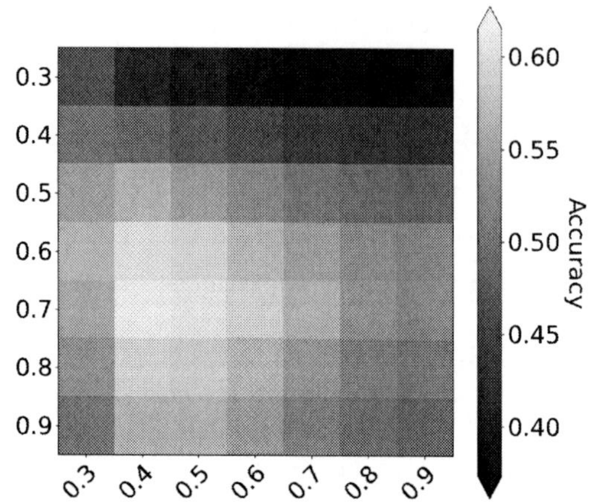

Figure 2: The influence of thresholds on accuracy for the SUPPORTS (x-axis) and REFUTES (y-axis) with fixed threshold for Universal Schema triple candidates.

6 Results and Discussion

Our main results are presented in Table 2, where we compare our system's performance against the current state-of-the-art system on FEVER, BEVERS (DeHaven and Scott, 2023), the FEVER-trained entailment-predictor (Diggelmann et al., 2020), and QACG (Pan et al., 2021)[5]. Also, we conduct additional ablation experiments to demonstrate the robustness of our system by varying the weighting factor and voting mechanism.

Finding 1 *Our zero-shot approach exhibited enhanced robustness against adversarial perturbations and manifested notable out-of-domain effectiveness in contrast to supervised approaches.*

As shown in Table 2, our zero-shot method demonstrates greater resilience against adversarial attacks compared to supervised methods, providing a significant advantage in real-world scenarios where the presence of misinformation and deceptive tactics can impede the performance of fact-checking systems.

By abstaining from using training data, our approach intuitively circumvents these issues and offers a more robust approach to fact-checking. Specifically, despite exhibiting lower performance than supervised systems on the original FEVER dataset, our models achieved highly competitive scores on the FEVER-Symmetric dataset, trailing

[5]We made efforts to establish contact with the authors of QACG; however, our attempts to elicit a response were unsuccessful. Therefore, a direct comparison with their approach is not feasible, except for the FEVER-Symmetric dataset, where they reported performance under the same setting as ours.

Model	FEVER		FEVER-Symmetric	FEVER 2.0	Climate-FEVER	
	Accuracy	FEVER Score	Accuracy	Accuracy	Accuracy	F1
Supervised						
BEVERS	**80.24**	**77.70**	75.9	63.4	-	-
Diggelmann et al. (2020)	77.69	-	-	-	38.78	32.85
Zero-shot						
Random Guess	33.33	-	50.00	50.00	33.33	33.33
QACG	-	-	77.1	-	-	-
NLI Model (base)	36.07	31.65	51.74	49.68	-	-
NLI Model (large)	58.12	54.38	78.94	70.38	44.37	44.24
Our system (base)	38.56	33.73	56.62	53.28	-	-
Our system (large)	60.40	56.79	**79.78**	72.92	**46.71**	**45.71**
Our system (large) + USchema	**61.30**	**57.84**	**79.78**	**73.34**	**46.71**	**45.71**

Table 2: Main results on FEVER (S/R/NEI), FEVER-Symmetric (S/R), FEVER 2.0 (S/R) and Climate-FEVER (S/R/NEI). BEVERS is the current state-of-the-art system on FEVER and Diggelmann et al. (2020) is the entailment-predictor based on ALBERT (large-v2). The accuracy on FEVER-Symmetric, FEVER 2.0 and Climate-FEVER datasets was achieved without fine-tuning, demonstrating the models' robustness.

Variant	Δ Accuracy
tf-idf	**+2.28**
Cosine similarity	+2.11
Max voting	+2.05
Majority voting	+2.13
Weighted sampling	+1.93

Table 3: Improvements of our system over baseline using different retrieval weighting factor and voting technique are steady.

Evidence	Δ Accuracy
Gold + Random	**+7.93**
Gold + Retrieved (tf-idf)	+3.74
Retrieved (tf-idf)	+2.28

Table 4: Improvements of our system over baseline using gold evidence vs. retrieved evidence.

the state-of-the-art by only approximately 2 percentage points. We attribute this positive outcome to our system's utilization of NLI models, which already demonstrate outstanding performance on this adversarial dataset. The results obtained on the FEVER 2.0 dataset align with FEVER-Symmetric and further strengthen our conclusions.

On Climate-FEVER, the supervised approach delineated by Diggelmann et al. (2020) achieved an accuracy of 38.78% and an F1 score of 32.85%. In comparison, our introduced zero-shot methodology showcased enhanced results, achieving an accuracy rate of 46.71% and an F1 score of 45.71%, which demonstrated a notable generalization ability. These findings suggest that our zero-shot method offers a promising avenue for improved performance in out-of-domain tasks.

Finding 2 *Our system, utilizing triple-level inference, consistently improves over the baseline results irrespective of the NLI model used.*

In our experiments, our approach was able to improve the performance of both the base size and large size NLI models by approximately 2.5%. These consistent improvements suggest that our approach can continue to benefit from the ongoing progress: as more advanced models are being developed, our system is expected to demonstrate even greater accuracy and reliability.

In addition, we performed ablation experiments to investigate the impact of various weighting factors and different voting mechanisms, as outlined in Section 3. The results, presented in Table 3, demonstrate that our system's improvements over the baseline NLI models in Table 2 are consistently observed across all variants, indicating the reliability and robustness of our approach.

Furthermore, we conducted experiments to evaluate the effect of evidence quality on claim verification, as presented in Table 4. The Gold + Random method involves using gold-standard evidence for SUPPORTS and REFUTES claims, while random evidence is used for NEI claims. The Gold + Retrieved method is similar, but uses retrieved evidence instead of random evidence for NEI claims while still utilizing gold-standard evidence for SUPPORTS and REFUTES claims. The results indicate

Claim	The Adventures of Pluto Nash was reviewed by Ron Underwood .
Evidence Sentences	1: The Adventures of Pluto Nash is a 2002 Australian-American science fiction action comedy film starring Eddie Murphy -LRB- in a dual role -RRB- and directed by Ron Underwood . 2: Ron " Thunderwood " Underwood is a musician and director from Phoenix , Arizona . ...
Evidence Triples	<a 2002 Australian - American science fiction action comedy film, starring, Eddie Murphy> ...
USchema Triples	<The Adventures of Pluto Nash, directed, by Ron Underwood> ...

Table 5: An example with Universal Schema triples. Due to space limitations, not all sentences and triples for this example are shown. The table focuses on the most critical ones that effectively demonstrate our points.

that the performance improvements of our system increases as the quality of evidence improves, suggesting that our zero-shot approach benefits more from less noisy evidence. This likely due to the fact that our system relies on a strict set of rules to classify claims, which may be more sensitive to the presence of noise in the evidence. Thus, our system is likely to benefit from the continued development of better evidence retrieval systems.

Finding 3 *Employing the Universal Schema model provides marginal gains by bridging the gaps between extracted claim and evidence triples.*

The Universal Schema model, despite its modest gains, contributes to enhancing the overall performance of our fact-checking system. In manual analysis of the results we found that integrating the Universal Schema model helps our approach in handling claims involving mutual exclusivity, resulting in increased accuracy. Mutual exclusivity denotes a situation in which two or more events cannot coexist simultaneously. To illustrate this, let us consider the claim in Table 5 *The Adventures of Pluto Nash was reviewed by Ron Underwood*, initially classified as NOT ENOUGH INFORMATION (NEI) in the absence of the Universal Schema model. This misclassification originated from the complexity of the retrieved evidence, which presented a complex sentence implying that Ron Underwood directed the movie, thereby refuting the claim. However, extracting the relation needed as evidence <*The Adventures of Pluto Nash, directed by, Ron Underwood*> posed challenges so it was not extracted. Consequently, due to the absence of this critical triple, the model erroneously labeled the claim as NEI. By incorporating the Universal Schema model, our system successfully recovered the missing evidence triple, while also recognizing the inherent mutual exclusivity between assuming both the director and reviewer roles for the same movie. As a result, using the Universal Schema model accurately predicted the REFUTES label.

We also observed that the Universal Schema model offers limited assistance when applied to the two adversarial datasets considered. This is due to the fact that, in both the FEVER-Symmetric and FEVER 2.0 setting, all the necessary evidence is provided, unlike real-world scenarios. Consequently, the value provided by the Universal Schema model, which primarily focuses on filling gaps, becomes minimal since no gaps exist in the presence of sufficient evidence.

7 Conclusion

We introduced a novel zero-shot fact-checking method, translating claims and evidence into semantic triples with external knowledge graphs. This method surpasses other zero-shot baselines, impressively without direct FEVER dataset training. Its resilience is evident, avoiding the typical performance dips seen in supervised models on adversarial datasets like FEVER-Symmetric and FEVER 2.0. Also on the Climate-FEVER dataset, our approach outshines even supervised counterparts, highlighting its generalization prowess. Augmented by pretrained NLI models, our system's robustness is further emphasized. As future steps, we aim to hone model interpretability, examine diverse knowledge graphs, and test our method's versatility on other fact-checking datasets.

Limitations

While our novel zero-shot learning method for fact-checking with semantic triples and knowledge graphs has shown promising results, there are several limitations that must be noted.

Firstly, our method's language capabilities have

been exclusively tested on the English language, which poses an inherent limitation. Though the method was not specifically designed and implemented for English, the experiments were solely conducted using English datasets. Consequently, the potential effectiveness of our approach with other languages remains unverified. Differences in linguistic features and semantic triple structures across languages might present unique challenges that we have yet to encounter or address.

Secondly, our approach relies heavily on Wikipedia as both the source for datasets used in evaluation and the basis for our knowledge graphs. While Wikipedia is a vast and continually updated source of knowledge, its use as the sole source of data introduces biases and limitations. Wikipedia's content is predominantly generated by its user community, which can lead to the inclusion of inaccuracies, cultural biases, or omissions. This limitation might affect the fact-checking capabilities of our model, as the reliability of its responses are directly proportional to the quality and accuracy of the information within Wikipedia.

Additionally, the reliance on a single source for data and knowledge graphs constrains the method's applicability in fact-checking scenarios where knowledge outside of Wikipedia's domain is required. It may also lead to an overfitting issue, as the model might be overly tuned to Wikipedia's style and structure, limiting its performance when applied to different or broader sources.

In future work, addressing these limitations by incorporating support for multiple languages and expanding the data sources beyond Wikipedia would be essential steps towards enhancing the effectiveness and generalizability of our approach.

Ethics Statement

The use of fact-checking datasets and systems has become increasingly important in combatting misinformation, and as such, it is necessary to consider the ethical implications of their use. One of the key concerns in this regard is the potential for biases in these datasets. Such biases can arise from various sources, including the selection and interpretation of sources, the types of claims being fact-checked, and the demographic characteristics of the individuals involved. These biases have the potential to perpetuate stereotypes and reinforce existing power dynamics, and thus it is the responsibility of researchers to ensure that they use representative and unbiased datasets to train and evaluate their models. Transparency regarding any potential biases in models is also essential, and steps must be taken to mitigate any negative impact. By addressing these ethical concerns, researchers can promote the integrity of fact-checking and contribute to a more informed and equitable public discourse.

Acknowledgements

Zhangdie Yuan and Andreas Vlachos are both supported by the ERC grant AVeriTeC (GA 865958).

References

Bill Adair, Chengkai Li, Jun Yang, and Cong Yu. 2017. Progress toward "the holy grail": The continued quest to automate fact-checking. In *Computation+ Journalism Symposium,(September)*.

Kurt Bollacker, Colin Evans, Praveen Paritosh, Tim Sturge, and Jamie Taylor. 2008. Freebase: A collaboratively created graph database for structuring human knowledge. In *Proceedings of the 2008 ACM SIGMOD International Conference on Management of Data*, SIGMOD '08, page 1247–1250, New York, NY, USA. Association for Computing Machinery.

Giovanni Luca Ciampaglia, Prashant Shiralkar, Luis M Rocha, Johan Bollen, Filippo Menczer, and Alessandro Flammini. 2015. Computational fact checking from knowledge networks. *PloS one*, 10(6):e0128193.

Mitchell DeHaven and Stephen Scott. 2023. Bevers: A general, simple, and performant framework for automatic fact verification. *arXiv preprint arXiv:2303.16974*.

Dorottya Demszky, Kelvin Guu, and Percy Liang. 2018. Transforming question answering datasets into natural language inference datasets. *arXiv preprint arXiv:1809.02922*.

Thomas Diggelmann, Jordan Boyd-Graber, Jannis Bulian, Massimiliano Ciaramita, and Markus Leippold. 2020. Climate-fever: A dataset for verification of real-world climate claims. *arXiv preprint arXiv:2012.00614*.

Zhijiang Guo, Michael Schlichtkrull, and Andreas Vlachos. 2022. A survey on automated fact-checking. *Transactions of the Association for Computational Linguistics*, 10:178–206.

Suchin Gururangan, Swabha Swayamdipta, Omer Levy, Roy Schwartz, Samuel Bowman, and Noah A. Smith. 2018. Annotation artifacts in natural language inference data. In *Proceedings of the 2018 Conference of the North American Chapter of the Association for Computational Linguistics: Human Language Technologies, Volume 2 (Short Papers)*, pages 107–112,

New Orleans, Louisiana. Association for Computational Linguistics.

Andreas Hanselowski, Hao Zhang, Zile Li, Daniil Sorokin, Benjamin Schiller, Claudia Schulz, and Iryna Gurevych. 2018. UKP-athene: Multi-sentence textual entailment for claim verification. In *Proceedings of the First Workshop on Fact Extraction and VERification (FEVER)*, pages 103–108, Brussels, Belgium. Association for Computational Linguistics.

Naeemul Hassan, Fatma Arslan, Chengkai Li, and Mark Tremayne. 2017. Toward automated fact-checking: Detecting check-worthy factual claims by claimbuster. In *Proceedings of KDD*.

Shengding Hu, Ning Ding, Huadong Wang, Zhiyuan Liu, Jingang Wang, Juanzi Li, Wei Wu, and Maosong Sun. 2021. Knowledgeable prompt-tuning: Incorporating knowledge into prompt verbalizer for text classification. *arXiv preprint arXiv:2108.02035*.

Weijie Liu, Peng Zhou, Zhe Zhao, Zhiruo Wang, Qi Ju, Haotang Deng, and Ping Wang. 2020. K-bert: Enabling language representation with knowledge graph. In *Proceedings of the AAAI Conference on Artificial Intelligence*, volume 34, pages 2901–2908.

Robert L Logan IV, Nelson F Liu, Matthew E Peters, Matt Gardner, and Sameer Singh. 2019. Barack's wife hillary: Using knowledge-graphs for fact-aware language modeling. *arXiv preprint arXiv:1906.07241*.

Ndapandula Nakashole and Tom M. Mitchell. 2014. Language-aware truth assessment of fact candidates. In *Proceedings of the 52nd Annual Meeting of the Association for Computational Linguistics (Volume 1: Long Papers)*, pages 1009–1019, Baltimore, Maryland. Association for Computational Linguistics.

Allen Newell, J. C. Shaw, and Herbert A. Simon. 1959. Report on a general problem-solving program. In *IFIP Congress*.

Liangming Pan, Wenhu Chen, Wenhan Xiong, Min-Yen Kan, and William Yang Wang. 2021. Zero-shot fact verification by claim generation. In *Proceedings of the 59th Annual Meeting of the Association for Computational Linguistics and the 11th International Joint Conference on Natural Language Processing (Volume 2: Short Papers)*, pages 476–483, Online. Association for Computational Linguistics.

Adam Poliak, Jason Naradowsky, Aparajita Haldar, Rachel Rudinger, and Benjamin Van Durme. 2018. Hypothesis only baselines in natural language inference. In *Proceedings of the Seventh Joint Conference on Lexical and Computational Semantics*, pages 180–191, New Orleans, Louisiana. Association for Computational Linguistics.

Nils Reimers and Iryna Gurevych. 2019. Sentence-BERT: Sentence embeddings using Siamese BERT-networks. In *Proceedings of the 2019 Conference on Empirical Methods in Natural Language Processing and the 9th International Joint Conference on Natural Language Processing (EMNLP-IJCNLP)*, pages 3982–3992, Hong Kong, China. Association for Computational Linguistics.

Steffen Rendle, Christoph Freudenthaler, Zeno Gantner, and Lars Schmidt-Thieme. 2009. Bpr: Bayesian personalized ranking from implicit feedback. In *Proceedings of the Twenty-Fifth Conference on Uncertainty in Artificial Intelligence*, UAI '09, page 452–461, Arlington, Virginia, USA. AUAI Press.

Sebastian Riedel, Limin Yao, Andrew McCallum, and Benjamin M. Marlin. 2013. Relation extraction with matrix factorization and universal schemas. In *Proceedings of the 2013 Conference of the North American Chapter of the Association for Computational Linguistics: Human Language Technologies*, pages 74–84, Atlanta, Georgia. Association for Computational Linguistics.

Tal Schuster, Darsh Shah, Yun Jie Serene Yeo, Daniel Roberto Filizzola Ortiz, Enrico Santus, and Regina Barzilay. 2019. Towards debiasing fact verification models. In *Proceedings of the 2019 Conference on Empirical Methods in Natural Language Processing and the 9th International Joint Conference on Natural Language Processing (EMNLP-IJCNLP)*, pages 3419–3425, Hong Kong, China. Association for Computational Linguistics.

Joe Stacey, Pasquale Minervini, Haim Dubossarsky, and Marek Rei. 2022. Logical reasoning with span-level predictions for interpretable and robust NLI models. In *Proceedings of the 2022 Conference on Empirical Methods in Natural Language Processing*, pages 3809–3823, Abu Dhabi, United Arab Emirates. Association for Computational Linguistics.

Gabriel Stanovsky, Julian Michael, Luke Zettlemoyer, and Ido Dagan. 2018. Supervised open information extraction. In *Proceedings of the 2018 Conference of the North American Chapter of the Association for Computational Linguistics: Human Language Technologies, Volume 1 (Long Papers)*, pages 885–895, New Orleans, Louisiana. Association for Computational Linguistics.

James Thorne, Andreas Vlachos, Christos Christodoulopoulos, and Arpit Mittal. 2018a. Fever: a large-scale dataset for fact extraction and verification. In *Proceedings of NAACL-HLT*.

James Thorne, Andreas Vlachos, Oana Cocarascu, Christos Christodoulopoulos, and Arpit Mittal. 2018b. The FEVER2.0 shared task. In *Proceedings of the Second Workshop on Fact Extraction and VERification (FEVER)*.

James Thorne, Andreas Vlachos, Oana Cocarascu, Christos Christodoulopoulos, and Arpit Mittal. 2019. The FEVER2.0 shared task. In *Proceedings of the Second Workshop on Fact Extraction and VERification (FEVER)*, pages 1–6, Hong Kong, China. Association for Computational Linguistics.

Denny Vrandečić and Markus Krötzsch. 2014. Wikidata: A free collaborative knowledgebase. *Commun. ACM*, 57(10):78–85.

Wenhui Wang, Furu Wei, Li Dong, Hangbo Bao, Nan Yang, and Ming Zhou. 2020. Minilm: Deep self-attention distillation for task-agnostic compression of pre-trained transformers. *Advances in Neural Information Processing Systems*, 33:5776–5788.

Xiaozhi Wang, Tianyu Gao, Zhaocheng Zhu, Zhengyan Zhang, Zhiyuan Liu, Juanzi Li, and Jian Tang. 2021a. Kepler: A unified model for knowledge embedding and pre-trained language representation. *Transactions of the Association for Computational Linguistics*, 9:176–194.

Xiaozhi Wang, Tianyu Gao, Zhaocheng Zhu, Zhengyan Zhang, Zhiyuan Liu, Juanzi Li, and Jian Tang. 2021b. Kepler: A unified model for knowledge embedding and pre-trained language representation. *Transactions of the Association for Computational Linguistics*, 9:176–194.

Dustin Wright, David Wadden, Kyle Lo, Bailey Kuehl, Arman Cohan, Isabelle Augenstein, and Lucy Lu Wang. 2022. Generating scientific claims for zero-shot scientific fact checking. *arXiv preprint arXiv:2203.12990*.

Alexander Yates, Michele Banko, Matthew Broadhead, Michael Cafarella, Oren Etzioni, and Stephen Soderland. 2007. TextRunner: Open information extraction on the web. In *Proceedings of Human Language Technologies: The Annual Conference of the North American Chapter of the Association for Computational Linguistics (NAACL-HLT)*, pages 25–26, Rochester, New York, USA. Association for Computational Linguistics.

Qingyu Zhou, Nan Yang, Furu Wei, Chuanqi Tan, Hangbo Bao, and Ming Zhou. 2018. Neural question generation from text: A preliminary study. In *Natural Language Processing and Chinese Computing: 6th CCF International Conference, NLPCC 2017, Dalian, China, November 8–12, 2017, Proceedings 6*, pages 662–671. Springer.

A Hyperparameters

For the universal schema model, the hyperparameters were manually tuned using the wikidata dev set, with a batch size of 32, a learning rate of 2e-5, an Adam epsilon of 1e-8, a weighted decay of 0.01 and a maximum gradient norm of 1.0. The model was trained for a maximum of 3 epochs, with early stopping based on the loss observed on the dev set. Given the large amount of training data and limited computing resources, we partition the data into sections of 10000000 randomly shuffled samples to make the task feasible. Each section is treated as a separate training batch for our model.

Fine-tuning Language Models for Triple Extraction with Data Augmentation

Yujia Zhang, Tyler Sadler, Mohammad Reza Taesiri, Wenjie Xu, Marek Z. Reformat
University of Alberta
{yujia10, tsadle, taesiri, wx4, reformat}@ualberta.ca

Abstract

Advanced language models with impressive capabilities to process textual information can more effectively extract high-quality triples, which are the building blocks of knowledge graphs. Our work examines language models' abilities to extract entities and the relationships between them. We use a diverse data augmentation process to fine-tune large language models to extract triples from the text. Fine-tuning is performed using a mix of trainers from HuggingFace and five public datasets, such as different variations of the WebNLG, SKE, DocRed, FewRel, and KELM. Evaluation involves comparing model output with test set triples based on several criteria, such as type, partial, exact, and strict accuracy. The obtained results outperform ChatGPT and even match or exceed the performance of GPT-4.

1 Introduction

Knowledge graphs (KGs) represent knowledge in a semantically rich and intuitive way, enabling one to better understand and utilize gathered information. A KG is a data structure representing real-world entities and the relationships between them in the format of a triple, e.g., ⟨*head entity, relation, tail entity* ⟩ or ⟨ *subject, predicate, object* ⟩ (Ji et al., 2021).

The majority of available knowledge is composed of unstructured textual data. The need to 'convert it' into a structured format via extracting entities and relationships between them drives the construction of KGs. Large language models, like ChatGPT or GPT-4, have a remarkable capacity for understanding and generating text. It makes them useful tools for automating the process of knowledge extraction from textual sources. They can capture nuances and complexities of language, allowing for a deeper comprehension of the text's meaning. Therefore, they can be employed to create KGs that accurately and fully capture complicated semantic relations and the meaning of texts.

Extracting triples from texts poses several challenges (Hofer et al., 2023). Finding accurate and comprehensive entities and representative relationships from the text can be difficult, especially with various language usage, implicit references, and context-dependent interpretations. Additionally, processing and analyzing enormous quantities of text can be computationally demanding and resource-intensive. Therefore, methods for capturing reliable contextual information are paramount for KG's growth and development. Advanced context-aware techniques must be developed to identify and separate contextual references, capture relationships, and identify implicit connections.

This work aims to tune large language models (LLMs) to perform triple extraction from text. We have conducted several experiments using various models and datasets of different quality and sizes. The construction of triples adhering to the DBpedia ontology format has been particularly interesting. The WebNLG dataset (Castro Ferreira et al., 2020), predominantly using the DBpedia vocabulary for its entities and properties or emulating its ontological style, serves as the basis for our training data.

We have introduced a set of procedures to generate various prompts, instructing models about different processes related to triple extraction and understanding. This has led to the augmentation of the original WebNLG data and the creation of various versions of training datasets.

Eleven models, each with seven billion parameters, have been trained. Their efficacy has been evaluated in comparison with GPT-3.5 and GPT-4 on WebNLG. Additionally, we have preliminary assessed larger models with thirteen, thirty, and thirty-three billion parameters and trained them similarly.

The ultimate objective is to propose and illustrate a training methodology capable of elevating domain-specific models to or beyond the proficiency of leading-edge models.

Proceedings of the 1st Workshop on Knowledge Graphs and Large Language Models (KaLLM 2024), pages 116–124
August 15, 2024 ©2024 Association for Computational Linguistics

The findings of the work that constitute our contributions are:

- the reasonably sized large language models, such as ones with seven billion parameters, can be successfully tuned to extract triples from text;
- the proposed procedures to build a variety of prompts lead to the generation of enlarged and enhanced (enriched with information that improves training) datasets;
- small, fine-tuned models can outperform the baselines set up by GPT family models: ChatGPT and GPT-4.
- high-quality data is essential for the triple generation task; many datasets in the triple extraction space focus on extracting only specific relationships from text rather than all possible relationships or do not follow particular vocabulary, like DBpedia ontology.

2 Related Work

In the field of triple extraction, LSTM is a conventional technique to explore. Seq2Rdf (Liu et al., 2018) employs an LSTM-based sequence-to-sequence model to map natural language text to RDF triples in one step, using pre-trained word and knowledge graph embeddings for initialization. However, it is limited to extracting single triples and cannot handle multi-triple extraction. The ChatIE framework (Wei et al., 2023) achieves zero-shot information extraction by promoting ChatGPT, without requiring any labeled data for training. It allows interactively querying the model to extract structured information piece by piece in a multi-turn conversational format. The ChatIE relies on LLM like ChatGPT which is not open source. The performance depends heavily on how well the prompts are engineered and provides many details.

The Head to Tail benchmark (Sun et al., 2023) provides a systematic way to evaluate how knowledgeable LLM are about facts in diverse domains(movies, books, academics). The benchmark is still limited in size and diversity compared to the vast world knowledge, 18k QA pairs may not comprehensively cover all entity types, relationships, and knowledge domains. Few-shot learning with GPT-3 (Wadhwa et al., 2023) achieves state-of-the-art performance on standard relation extraction

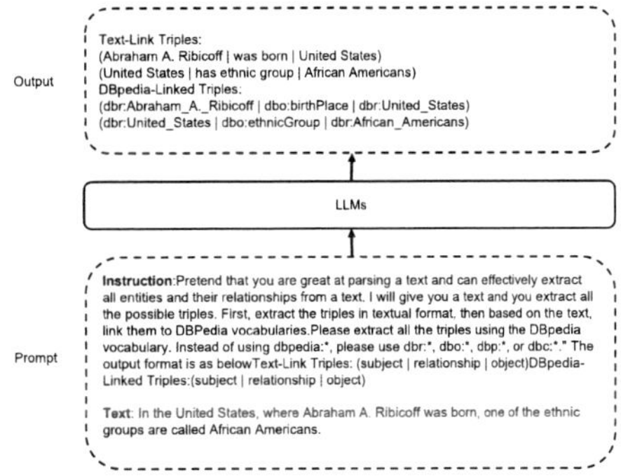

Figure 1: Example of triple extraction prompt workflow

datasets, surpassing existing fully supervised models. Fine-tuning Flan-T5 on explanations generated by GPT-3 further enhances performance. Treating relation extraction as a text-generation task provides flexibility in expressing entities and relations. However, GPT-3 is opaque, not open source, and significantly costly.

3 Problem and Experimental Setup

The paper focuses on extracting information from plain text. It is the task of building triples of the form $\langle$*subject, predicate, object*$\rangle$ based on the content of a sentence. Triple extraction is a domain-independent task. Two entities of a triple, i.e., subject and object, appear in the text, while a relation between these two entities is often deduced by 'understanding the meaning' of the sentence. All the components of a triple are extracted at the same time.

Here is a more formal description of the task. Given a set of sentences $D := \{w_1, w_2, ..., w_n\}$, we want to obtain a set of facts built from and based on these sentences. Let this set be $Facts := \{fact_1, fact_2, ..., fact_n\}$, and each fact is denoted as $\langle s, p, o \rangle, s \in S, p \in P, o \in O$, where S, P, O are sets of subjects, predicates, and objects respectively.

These triples are the basic units of knowledge graphs, resulting from the development of the Semantic Web concept. The classes (types of entities) and properties (relationships and attributes) used to describe triples' components are defined using ontologies. One of the most well-known ontologies is the one used by DBpedia (Lehmann et al., 2015).

Within the DBpedia dataset, triples are generated and represented using the DBpedia ontology as the schema. This ontology consists of 320 classes organized into a subsumption hierarchy and 1650 dis-

Llama2	You are an AI assistant who is an expert in knowledge graphs. You will be given an instruction and text. Generate a response to appropriately complete the instruction's request. {**instruction**}{**input**}{**output**}
LLongOrca	Below is an instruction that describes a task, paired with an input that provides further context. Write a output that appropriately completes the request. {**instruction**}{**input**}{**output**}
other models	### Instruction:{**instruction**} ### Input: {**input**} {**output**}

Table 1: Generic prompt template for different models.

tinct properties describing relations between them. The subsumption hierarchy is purposefully maintained relatively shallow, with a maximum depth of five to accommodate use cases where the ontology is traversed or visualized. Online browsing of the entire DBpedia ontology is available at [1].

3.1 Datasets

WebNLG The WebNLG corpus (Castro Ferreira et al., 2020) is made up of sets of triplets describing facts (entities and their relationships) and the matching facts expressed in natural language, in other words, text from which the triples are extracted. It includes 13,211 training data and 2,155 test data.

FewREL Few-Shot Relation Classification Dataset (FewRel)(Han et al., 2018) composes 70,000 instances from Wikipedia and 100 relations. The dataset is divided into three subsets: training set (64 relations), validation set (16 relations), and test set (20 relations).

DocRED Document-Level Relation Extraction Dataset (DocRED) (Yao et al., 2019) is created from Wikipedia and Wikidata in relation extraction data. Annotated on 5,053 Wikipedia articles, DocRED comprises 132,375 entities and 56,354 relational facts. The collection offers large-scale distantly supervised data over 101,873 documents in addition to the human-annotated data.

KELM The English Wikidata KG and the corresponding natural text sentences make up the large-scale synthetic corpus known as KELM(Agarwal et al., 2020). It has roughly 15 million artificially generated sentences produced by a refined T5 model. A list of triples of the format [subject, relation, object] is contained in each linearized KG graph in KELM. A subset of KELM, named KELM-sub, is used which contains 400,000/5,000 samples as train/test set.

SKE Baidu has released a Chinese dataset called SKE2019. The train set contains 194,747 sentences, whereas the validated set contains 21,639 sentences. SKE21 (Xie et al., 2021) has been released by manually labeling 1150 sentences from the test set with 2765 annotated triples. It contains 194,747 training data, 21,639 validation data, and 1,150 testing data. [2]

3.2 Large Language Models

LLMs like ChatGPT and GPT-4, pre-trained on a large-scale corpus, are composed of decoder modules based on the Transformer design, which incorporates a self-attention mechanism. However, it is difficult to conduct further research due to the close-source nature of models. Then, open-source decoder-only LLMs like Alpaca and Vicuna are released, which are fine-tuned based on LLaMA (Touvron et al., 2023a) and achieve competitive performance with ChatGPT and GPT-4.

ChatGPT-3.5 and GPT-4 Human-like conversations are the main purpose of ChatGPT, an advanced LLM created by OpenAI. To improve ChatGPT's alignment with human tastes and values, it uses RLHF (Christiano et al., 2017) during the fine-tuning process. GPT-4, an advanced big language model created by OpenAI, is expanding on the achievements of its forerunners, such as GPT-3 and ChatGPT.

Vicuna-13B (Chiang et al., 2023),Wizard (Xu et al., 2023), Orca (Mukherjee et al., 2023), **LLaMA** (Touvron et al., 2023a)(Touvron et al., 2023b), LlongOrca (Lian et al., 2023), **SOLAR** 10.7B (Kim et al., 2023)**Mixtral** Mixtral[3], Mistral mode[4], **Platypus** Platypus-30B (Lee et al., 2023) is the open-source model we choose from HuggingFace.

[1] http://mappings.dbpedia.org/server/ontology/classes/

[2] http://ai.baidu.com/broad/download?dataset=sked

[3] https://mistral.ai/news/mixtral-of-experts/

[4] https://huggingface.co/ignos/Mistral-T5-7B-v1

Data Format			
Data Augmentation (name)	Parts of prompt		Response
	instruction	**input**	**output**
Text2triples	Think of yourself as efficient in deconstructing a text and precisely identifying all the entities and their interrelations. I'll furnish you with a text and your job is to gather all potential triples, adhering to the pattern: (subject|relationship|object).	Sentence	Triples
Explanation	"Assume you're highly competent in scrutinizing a piece of text and successfully distilling all its entities along with their connections. I'll provide a text, and you are to extract every possible triplet, following the convention: (subject|relationship| object). Detail the entire process systematically."	Sentence	To extract triplets from the given text, we need to identify the subject, predicate, and object. Subject: "Aarhus Airport" Predicate: "cityServed" Object: "Aarhus, Denmark" The property "cityServed" is derived from the context of the sentence, where it implies that the airport serves the city of Aarhus. Therefore, here is the answer in the correct format: Aarhus_Airport | cityServed| "Aarhus, Denmark")
Triples2text	Picture yourself as an expert in scrutinizing a text, effectively extracting all entities and their relationships and then constructing text based on the given triples. Once I supply you with triples in the (subject|relationship|object) format, your duty is to reexamine these triples and create text that imparts their semantic interpretation.	Triples	Sentence
Reflection	Picture yourself as being highly skilled in text dissection, with the ability to efficiently identify all entities and their ties. When provided a text along with triples in the (subject|relationship|object) format, you are to check these triples in light of the text and correct any inaccuracies.	Sentence Triples	Corrected triples

Table 2: The overall Data Augmentation Tricks

3.3 Prompt Engineering & Data Preparation

Prompt engineering is an in-context method for learning language models. In a nutshell, a prompt is a sequence of natural language inputs for a model, consisting of an instruction, context, and input text. The instruction guides the model to perform a specific task, while the context provides additional information; the input text is the text to be processed by the model. An example of the triple extraction prompt is shown in Figure 1.

In this work, we used different prompt formats for various models, ensuring that both fine-tuning and inference employed the same prompt format. The three types of prompts are detailed in Table 1. The components {**instruction**}, {**input**}, and {**output**} are replaced with information/data specific to the proposed Data Formats, Table 2.

The experiments have been conducted with the training datasets built with different versions of Data Formats. Such an approach allowed us to increase the size of training datasets by 3- and 4-fold. The process of building different datasets is illustrated at the top of Figure 2. Examples of data formats are included in Table 2. Each format has its style of the *instruction*, *input*, as well as *output*. The tasks associated with each Data Format differed from explaining the extraction process via reconstructing a sentence from triples to evaluating triples. The data formats were used to construct various Training Datasets, Table 3.

The first Training Dataset is called **WebNLG-combined dataset**. It contains 39,633 entries in three categories/subsets, each of 13,211 entries. The first subset includes *Test2triples*, i.e., sets of sentences together with the triples extracted from them. The second subset is the extension of the first one. We have added *Explanation* of the triple extraction process. The explanations were generated by prompting GPT-3.5 with the input text and the ground truth triples to elucidate the extraction process. The explanations comprise entity identification, property analysis, source derivation, entity relationships, and the resultant triples. The third is *Triple2text* subset. It sets the ground truth triples as the model input and the original text as the target output. The aim is to enhance reasoning capabilities and improve triple generation performance.

The second generated Training Data is named **WebNLG-combined-with-reflections** with 52,844 entries. We have extended the WebNLG-combined dataset with so-called *Reflection* data. These data were generated by a *Vicuna* model previously trained for the triple extraction task using *Test2triples* and *Explanation*. The model was fed with the text and triples generated from it, and the task was either amending the triples or confirming their correctness. The anticipated output was either

Training Dataset Name	Used Data Format(s)	Size
WebNLG (original)	*Text2triples*	N
WebNLG-combined	*Text2triples + Explanations + Triples2text*	3*N
WebNLG-combined-with-reflections	*Text2triples + Explanations + Triples2text + Reflection*	4*N
WebNLG-reflections-updated-instructions	*Text2triples + Explanations + Triples2text + Reflection* + new_instructions	4*N

Table 3: Variants of WebNLG training data

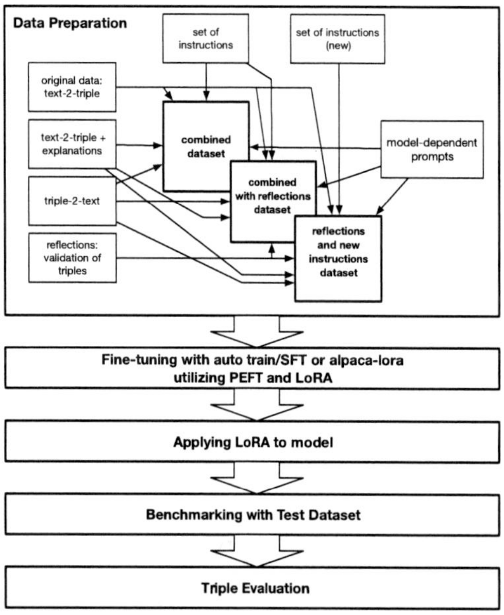

Figure 2: Experimental Workflow

a confirmation that a given input triple was accurate or its correct version.

For both datasets mentioned above, the **instruction** was randomly selected from the previously generated set of twenty distinct instructions. These instructions were a mix of human-authored instructions and variations generated by GPT-4 to enhance diversity. All instructions underwent thorough evaluation before they were used.

The **WebNLG-reflections-updated-instructions** dataset was the WebNLG-combined-with-reflections dataset when a new set of instructions was used. This time, there are eleven instructions: ten newly constructed and one from the original set. Again, this new set of instructions is a mixture of human-written and rephrased by GPT-4.

3.4 Overall Experiments Setup

The workflow of experimental steps and some details about the components forming different Training Datasets are shown in Figure 2. Once the datasets were prepared, the models have been tuned and benchmarked using the testing dataset. The final step was an evaluation of the results (for details, see next section).

To prepare models for the process of triple extraction, we utilized HuggingFace libraries to perform supervised finetuning utilizing Parameter-Efficient Finetuning (PEFT) (Liu et al., 2022) and Low-Rank Adaptation (LoRA) (Hu et al., 2021) on the WebNLG dataset. We used two prewritten trainers, *finetune script* from *alpaca-Lora* and *autotrain-advanced* from HuggingFace. The *finetune script* was slightly modified to change evaluation steps and to ensure the graphics processing unit (GPU) cache was cleared after all evaluations and checkpoints were saved. All models were trained using two Nvidia 3090 24GB GPUs and a cutoff length 1024, with varying configurations of packages and datasets based on the trainer used.

For the *finetune script*, we set an approximately 85:15 split between training and validation data. The validation set size is 6,000 for *WebNLG-combined* and 8,000 for *WebNLG-combined-with-reflections*.

For *autotrain-advanced*, Supervised Fine-tuning (SFT) Trainer is used from the Transformer Reinforcement Learning (TRL) package that is included as an option for training in autotrain-advanced (von Werra et al., 2020). The *WebNLG-reflections-updated-instructions* dataset is used. It contained different instructions for each training task, including additional details about formatting triples and better explaining the model's role.

We trained a collection of eleven models chosen based on relative performance on the HuggingFace LLM leaderboard, and compare their performance between each other and GPT-4. After training, the LoRA weights are combined with the base model to obtain our fine-tuned model output. These exported weights are used to run inference on the model.

4 Evaluation Procedure and Results

4.1 Evaluation Procedure

The evaluation framework comprises two phases: Inference, generating the model's output on the test set, and evaluation, comparing this output against

	Type			Partial			Exact			Strict		
Model	Prec.	Rec.	F1	Prec.	Rec.	F1	Prec.	Rec.	F1	Prec.	Rec.	F1
GPT-4 50 samples	0.706	0.729	0.714	0.684	0.707	0.692	0.651	0.668	0.657	0.640	0.652	0.645
GPT-4-0314	0.693	0.711	0.700	0.668	0.688	0.675	0.634	0.649	0.640	0.626	0.634	0.629
ChatGPT-3.5-2023	0.592	0.610	0.599	0.570	0.588	0.577	0.533	0.548	0.539	0.521	0.532	0.525
GPT-4 Full	0.567	0.624	0.587	0.536	0.580	0.552	0.478	0.506	0.488	0.455	0.482	0.465
Vicuna-7b	0.715	0.729	0.721	0.702	0.714	0.706	0.683	0.693	0.687	0.680	0.689	0.683
WizardLM-7b	0.700	0.715	0.706	0.688	0.701	0.693	0.671	0.682	0.675	0.667	0.677	0.671
Orca-mini-7b	0.683	0.700	0.690	0.670	0.686	0.677	0.652	0.664	0.657	0.647	0.658	0.652
Orca-mini-2-7b	0.711	0.726	0.717	0.698	0.710	0.703	0.681	0.690	0.684	0.677	0.687	0.681
Orca-mini-3-7b	**0.746**	**0.762**	**0.753**	**0.732**	**0.746**	**0.738**	**0.715**	**0.726**	**0.719**	**0.712**	**0.723**	**0.717**
Llama-2-7b	0.705	0.714	0.708	0.689	0.698	0.693	0.669	0.677	0.673	0.666	0.673	0.669
Llama-2-chat-7b	0.685	0.700	0.691	0.670	0.684	0.675	0.650	0.660	0.654	0.645	0.654	0.649
LlongOrca-7b	0.710	0.722	0.715	0.697	0.707	0.701	0.680	0.689	0.684	0.677	0.685	0.680
SOLAR-Instruct-10b	0.729	0.741	0.734	0.716	0.727	0.720	0.699	0.708	0.703	0.697	0.705	0.700
Mistral-t5-7b	0.731	0.746	0.738	0.716	0.729	**0.721**	0.697	0.708	0.702	0.695	0.704	0.698
Mixtral-8x7b	0.730	0.739	0.734	0.716	0.725	0.720	0.699	0.706	0.702	0.696	0.702	0.698
Vicuna-33b	**0.750**	**0.762**	**0.755**	**0.738**	**0.749**	**0.742**	**0.723**	**0.732**	**0.727**	**0.720**	**0.729**	**0.724**
Platypus-30b	**0.747**	**0.762**	**0.753**	**0.732**	**0.746**	**0.738**	**0.715**	**0.726**	**0.720**	**0.713**	**0.724**	**0.718**

Table 4: WebNLG-reflections-updated-instructions performance results

ground truth triples. All models were benchmarked with a maximum token limit of 1,024, and the output was generated without streaming. For evaluation, the numerical results such as precision, recall, and F1, and saved as the output file. The test set includes the same instructions in our training data and includes 2,155 instances of directly extracting triples from text.

The scores are calculated using the evaluate package (Segura-Bedmar et al., 2013). It calculates metrics based on four different criteria. First is *type evaluation (TE)* where only the tags must match to be considered correct. These tags are SUB, PRED, and OBJ for the subject, predicate, and object. *Partial evaluation (PE)* requires the triples to match partially or completely, irrespective of tag, to be considered partially or completely correct. *Exact evaluation (EE)* requires the triples to match exactly, irrespective of tag, to be considered correct. *Strict evaluation (SE)* requires both the triples and tag to match to be considered correct. Each evaluation type assigns a label of correct (COR), incorrect (InCOR), missed (MIS), or spurious (SPU), based on the triples and tags. Partial (PAR) is assigned only for the partial evaluation type. MIS and SPU are across all evaluation types, with MIS being assigned for each part of a reference triple when there is no matching candidate, and SPU assigned for each part of a candidate triple when there is no matching reference. The following formulas are calculations of precision (P), recall (R), and F1. The type and partial scores are calculated with the "partial" formulas and exact and strict scores are calculated with the "exact" formulas:

$$\begin{aligned} Possible &= COR + InCOR + PAR + MIS \\ &= TP + FN \\ Actual &= COR + InCOR + PAR + SPU \\ &= TP + FP \end{aligned}$$

$$P_{TE|PE} = \frac{COR + 0.5 * PAR}{Actual}$$

$$R_{TE|PE} = \frac{COR + 0.5 * PAR}{Possible}$$

$$\mathrm{P}_{EE|SE} = \frac{COR}{Actual} = \frac{COR}{COR + InCOR + SPU}$$

$$\mathrm{R}_{EE|SE} = \frac{COR}{Possible} = \frac{COR}{COR + InCOR + MIS}$$

4.2 Results

WebNLG Dataset. The obtained results for the fine-tuned models are included in Table 4. It can be observed that small 7b models *Orca-mini3-7b* and *Mistral-t5-7b* have the best performances even when compared with GPT-4. The *Orca-mini3-7b* model achieved the highest F1 scores for all evaluations, outperforming all 7b models in our comparative analysis.

Small variations have been observed between training methods and datasets. In general, models show slight improvement from WebNLG-combined to WebNLG-combined-with-reflections and then to WebNLG-reflections-updated-instructions. Additionally, modifying the instructions shows a decrease in training loss. GPT models had a bigger drop in performance going to the exact and strict metrics compared to our models, which resulted in our models performing relatively better on the exact and strict metrics.

Ablation Study. We performed ablation studies to evaluate the impact of different data augmentation strategies on the performance of these models. Figure 3 shows the effects of various data augmentation techniques on the models' performance. We show the performance results obtained for two models – *Orca* and *Vicuna* – and four Training Datasets: the original WebNLG dataset, the WebNLG-combined dataset, the WebNLG-combined-with-reflections dataset, and the WebNLG-reflections-updated-instructions dataset, Table 3. We report the precision, recall, and F1 values for the most demanding task of generating triples identical to those provided as the target. It is easily seen that the results obtained for the last Training Dataset are the best.

Other Datasets. Two models *Orca-mini-3* and *Llama-2-13b* have been finetuned on different datasets, Table 5. The best scores have been obtained for the **KELM** dataset. The *Llama-2-13b* finetuned on another dataset **DocRED** performed very poorly and was completely unable to learn proper formatting of triples.

The main issue with inference on other data is related to the type of triple properties and how many triples are extracted from a single sentence. For example, the analysis of the DocRED dataset revealed that it is focused mainly on such relations as *country* and *location* while ignoring any other relations. In DocRed, a few triples are extracted from paragraph sentences. There is much looping in the models' output; models do not efficiently learn triple formats. Some outputs were of the form (subject | predicate | object). Further, there are only about 3,000 entries in annotated training data. For yet another dataset – **FewRel** – the issue seems to be related to the model not knowing when to generate triples following the DBpedia and when using Wikidata formats.

5 Discussion and Limitations

The obtained results and their analysis have led to a few observations that confirmed known facts about tuning large models and allowed to draw some new ones. We can categorize them into three parts: data size, model selection, and interaction with a model (prompt and data preparation).

Size and Quality of Datasets. It is a well-known fact that larger datasets lead to better results. Such an obvious statement is also true for the triple extraction process. It is seen in Table 5. The results obtained for KELM data – 400,000 samples in the training set – confirm that. The model was tuned with a simple prompt containing text-2-triple and instructions. Comparing that with our primary focused data, WebNLG, which includes only 13,211 training datasets, shows a significant advantage of large datasets.

Once we collected results for the other two datasets - DocRED and FewRel - we investigated the content of the training datasets. It has become apparent that the reference triples that were supposed to be constructed from sentences were of poor quality: limited to a few relations, incoherent structure, a limited number of triples (quite often just one) form small paragraphs.

Model Selection/Multilingual Triples. In our experiments, one of the datasets – SKE – is a set of Chinese sentences and extracted from them triples. The difference in results obtained from *orca-mini-3-7b* and *llama-2-13b* is very large. A quick investigation revealed that the dataset used to train the *orca-mini-3-7* model contained a large amount of Chinese text. Again, it confirms a commonsense fact that if a language model is not exposed to a text in a given language, its performance, related to this language, is not satisfactory.

Prompt and Data Preparation. The most interesting and important observation coming from our experiments is a high significance of the creative approach to constructing prompts and 'augmentation' of the training datasets.

As indicated earlier, the task of extracting triples from WebNLG data involves the usage of DBpedia vocabulary. In particular, properties/relations of the extracted triples have/should be in the DBpedia format. The WebNLG dataset has been analyzed to ensure the training data is of high quality. DBpedia ontology has been used to determine if the triples/relations were consistent.

The consistent structure of triples is essential so the model can effectively learn how to form triples properly. Exposure to different properties is also of high importance. The properties seen in the training and testing sets overlapped, with thirty-six properties unique to the test set. All properties were checked to ensure they were present in DBpedia.

A small amount of training data, just 13,211, has forced us to generate larger datasets from the original set via setting different tasks related to processing and extraction of triples. Section 3 details how various versions of Training Datasets were created. We enhanced the data with explanations of triple generation processes generated by GPT-3.5 and previously tuned model, generation of sentences based on sets of triples, and simple evaluation of extracted triples. These activities have improved

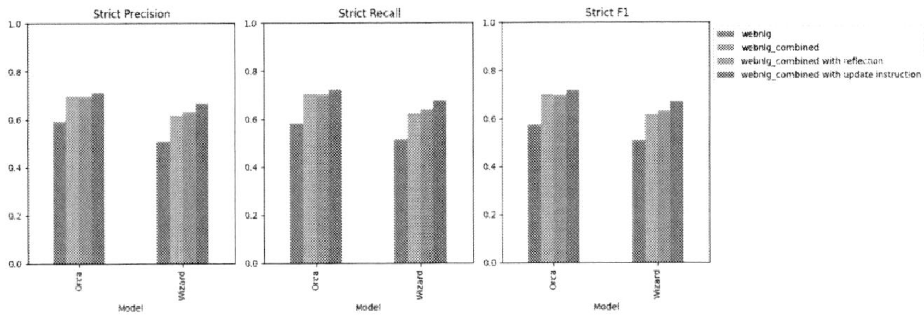

Figure 3: Results of ablation studies on two modes: Orca and Wizard

		Type			Partial			Exact			Strict		
Data	Model	Prec.	Rec.	F1	Prec.	Rec.	F1	Prec.	Rec.	F1	Prec.	Rec.	F1
SKE	orca-mini-3	0.828	0.828	0.828	0.829	0.829	0.829	0.829	0.829	0.829	0.827	0.827	0.827
	llama-2-13b	0.129	0.127	0.127	0.130	0.128	0.129	0.127	0.127	0.127	0.124	0.124	0.124
DocRED	orca-mini-3	0.057	0.054	0.052	0.050	0.050	0.048	0.031	0.031	0.030	0.024	0.025	0.024
	llama-2-13b	0.096	0.037	0.051	0.051	0.022	0.028	0.002	0.002	0.002	0.002	0.002	0.002
FewRel	orca-mini-3	0.314	0.402	0.342	0.354	0.425	0.376	0.312	0.362	0.327	0.240	0.286	0.254
	llama-2-13b	0.304	0.378	0.325	0.344	0.405	0.361	0.297	0.340	0.310	0.224	0.263	0.236
KELM	orca-mini-3-7b	0.867	0.899	0.879	0.848	0.873	0.857	0.823	0.841	0.830	0.820	0.837	0.826
	Llama-2-13b	0.861	0.865	0.852	0.825	0.836	0.825	0.779	0.796	0.785	0.769	0.786	0.776
raw_Webnlg	orca-mini-3-7b	0.618	0.638	0.626	0.598	0.615	0.605	0.574	0.588	0.579	0.593	0.583	0.575
	Llama-2-13b	0.62	0.637	0.626	0.602	0.618	0.608	0.581	0.593	0.586	0.577	0.588	0.581

Table 5: Performance on other datasets

our best model's performance, i.e., *orca-mini-3-7b*.

Limitations There are some limitations of fine-tuned models. They hallucinated on occasion, especially when they generated responses for more well-known topics, such as when we asked them to generate a response to the Jeff Bezos Wikipedia article. The models frequently hallucinated the birthplace of Bezos, providing false information about the location. Also, models had looping issues, where they would continually generate output until they reached the token limit.

6 Conclusion

The paper aims to investigate different scenarios of a triple extraction task. Various models and a few datasets have been used in the experiments. A prime contribution is the development of a procedure/methodology for augmenting the original dataset. The additions included several tasks indirectly related to the triple extraction process: explaining the extraction steps, reconstructing sentences from triples, and determining the correctness of extracted triples. It resulted in enlarged training datasets (3- or 4-fold). As an outcome, the performance of 7b tuned models is comparable to or even better than that of well-known models from the GPT family.

The applied procedures concentrated on generating triples containing elements compatible with a specific vocabulary, in our case, DBpedia. While our models suffer from occasional looping and hallucinations, they effectively extract triples following DBpedia ontology from sentences. The results demonstrate that achieving and exceeding GPT performance with fine-tuned models is possible without large datasets.

References

Oshin Agarwal, Heming Ge, Siamak Shakeri, and Rami Al-Rfou. 2020. Knowledge graph based synthetic corpus generation for knowledge-enhanced language model pre-training. *arXiv preprint arXiv:2010.12688*.

Thiago Castro Ferreira, Claire Gardent, Nikolai Ilinykh, Chris van der Lee, Simon Mille, Diego Moussallem, and Anastasia Shimorina. 2020. The 2020 bilingual, bi-directional WebNLG+ shared task: Overview and evaluation results (WebNLG+ 2020). In *3rd International Workshop on Natural Language Generation from the Semantic Web*, pages 55–76, Dublin, Ireland (Virtual). Association for Computational Linguistics.

Wei-Lin Chiang, Zhuohan Li, Zi Lin, Ying Sheng, Zhanghao Wu, Hao Zhang, Lianmin Zheng, Siyuan Zhuang, Yonghao Zhuang, Joseph E. Gonzalez, Ion Stoica, and Eric P. Xing. 2023. Vicuna: An open-source chatbot impressing gpt-4 with 90%* chatgpt quality.

Paul F Christiano, Jan Leike, Tom Brown, Miljan Martic, Shane Legg, and Dario Amodei. 2017. Deep reinforcement learning from human preferences. *Advances in neural information processing systems*, 30.

Xu Han, Hao Zhu, Pengfei Yu, Ziyun Wang, Yuan Yao, Zhiyuan Liu, and Maosong Sun. 2018. Fewrel: A large-scale supervised few-shot relation classification dataset with state-of-the-art evaluation. *arXiv preprint arXiv:1810.10147*.

Marvin Hofer, Daniel Obraczka, Alieh Saeedi, Hanna Köpcke, and Erhard Rahm. 2023. Construction of knowledge graphs: State and challenges. *arXiv preprint arXiv:2302.11509*.

Edward J. Hu, Yelong Shen, Phillip Wallis, Zeyuan Allen-Zhu, Yuanzhi Li, Shean Wang, and Weizhu Chen. 2021. Lora: Low-rank adaptation of large language models. *CoRR*.

Shaoxiong Ji, Shirui Pan, Erik Cambria, Pekka Marttinen, and S Yu Philip. 2021. A survey on knowledge graphs: Representation, acquisition, and applications. *IEEE transactions on neural networks and learning systems*, 33(2):494–514.

Dahyun Kim, Chanjun Park, Sanghoon Kim, Wonsung Lee, Wonho Song, Yunsu Kim, Hyeonwoo Kim, Yungi Kim, Hyeonju Lee, Jihoo Kim, et al. 2023. Solar 10.7 b: Scaling large language models with simple yet effective depth up-scaling. *arXiv preprint arXiv:2312.15166*.

Ariel N Lee, Cole J Hunter, and Nataniel Ruiz. 2023. Platypus: Quick, cheap, and powerful refinement of llms. *arXiv preprint arXiv:2308.07317*.

Jens Lehmann, Robert Isele, Max Jakob, Anja Jentzsch, Dimitris Kontokostas, Pablo N Mendes, Sebastian Hellmann, Mohamed Morsey, Patrick Van Kleef, Sören Auer, et al. 2015. Dbpedia–a large-scale, multilingual knowledge base extracted from wikipedia. *Semantic web*, 6(2):167–195.

Wing Lian, Bleys Goodson, Guan Wang, Eugene Pentland, Austin Cook, Chanvichet Vong, and "Teknium". 2023. Llongorca7b: Llama2-7b model instructtuned for long context on filtered openorcav1 gpt-4 dataset. `https://https://huggingface.co/Open-Orca/LlongOrca-7B-16k`,.

Haokun Liu, Derek Tam, Mohammed Muqeeth, Jay Mohta, Tenghao Huang, Mohit Bansal, and Colin A Raffel. 2022. Few-shot parameter-efficient fine-tuning is better and cheaper than in-context learning. *Advances in Neural Information Processing Systems*, 35:1950–1965.

Yue Liu, Tongtao Zhang, Zhicheng Liang, Heng Ji, and Deborah L. McGuinness. 2018. Seq2rdf: An end-to-end application for deriving triples from natural language text.

Subhabrata Mukherjee, Arindam Mitra, Ganesh Jawahar, Sahaj Agarwal, Hamid Palangi, and Ahmed Awadallah. 2023. Orca: Progressive learning from complex explanation traces of gpt-4.

Isabel Segura-Bedmar, Paloma Martínez Fernández, and María Herrero Zazo. 2013. Semeval-2013 task 9: Extraction of drug-drug interactions from biomedical texts (ddiextraction 2013). Association for Computational Linguistics.

Kai Sun, Yifan Ethan Xu, Hanwen Zha, Yue Liu, and Xin Luna Dong. 2023. Head-to-tail: How knowledgeable are large language models (llm)? a.k.a. will llms replace knowledge graphs?

Hugo Touvron, Thibaut Lavril, Gautier Izacard, Xavier Martinet, Marie-Anne Lachaux, Timothée Lacroix, Baptiste Rozière, Naman Goyal, Eric Hambro, Faisal Azhar, Aur'elien Rodriguez, Armand Joulin, Edouard Grave, and Guillaume Lample. 2023a. Llama: Open and efficient foundation language models. *ArXiv*, abs/2302.13971.

Hugo Touvron, Louis Martin, Kevin Stone, Peter Albert, Amjad Almahairi, Yasmine Babaei, Nikolay Bashlykov, Soumya Batra, Prajjwal Bhargava, Shruti Bhosale, et al. 2023b. Llama 2: Open foundation and fine-tuned chat models, 2023. *URL https://arxiv.org/abs/2307.09288*.

Leandro von Werra, Younes Belkada, Lewis Tunstall, Edward Beeching, Tristan Thrush, Nathan Lambert, and Shengyi Huang. 2020. Trl: Transformer reinforcement learning. `https://github.com/huggingface/trl`.

Somin Wadhwa, Silvio Amir, and Byron C. Wallace. 2023. Revisiting relation extraction in the era of large language models.

Xiang Wei, Xingyu Cui, Ning Cheng, Xiaobin Wang, Xin Zhang, Shen Huang, Pengjun Xie, Jinan Xu, Yufeng Chen, Meishan Zhang, Yong Jiang, and Wenjuan Han. 2023. Zero-shot information extraction via chatting with chatgpt.

Chenhao Xie, Jiaqing Liang, Jingping Liu, Chengsong Huang, Wenhao Huang, and Yanghua Xiao. 2021. Revisiting the negative data of distantly supervised relation extraction. *arXiv preprint arXiv:2105.10158*.

Can Xu, Qingfeng Sun, Kai Zheng, Xiubo Geng, Pu Zhao, Jiazhan Feng, Chongyang Tao, and Daxin Jiang. 2023. Wizardlm: Empowering large language models to follow complex instructions. *arXiv preprint arXiv:2304.12244*.

Yuan Yao, Deming Ye, Peng Li, Xu Han, Yankai Lin, Zhenghao Liu, Zhiyuan Liu, Lixin Huang, Jie Zhou, and Maosong Sun. 2019. Docred: A large-scale document-level relation extraction dataset. *arXiv preprint arXiv:1906.06127*.

Improving LLM-based KGQA for multi-hop Question Answering with implicit reasoning in few-shot examples

Mili Shah, Joyce Cahoon, Mirco Milletari, Jing Tian
Fotis Psallidas, Andreas Mueller, Nick Litombe
Microsoft
milishah, jcahoon, mimillet, jingtian, fopsalli, amueller, nicklitombe@microsoft.com

Abstract

Large language models (LLMs) have shown remarkable capabilities in generating natural language texts for various tasks. However, using LLMs for question answering on knowledge graphs still remains a challenge, especially for questions requiring multi-hop reasoning. In this paper, we present a novel planned query guidance approach that improves large language model (LLM) performance in multi-hop question answering on knowledge graphs (KGQA). We do this by designing few-shot examples that implicitly demonstrate a systematic reasoning methodology to answer multi-hop questions. We evaluate our approach for two graph query languages, Cypher and SPARQL, and show that the queries generated using our strategy outperform the queries generated using a baseline LLM and typical few-shot examples by up to 24.66% and 7.7% in execution match accuracy for the MetaQA and the Spider benchmarks respectively. We also conduct an ablation study to analyze the incremental effects of the different techniques of designing few-shot examples. Our results suggest that our approach enables the LLM to effectively leverage the few-shot examples to generate queries for multi-hop KGQA.

1 Introduction

Question answering on knowledge graphs (KGQA) is a challenging task that requires understanding the natural language query, mapping it to the KG schema, and generating a graph query that can retrieve the correct answer from the KG. We focus on two graph query languages in this work, namely Cypher[1], a well-known graph query language developed by Neo4j[2], and SPARQL, a popular language for querying RDF[3] databases. In this study, we focus on the task of answering a question from a knowledge graph by generating Cypher and SPARQL queries to query the knowledge graph.

Large language models (LLMs), such as GPT-4 (OpenAI et al., 2024), have shown remarkable capabilities in generating natural language texts for various tasks. Recent studies have explored the capability of LLMs in Cypher generation (Guo et al., 2023; Jiang et al., 2023b; An et al., 2023) as well as SPARQL generation (Jiang et al., 2023a; Li et al., 2023; Gu and Su, 2022; Ye et al., 2021). However, using LLMs for multi-hop KGQA still remains a challenge, as they need to generate queries that can capture the multi-hop reasoning logic. Furthermore, models are limited by the availability of labeled data for KGQA, which is costly and time-consuming to obtain.

Therefore, it is desirable to leverage the few-shot learning ability of LLMs, which allows them to adapt to new tasks with only a few examples, and design effective few-shot examples that can guide the LLM to generate more accurate queries for multi-hop KGQA. The utilization of few-shot learning in LLMs has shown promise in various domains to address the limitations of data scarcity and improve model generalization. Several studies demonstrated the value of few-shot learning in various domains for improving the performance of LLMs (Shirafuji et al., 2023; Huang et al., 2024; Ahmed and Devanbu, 2023). However, to the best of our knowledge, the influence of few-shot examples design in KGQA, particularly for generating Cypher and SPARQL queries, has not been extensively studied.

Existing KGQA models like TransferNet(Shi et al., 2021), which excels in multi-hop reasoning over relation graphs, UniKGQA(Jiang et al., 2022), known for its unified retrieval and reasoning framework, and NuTrea(Choi et al., 2023), which leverages neural tree search for context-rich embeddings, outperform our proposed LLM-based

[1] https://neo4j.com/docs/cypher-manual/current/introduction/

[2] https://neo4j.com/

[3] Resource Description Framework

Proceedings of the 1st Workshop on Knowledge Graphs and Large Language Models (KaLLM 2024), pages 125–135
August 15, 2024

Question: "the films that share actors with the film [Dil Chahta Hai] were released in which years"

Answer: "1997|1998|2003|2001|2006|2004|2005|2014|2008|2009|2010|2012"

Figure 1: An example of a 3-hop question-answer pair in MetaQA.

approach, achieving up to 100% in the Hits@1 metric. However, these methods incur higher complexity and cost, as they require extensive training on specific knowledge graphs. In contrast, simple LLM-based methods can achieve competitive performance with a well-designed few-shot example set, bypassing the need for exhaustive training or customization. This efficiency makes the study of few-shot example design for LLM-based KGQA a crucial research area, promising swift adaptability and innovation in question-answering systems.

In this paper, we propose a novel approach to improve the performance of LLM-based Cypher and SPARQL generation for multi-hop KGQA. We do this by designing few-shot examples that implicitly demonstrate a systematic reasoning methodology to answer multi-hop questions. This guides the LLM to follow a similar reasoning process for new questions, without explicitly specifying the steps. We hypothesize that such few-shot examples can enhance the LLM's understanding of the question, the KG schema, and the syntax of the graph query language, enabling it to generate more accurate queries for multi-hop KGQA.

We evaluate our approach on two popular benchmark datasets, MetaQA (Zhang et al., 2018) and Spider (Kosten et al., 2023), both of which feature natural language questions across various levels of difficulty for multi-hop querying. We start by conducting an ablation study to analyze the effects of different components of our few-shot examples design on Cypher. We then show how our methodology transfers to SPARQL. Our results demonstrate that this strategy can enhance execution match accuracy over that of conventional methods used in few-shot examples.

2 Methodology

This work focuses on the methodology of crafting few-shot examples for improved performance of LLMs for the task of Cypher and SPARQL generation for KGQA. For this task, a few-shot example is composed of a natural language question, accompanied by an expected response of a Cypher or SPARQL query that can be run on an associated KG to answer the natural language question.

We propose a method for designing Cypher and SPARQL queries for few-shot examples that clearly demonstrates to the LLM the reasoning required to answer multi-hop questions. Techniques like chain-of-thought prompting (Wei et al., 2022) use textual explanations to teach step-by-step reasoning to LLMs. Our methodology employs a code style that implicitly shows how to take each hop step-by-step. Figure 2 is an example of a Cypher query written in such a style to be used as a few-shot example.

Contrast the query in Figure 2 with a typical or conventional style[4] used by developers to write Cypher queries in Figure 3. Certain prevalent practices characterize this conventional style of crafting such graph queries. These include the utilization of succinct and non-descriptive variable names, the consolidation of all traversal hops into a single chain in a single MATCH clause, and the immediate specification of string literals for entity matching within the variable declaration itself in the MATCH clause (e.g., {name: "Dil Chahta Hai"}).

Our proposed approach outlines practical methods for crafting few-shot examples to generate graph queries, like Cypher and SPARQL:

1. **Structured Traversal Clarity**: Each hop should be articulated on a separate line to mirror the logical sequence of traversals, strictly adhering to the correct order of entities and relationships encountered. This makes the traversal reasoning clear and easy to follow. This approach enhances the clarity of traversal reasoning, ensuring that each step is both transparent and sequentially accurate.

2. **Logical Continuity in Chaining**: Maintain an unbroken logical chain where the endpoint

[4] https://neo4j.com/docs/cypher-manual/current/styleguide/, https://neo4j.com/docs/cypher-manual/current/queries/basic/#find-connected-nodes, https://gist.github.com/wjgilmore/8ba5f31ef1435dc04c52, https://gist.github.com/wjgilmore/8ba5f31ef1435dc04c52

```
MATCH (dilMovie:`movie`)-[:starred_actors]->(actor:`actor`)
MATCH (actor:`actor`)<-[:starred_actors]-(otherMovie:`movie`)
MATCH (otherMovie:`movie`)-[:release_year]->(year:`year`)
WHERE toLower(dilMovie.name)='dil chahta hai'
AND dilMovie <> otherMovie
RETURN year LIMIT 200
```

Figure 2: A sample of a Cypher query used in a few-shot example designed using our approach. Implicit reasoning is demonstrated by writing each hop line-by-line, with an easy-to-understand code style following the correct chain of hops, and separating reasoning of hops from the constraints into the WHERE clause. The natural language question corresponding to this Cypher query from the MetaQA dataset is "the films that share actors with the film Dil Chahta Hai were released in which years".

```
MATCH (yr:`year`)<-[:release_year]-(m:`movie`)-[:starred_actors]->(:`actor`)<-
[:starred_actors]-(m2:`movie` {name: 'Dil Chahta Hai'})
WHERE m <> m2
RETURN yr LIMIT 200
```

Figure 3: A sample of a Cypher query written in a commonly used style. The natural language question corresponding to this Cypher query from the MetaQA dataset is "the films that share actors with the film Dil Chahta Hai were released in which years".

of one hop is the starting point for the next, ensuring a coherent flow of entities throughout the query. Ensuring a coherent progression of entities throughout the query facilitates the LLM's ability to mirror the thought process when identifying subsequent steps.

3. **Distinct Separation of Logic**: In the case of Cypher, employ MATCH clauses exclusively for hops, while isolating all constraints, such as string literals for entity matching, within WHERE clauses to promote clarity; and in the case of SPARQL, utilize WHERE clauses for hops and separate constraints within the FILTER clause. This approach delineates the decision-making process for selecting hops from other constraints, thus sharpening the focus on the hop selection mechanism.

4. **Descriptive Variable Naming**: Adopt variable names that are both illustrative and consistent, reflecting the entity type and any applicable constraints, such as "dilMovie" to denote a 'movie' entity constrained by the title "Dil Chahta Hai". This approach enhances the traversal's logical coherence as well as aids the LLM in retaining the constraints for inclusion in the WHERE clause.

5. **Examples with increasing complexity**: Present multiple examples that escalate in complexity, such as starting with a simple 1-hop query and advancing through to more complex 2-hop and 3-hop queries, to reinforce the learning of the reasoning pattern.

6. **Consistency**: Ensure that the structure and presentation of all few-shot examples remain uniform, facilitating easier pattern recognition and learning.

3 Experimental setup

3.1 Cypher

3.1.1 Dataset

We evaluate our approach on a widely used benchmark for multi-hop KGQA, MetaQA (Zhang et al., 2018). MetaQA comprises of a movie knowledge graph with 43k entities and 9 relationship types, along with question-answer pairs. The dataset contains 161 1-hop question templates (31% of total question templates), 210 2-hop question templates (40% of total question templates), and 150 3-hop question templates (29% of total question templates). The corresponding answers are a list of entities from the KG. Figure 1 shows an example of a 3-hop question-answer pair.

3.1.2 Baselines

We compare our proposed approach with an LLM-based Cypher generation module[5] developed by

[5]https://python.langchain.com/docs/use_cases/graph/integrations/graph_cypher_qa

Question Type	Our proposed approach	LangChain's Cypher generation module	Examples with conventional style
3-hop (150 questions)	**97.33%**	67.33%	72.67%
2-hop (210 questions)	**100%**	89.52%	93.33%
1-hop (161 questions)	**92.54%**	88.81%	91.30%

Table 1: KGQA results for the MetaQA dataset comparing our approach (with systematic few-shot examples implicitly demonstrating reasoning), with two baselines, the first being the Cypher generation module available in LangChain, and the second being an approach where Cypher queries in few-shot examples are written in a typical fashion. The metric shown is execution match accuracy.

Variation of few-shot example design	Execution match accuracy
Conventionally written examples (baseline)	72.67%
Only one example written conventionally	83.33%
Non-descriptive variable names	87.33%
All hops in one line	94.67%
Only one example written with our design	95.33%
Chain direction not maintained	95.33%
Examples written with our design	**97.33%**

Table 2: Ablation experiments on 3-hop questions of the MetaQA dataset. Appendix D provides the few-shot examples used for each of these experiments.

Neo4j and made available in LangChain. This is a commonly used module for the task of KGQA.

We also compare against a second baseline of few-shot examples with Cypher queries written in a typical or conventional fashion. An example of a Cypher query written in such a style is shown in Figure 3. Section 2 details some features that characterize this conventional style. This baseline enables us to determine the influence of the design of few-shot examples.

3.1.3 Query Generation and Post-Processing pipeline

Our experiments employ GPT-4 (OpenAI et al., 2024) as the LLM across all methods under examination to generate Cypher queries given natural language questions.

We run these generated Cypher queries on MetaQA KG hosted in Neo4j.

A Cypher query corrector module[6] is incorporated as a post-processing step to rectify common errors in the directionality of relationships within the Cypher queries. For instance, it corrects MATCH (dilMovie:'movie')<–[:starred_actors]–(actor:'actor') to MATCH (dilMovie:'movie ')–[:starred_actors]–>(actor:'actor'). To ensure consistency and fairness in our comparative analysis, the Cypher query corrector module is applied across all experimental conditions, encompassing the proposed approach, the baselines, and all the ablation studies.

[6]https://api.python.langchain.com/en/latest/chains/langchain.chains.graph_qa.cypher_utils.CypherQueryCorrector.html

3.1.4 Prompt

For both the proposed approach and the baseline with typically written Cypher queries, we specify three few-shot examples. The ablation studies employ variations of few-shot examples. All other prompt components, namely the instructions and the graph schema, remain consistent across these two methods as well as ablation studies. The complete prompt utilized for our proposed approach, including all the few-shot examples, is detailed in Appendix A. The few-shot examples employed for the baseline featuring typically written examples are enumerated in Appendix C.

For the baseline that relies on LangChain's Cypher generation module, we use the default prompt generated by the module. Notably, it does not involve any few-shot examples. The complete prompt is attached in Appendix B.

3.2 SPARQL

3.2.1 Dataset

In order to evaluate how well this style of few-shot expression generalizes and transfers to other graph

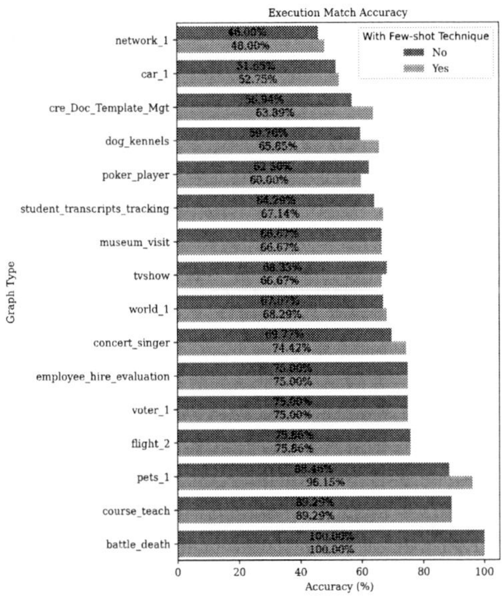

Figure 4: Execution match accuracy of our methodology for generating SPARQL queries on the Spider benchmark.

query languages, we tested its applicability on the SPARQL version of the Spider benchmark (Kosten et al., 2023). This version of Spider is useful as it already includes few-shot examples for training, precluding the need for us to handcraft examples as done for our Cypher module. We leverage a static prompt as attached in Appendix E to convert these few-shot examples into the style as outlined in Section 2.

3.2.2 Baselines

We compare the performance of the few-shots re-expressed in the format discussed against the performance without these few-shot examples. The prompt follows that as utilized for Cypher generation, except the graph schema is provided in RDF format. Similar to the Cypher pipelines above, we also include a corrector module as a post-processing step across these strategies to ensure that the SPARQL generated is syntactically valid.

3.3 Evaluation metric

The success of the generated queries is determined by the accuracy of the output, specifically, whether the entities in the generated answers precisely align with those anticipated in the expected answers. Execution match is reported in terms of the number of samples meeting this criterion.

4 Results

4.1 On Cypher generation

We observe in Table 1 that our approach outperforms both the LLM-based KGQA system in LangChain and the baseline of few-shot examples in terms of exact match accuracy across all hop levels. The increase in performance is especially pronounced in 3-hop questions, supporting our hypothesis that our methodology is able to effectively demonstrate to the LLM the reasoning required to answer complex multi-hop questions.

Notably, our proposed approach shows better performance in 3-hop and 2-hop questions over 1-hop questions. Manual examination revealed that most of the failures in 1-hop questions can be attributed to confusion between selecting the correct entity-type to traverse between "imdbvotes" and "imdbrating" for questions like "how famous of a film was [Pumping Iron]" or "what do people think of [Beau Travail] ".

The results in Table 2 show that including three examples instead of one in a typically written style leads to regression in performance, and thus demonstrates the importance of well-designed examples. Other ablation experiments show that other features of example design in our approach like using descriptive variable names, writing the hops in order of traversal, etc. contribute positively to performance. Few-shot examples used for each ablation experiment are listed in Appendix D.

4.2 On SPARQL generation

Figure 4 highlights the performance of our few-shot design against the baseline across 16 different knowledge graphs from the SPARQL version of the Spider benchmark (Kosten et al., 2023). There is a modest increase in execution match accuracy for SPARQL, with the most significant improvement—a 7.7% lift—observed in the subset of questions related to the pets_1 graph. There are six graphs where our methodology shows no improvement in execution match accuracy, and two graphs, `tvshow` and `poker_player`, where it leads to regressions. This outcome primarily stems from the use of few-shot examples that do not quite match the query complexity for the question set associated with those graphs, as classified by the original benchmark's measure of query hardness, which includes queries with 10+ hops. Conducting a paired difference t-test on these results yields a test statistic of 2.33 with a corresponding p-value of 0.03, indicating that the minor lift provided by our methodology is statistically significant.

5 Discussion

Our findings demonstrate the effectiveness of our proposed approach in improving the performance of LLM-based KGQA systems, particularly in addressing the challenge of multi-hop reasoning. By designing few-shot examples that implicitly demonstrate systematic reasoning to guide LLMs in generating Cypher and SPARQL queries, we have shown enhancements in accuracy, thereby highlighting the potential of this methodology for advancing the field of KGQA. Future research directions include testing our proposed approach on knowledge graphs with increasingly complex schemas, addressing challenges such as accurate attribute selection, aggregations and function usage in these graph query languages, and assessing the efficacy of using this few-shot example design in more graph languages and code generation tasks. Additionally, there is potential to develop techniques that automatically generate few-shot examples for a broad range of LLMs, streamlining the creation process and enhancing adaptability across various domains.

References

Toufique Ahmed and Premkumar Devanbu. 2023. Few-shot training llms for project-specific code-summarization. In *Proceedings of the 37th IEEE/ACM International Conference on Automated Software Engineering*, ASE '22, New York, NY, USA. Association for Computing Machinery.

Yuan An, Jane Greenberg, Alex Kalinowski, Xintong Zhao, Xiaohua Hu, Fernando J. Uribe-Romo, Kyle Langlois, Jacob Furst, and Diego A. Gómez-Gualdrón. 2023. Knowledge graph question answering for materials science (kgqa4mat): Developing natural language interface for metal-organic frameworks knowledge graph (mof-kg). *Preprint*, arXiv:2309.11361.

Hyeong Kyu Choi, Seunghun Lee, Jaewon Chu, and Hyunwoo J Kim. 2023. Nutrea: Neural tree search for context-guided multi-hop kgqa. In *Advances in Neural Information Processing Systems*, volume 36, pages 35954–35965. Curran Associates, Inc.

Yu Gu and Yu Su. 2022. Arcaneqa: Dynamic program induction and contextualized encoding for knowledge base question answering. *arXiv preprint arXiv:2204.08109*.

Jiayan Guo, Lun Du, Hengyu Liu, Mengyu Zhou, Xinyi He, and Shi Han. 2023. Gpt4graph: Can large language models understand graph structured data ? an empirical evaluation and benchmarking. *Preprint*, arXiv:2305.15066.

Xijie Huang, Li Lyna Zhang, Kwang-Ting Cheng, Fan Yang, and Mao Yang. 2024. Fewer is more: Boosting llm reasoning with reinforced context pruning. *Preprint*, arXiv:2312.08901.

Jinhao Jiang, Kun Zhou, Zican Dong, Keming Ye, Wayne Xin Zhao, and Ji-Rong Wen. 2023a. Structgpt: A general framework for large language model to reason over structured data. *arXiv preprint arXiv:2305.09645*.

Jinhao Jiang, Kun Zhou, Zican Dong, Keming Ye, Xin Zhao, and Ji-Rong Wen. 2023b. StructGPT: A general framework for large language model to reason over structured data. In *Proceedings of the 2023 Conference on Empirical Methods in Natural Language Processing*, pages 9237–9251, Singapore. Association for Computational Linguistics.

Jinhao Jiang, Kun Zhou, Wayne Xin Zhao, and Ji-Rong Wen. 2022. Unikgqa: Unified retrieval and reasoning for solving multi-hop question answering over knowledge graph. *arXiv preprint arXiv:2212.00959*.

Catherine Kosten, Philippe Cudré-Mauroux, and Kurt Stockinger. 2023. Spider4sparql: A complex benchmark for evaluating knowledge graph question answering systems. In *2023 IEEE International Conference on Big Data (BigData)*, pages 5272–5281. IEEE.

Tianle Li, Xueguang Ma, Alex Zhuang, Yu Gu, Yu Su, and Wenhu Chen. 2023. Few-shot in-context learning for knowledge base question answering. *arXiv preprint arXiv:2305.01750*.

OpenAI, Josh Achiam, Steven Adler, Sandhini Agarwal, Lama Ahmad, Ilge Akkaya, Florencia Leoni Aleman, Diogo Almeida, Janko Altenschmidt, Sam Altman, Shyamal Anadkat, Red Avila, Igor Babuschkin, Suchir Balaji, Valerie Balcom, Paul Baltescu, Haiming Bao, Mohammad Bavarian, Jeff Belgum, Irwan Bello, Jake Berdine, Gabriel Bernadett-Shapiro, Christopher Berner, Lenny Bogdonoff, Oleg Boiko, Madelaine Boyd, Anna-Luisa Brakman, Greg Brockman, Tim Brooks, Miles Brundage, Kevin Button, Trevor Cai, Rosie Campbell, Andrew Cann, Brittany Carey, Chelsea Carlson, Rory Carmichael, Brooke Chan, Che Chang, Fotis Chantzis, Derek Chen, Sully Chen, Ruby Chen, Jason Chen, Mark Chen, Ben Chess, Chester Cho, Casey Chu, Hyung Won Chung, Dave Cummings, Jeremiah Currier, Yunxing Dai, Cory Decareaux, Thomas Degry, Noah Deutsch, Damien Deville, Arka Dhar, David Dohan, Steve Dowling, Sheila Dunning, Adrien Ecoffet, Atty Eleti, Tyna Eloundou, David Farhi, Liam Fedus, Niko Felix, Simón Posada Fishman, Juston Forte, Isabella Fulford, Leo Gao, Elie Georges, Christian Gibson, Vik Goel, Tarun Gogineni, Gabriel Goh, Rapha Gontijo-Lopes, Jonathan Gordon, Morgan Grafstein, Scott

Gray, Ryan Greene, Joshua Gross, Shixiang Shane Gu, Yufei Guo, Chris Hallacy, Jesse Han, Jeff Harris, Yuchen He, Mike Heaton, Johannes Heidecke, Chris Hesse, Alan Hickey, Wade Hickey, Peter Hoeschele, Brandon Houghton, Kenny Hsu, Shengli Hu, Xin Hu, Joost Huizinga, Shantanu Jain, Shawn Jain, Joanne Jang, Angela Jiang, Roger Jiang, Haozhun Jin, Denny Jin, Shino Jomoto, Billie Jonn, Heewoo Jun, Tomer Kaftan, Łukasz Kaiser, Ali Kamali, Ingmar Kanitscheider, Nitish Shirish Keskar, Tabarak Khan, Logan Kilpatrick, Jong Wook Kim, Christina Kim, Yongjik Kim, Jan Hendrik Kirchner, Jamie Kiros, Matt Knight, Daniel Kokotajlo, Łukasz Kondraciuk, Andrew Kondrich, Aris Konstantinidis, Kyle Kosic, Gretchen Krueger, Vishal Kuo, Michael Lampe, Ikai Lan, Teddy Lee, Jan Leike, Jade Leung, Daniel Levy, Chak Ming Li, Rachel Lim, Molly Lin, Stephanie Lin, Mateusz Litwin, Theresa Lopez, Ryan Lowe, Patricia Lue, Anna Makanju, Kim Malfacini, Sam Manning, Todor Markov, Yaniv Markovski, Bianca Martin, Katie Mayer, Andrew Mayne, Bob McGrew, Scott Mayer McKinney, Christine McLeavey, Paul McMillan, Jake McNeil, David Medina, Aalok Mehta, Jacob Menick, Luke Metz, Andrey Mishchenko, Pamela Mishkin, Vinnie Monaco, Evan Morikawa, Daniel Mossing, Tong Mu, Mira Murati, Oleg Murk, David Mély, Ashvin Nair, Reiichiro Nakano, Rajeev Nayak, Arvind Neelakantan, Richard Ngo, Hyeonwoo Noh, Long Ouyang, Cullen O'Keefe, Jakub Pachocki, Alex Paino, Joe Palermo, Ashley Pantuliano, Giambattista Parascandolo, Joel Parish, Emy Parparita, Alex Passos, Mikhail Pavlov, Andrew Peng, Adam Perelman, Filipe de Avila Belbute Peres, Michael Petrov, Henrique Ponde de Oliveira Pinto, Michael, Pokorny, Michelle Pokrass, Vitchyr H. Pong, Tolly Powell, Alethea Power, Boris Power, Elizabeth Proehl, Raul Puri, Alec Radford, Jack Rae, Aditya Ramesh, Cameron Raymond, Francis Real, Kendra Rimbach, Carl Ross, Bob Rotsted, Henri Roussez, Nick Ryder, Mario Saltarelli, Ted Sanders, Shibani Santurkar, Girish Sastry, Heather Schmidt, David Schnurr, John Schulman, Daniel Selsam, Kyla Sheppard, Toki Sherbakov, Jessica Shieh, Sarah Shoker, Pranav Shyam, Szymon Sidor, Eric Sigler, Maddie Simens, Jordan Sitkin, Katarina Slama, Ian Sohl, Benjamin Sokolowsky, Yang Song, Natalie Staudacher, Felipe Petroski Such, Natalie Summers, Ilya Sutskever, Jie Tang, Nikolas Tezak, Madeleine B. Thompson, Phil Tillet, Amin Tootoonchian, Elizabeth Tseng, Preston Tuggle, Nick Turley, Jerry Tworek, Juan Felipe Cerón Uribe, Andrea Vallone, Arun Vijayvergiya, Chelsea Voss, Carroll Wainwright, Justin Jay Wang, Alvin Wang, Ben Wang, Jonathan Ward, Jason Wei, CJ Weinmann, Akila Welihinda, Peter Welinder, Jiayi Weng, Lilian Weng, Matt Wiethoff, Dave Willner, Clemens Winter, Samuel Wolrich, Hannah Wong, Lauren Workman, Sherwin Wu, Jeff Wu, Michael Wu, Kai Xiao, Tao Xu, Sarah Yoo, Kevin Yu, Qiming Yuan, Wojciech Zaremba, Rowan Zellers, Chong Zhang, Marvin Zhang, Shengjia Zhao, Tianhao Zheng, Juntang Zhuang, William Zhuk, and Barret Zoph. 2024. Gpt-4 technical report. *Preprint*, arXiv:2303.08774.

Jiaxin Shi, Shulin Cao, Lei Hou, Juanzi Li, and Hanwang Zhang. 2021. TransferNet: An effective and transparent framework for multi-hop question answering over relation graph. In *Proceedings of the 2021 Conference on Empirical Methods in Natural Language Processing*, pages 4149–4158, Online and Punta Cana, Dominican Republic. Association for Computational Linguistics.

A. Shirafuji, Y. Oda, J. Suzuki, M. Morishita, and Y. Watanobe. 2023. Refactoring programs using large language models with few-shot examples. In *2023 30th Asia-Pacific Software Engineering Conference (APSEC)*, pages 151–160, Los Alamitos, CA, USA. IEEE Computer Society.

Jason Wei, Xuezhi Wang, Dale Schuurmans, Maarten Bosma, Brian Ichter, Fei Xia, Ed H. Chi, Quoc V. Le, and Denny Zhou. 2022. Chain-of-thought prompting elicits reasoning in large language models. In *NeurIPS*.

Xi Ye, Semih Yavuz, Kazuma Hashimoto, Yingbo Zhou, and Caiming Xiong. 2021. Rng-kbqa: Generation augmented iterative ranking for knowledge base question answering. *arXiv preprint arXiv:2109.08678*.

Yuyu Zhang, Hanjun Dai, Zornitsa Kozareva, Alexander J. Smola, and Le Song. 2018. Variational reasoning for question answering with knowledge graph. In *Proceedings of the Thirty-Second AAAI Conference on Artificial Intelligence and Thirtieth Innovative Applications of Artificial Intelligence Conference and Eighth AAAI Symposium on Educational Advances in Artificial Intelligence*, AAAI'18/IAAI'18/EAAI'18. AAAI Press.

A An example of a full prompt employing our design

```
[
  {
    "role": "system",
    "content": "You are a Cypher query
    generation engine for a Neo4j graph with the
     schema described below. You will create
    Cypher queries that helps users navigate the
    graph.

---
Node types:
- writer
- movie
- actor
- director
- tag
- year
- language
- genre
```

```
- imdbrating
- imdbvotes

Relations schema:
movie –> directed_by –> actor
movie –> directed_by –> director
movie –> directed_by –> writer
movie –> has_genre –> genre
movie –> has_imdb_rating –> imdbrating
movie –> has_imdb_votes –> imdbvotes
movie –> has_tags –> tag
movie –> in_language –> language
movie –> release_year –> year
movie –> starred_actors –> actor
movie –> starred_actors –> director
movie –> starred_actors –> writer
movie –> written_by –> actor
movie –> written_by –> director
movie –> written_by –> writer
–––"
  },
  {
    "role": "user",
    "content": "Write a Cypher query for: \"what
     films can be described by occupation\""
  },
  {
    "role": "assistant",
    "content": "‘‘‘
MATCH (movie:‘movie‘)–[:has_tags]–>(
    occupationTag:‘tag‘)
WHERE toLower(occupationTag.name)='
    occupation'
RETURN movie LIMIT 200
‘‘‘"
  },
  {
    "role": "user",
    "content": "Write a Cypher query for: \"
    which person wrote the films directed by
    Yuriy Norshteyn\""
  },
  {
    "role": "assistant",
    "content": "‘‘‘
MATCH (yuriyDirector:‘director‘)<–[:
    directed_by]–(movie:‘movie‘)
MATCH (movie:‘movie‘)–[:written_by]–>(writer
    :‘writer‘)
WHERE toLower(yuriyDirector.name)='yuriy
    norshteyn'
RETURN writer LIMIT 200
‘‘‘"
  },
  {
    "role": "user",
    "content": "Write a Cypher query for: \"the
    films that share actors with the film Dil
    Chahta Hai were released in which years\""
  },
  {
    "role": "assistant",
    "content": "‘‘‘
MATCH (dilMovie:‘movie‘)–[:starred_actors
    ]–>(actor:‘actor‘)
MATCH (actor:‘actor‘)<–[:starred_actors]–(
    otherMovie:‘movie‘)
MATCH (otherMovie:‘movie‘)–[:release_year
    ]–>(year:‘year‘)
WHERE toLower(dilMovie.name)='dil chahta
    hai'
AND dilMovie <> otherMovie
RETURN year LIMIT 200
‘‘‘"
  },
  {
    "role": "user",
    "content": "Write a Cypher query for: \"what
     types are the films starred by actors in The
    Gypsy Moths\""
  }
]
```

B An example of a full prompt used in the baseline using LangChain's Cypher generation module

```
Task:Generate Cypher statement to query a graph
    database.
Instructions:
Use only the provided relationship types and
    properties in the schema.
Do not use any other relationship types or
    properties that are not provided.
Schema:
Node properties are the following:
writer {name: STRING, node_id: STRING},
    movie {name: STRING, node_id: STRING},
    actor {name: STRING, node_id: STRING},
    director {name: STRING, node_id: STRING
    },tag {name: STRING, node_id: STRING},
    year {name: STRING, node_id: STRING},
    language {name: STRING, node_id:
    STRING},genre {name: STRING, node_id:
```

STRING},imdbrating {name: STRING, node_id: STRING},imdbvotes {name: STRING, node_id: STRING}
Relationship properties are the following:
directed_by {source: STRING},written_by {source: STRING},starred_actors {source: STRING},release_year {source: STRING}, in_language {source: STRING},has_tags {source: STRING},has_genre {source: STRING},has_imdb_votes {source: STRING},has_imdb_rating {source: STRING}
The relationships are the following:
(:movie)–[:has_tags]–>(:tag),(:movie)–[:directed_by]–>(:writer),(:movie)–[:directed_by]–>(:actor),(:movie)–[:directed_by]–>(:director),(:movie)–[:written_by]–>(:writer),(:movie)–[:written_by]–>(:actor),(:movie)–[:written_by]–>(:director),(:movie)–[:in_language]–>(:language),(:movie)–[:release_year]–>(:year),(:movie)–[:has_genre]–>(:genre),(:movie)–[:starred_actors]–>(:actor),(:movie)–[:starred_actors]–>(:director),(:movie)–[:starred_actors]–>(:writer),(:movie)–[:has_imdb_rating]–>(:imdbrating),(:movie)–[:has_imdb_votes]–>(:imdbvotes)
Note: Do not include any explanations or apologies in your responses.
Do not respond to any questions that might ask anything else than for you to construct a Cypher statement.
Do not include any text except the generated Cypher statement.
The question is:
the movies that share actors with the movie [Indiana Jones and the Last Crusade] were in which languages

C Few-shot examples provided to LLM for the baseline of typically written examples

Question: what films can be described by occupation
Cypher query: ‘‘‘
MATCH (s:‘movie‘)–[r:has_tags]–>(o:‘tag‘)
WHERE toLower(o.name)='occupation' RETURN s LIMIT 200
‘‘‘

Question: which person wrote the films directed by Yuriy Norshteyn
Cypher query: ‘‘‘
MATCH (d:‘director‘ {name:'Yuriy Norshteyn'})<–[:directed_by]–(m:‘movie‘)–[:written_by]–>(w:‘writer‘) RETURN w LIMIT 200
‘‘‘

Question: the films that share actors with the film Dil Chahta Hai were released in which years
Cypher query: ‘‘‘
MATCH (yr:‘year‘)<–[:release_year]–(m:‘movie‘)–[:starred_actors]–>(:‘actor‘)<–[:starred_actors]–(m2:‘movie‘ {name: 'Dil Chahta Hai'})
WHERE m <> m2
RETURN yr LIMIT 200
‘‘‘

D Few-shot examples provided to LLM for ablation experiments

D.1 Ablation experiment "One typical example only"

Question: the films that share actors with the film Dil Chahta Hai were released in which years
Cypher query: ‘‘‘
MATCH (yr:‘year‘)<–[:release_year]–(m:‘movie‘)–[:starred_actors]–>(:‘actor‘)<–[:starred_actors]–(m2:‘movie‘ {name: 'Dil Chahta Hai'})
WHERE m <> m2
RETURN yr LIMIT 200
‘‘‘

D.2 Ablation experiment "Non-descriptive variable names"

Question: what films can be described by occupation
Cypher query: ‘‘‘
MATCH (m:‘movie‘)–[:has_tags]–>(t:‘tag‘)
WHERE toLower(t.name)='occupation'
RETURN m LIMIT 200
‘‘‘

Question: which person wrote the films directed by Yuriy Norshteyn
Cypher query: ‘‘‘
MATCH (d:‘director‘)<–[:directed_by]–(m:‘movie‘)

```
MATCH (m:‘movie‘)–[:written_by]–>(w:‘writer‘)
WHERE toLower(d.name)=’yuriy norshteyn’
RETURN w LIMIT 200
‘‘‘
```

Question: the films that share actors with the film Dil Chahta Hai were released in which years

Cypher query: ‘‘‘

```
MATCH (m:‘movie‘)–[:starred_actors]–>(a:‘actor‘)
MATCH (a:‘actor‘)<–[:starred_actors]–(m2:‘movie‘)
MATCH (m2:‘movie‘)–[:release_year]–>(y:‘year‘)
WHERE toLower(m.name)=’dil chahta hai’
AND m <> m2
RETURN y LIMIT 200
‘‘‘
```

D.3 Ablation experiment "All hops in one line"

Question: what films can be described by occupation

Cypher query: ‘‘‘

```
MATCH (movie:‘movie‘)–[:has_tags]–>(occupationTag:‘tag‘)
WHERE toLower(occupationTag.name)=’occupation’
RETURN movie LIMIT 200
‘‘‘
```

Question: which person wrote the films directed by Yuriy Norshteyn

Cypher query: ‘‘‘

```
MATCH (yuriyDirector:‘director‘)<–[:directed_by]–(movie:‘movie‘)–[:written_by]–>(writer:‘writer‘)
WHERE toLower(yuriyDirector.name)=’yuriy norshteyn’
RETURN writer LIMIT 200
‘‘‘
```

Question: the films that share actors with the film Dil Chahta Hai were released in which years

Cypher query: ‘‘‘

```
MATCH (dilMovie:‘movie‘)–[:starred_actors]–>(actor:‘actor‘)<–[:starred_actors]–(otherMovie:‘movie‘)–[:release_year]–>(year:‘year‘)
WHERE toLower(dilMovie.name)=’dil chahta hai’
AND dilMovie <> otherMovie
RETURN year LIMIT 200
‘‘‘
```

D.4 Ablation experiment "One example only employing our design"

Question: the films that share actors with the film Dil Chahta Hai were released in which years

Cypher query: ‘‘‘

```
MATCH (dilMovie:‘movie‘)–[:starred_actors]–>(actor:‘actor‘)
MATCH (actor:‘actor‘)<–[:starred_actors]–(otherMovie:‘movie‘)
MATCH (otherMovie:‘movie‘)–[:release_year]–>(year:‘year‘)
WHERE toLower(dilMovie.name)=’dil chahta hai’
AND dilMovie <> otherMovie
RETURN year LIMIT 200
‘‘‘
```

D.5 Ablation experiment "Chain direction not maintained"

Question: what films can be described by occupation

Cypher query: ‘‘‘

```
MATCH (movie:‘movie‘)–[:has_tags]–>(occupationTag:‘tag‘)
WHERE toLower(occupationTag.name)=’occupation’
RETURN movie LIMIT 200
‘‘‘
```

Question: which person wrote the films directed by Yuriy Norshteyn

Cypher query: ‘‘‘

```
MATCH (movie:‘movie‘)–[:directed_by]–>(yuriyDirector:‘director‘)
MATCH (movie:‘movie‘)–[:written_by]–>(writer:‘writer‘)
WHERE toLower(yuriyDirector.name)=’yuriy norshteyn’
RETURN writer LIMIT 200
‘‘‘
```

Question: the films that share actors with the film Dil Chahta Hai were released in which years

Cypher query: ‘‘‘

```
MATCH (dilMovie:‘movie‘)–[:starred_actors]–>(actor:‘actor‘)
```

```
MATCH (otherMovie:‘movie‘)–[:starred_actors]->(actor:‘actor‘)
MATCH (otherMovie:‘movie‘)–[:release_year]->(year:‘year‘)
WHERE toLower(dilMovie.name)='dil chahta hai'
AND dilMovie <> otherMovie
RETURN year LIMIT 200
```

E Transferring methodology to SPARQL

E.1 Full prompt to transfer few-shot style

You are an expert at graph languages like CYPHER and SPARQL. You want rewrite graph queries so that each query is more readable and understandable. An example is given below:

```
## OLD QUERY
MATCH (yr:‘year‘)<–[:release_year]–(m:‘movie‘)–[:starred_actors]–>(a:‘actor‘)<–[:starred_actors]–(m2:‘movie‘ {{name: 'Dil Chahta Hai'}})
WHERE m <> m2
RETURN yr LIMIT 200

## NEW QUERY
MATCH (dilMovie:‘movie‘)–[:starred_actors]->(actor:‘actor‘)
MATCH (actor:‘actor‘)<–[:starred_actors]–(otherMovie:‘movie‘)
MATCH (otherMovie:‘movie‘)–[:release_year]->(year:‘year‘)
WHERE toLower(dilMovie.name)='dil chahta hai'
AND dilMovie <> otherMovie
RETURN year LIMIT 200
```

Help me rewrite the following query to make it more readable and understandable. Make sure that:

1. Each hop is articulated on a separate line to mirror the logical sequence of traversals, strictly adhering to the correct order of entities and relationships encountered
2. Maintain an unbroken logical chain where the endpoint of one hop is the starting point for the next, ensuring a coherent flow of entities throughout the query
3. Adopt variable names that are both illustrative and consistent, reflecting the entity type and any applicable constraints, like 'dilMovie' to denote a 'movie entity constrained by the title 'Dil Chahta Hai'

Please help me rewrite the following query in the style discussed above.

Author Index

Association for Computational Linguistics
209 N. Eighth Street
Stroudsburg, Pennsylvania 18360

ISBN 979-8-3313-0165-1

CURRAN ASSOCIATES INC.
proceedings.com